The Politics of Constructing the International Criminal Court

The Politics of Constructing the International Criminal Court

NGOs, Discourse, and Agency

Michael J. Struett

THE POLITICS OF CONSTRUCTING THE INTERNATIONAL CRIMINAL COURT
Copyright © Michael J. Struett, 2008.
All rights reserved. No part of this book may be used or reproduced in any manner whatsoever without written permission except in the case of brief quotations embodied in critical articles or reviews.

First published in 2008 by
PALGRAVE MACMILLAN™
175 Fifth Avenue, New York, N.Y. 10010 and
Houndmills, Basingstoke, Hampshire, England RG21 6XS.
Companies and representatives throughout the world.

PALGRAVE MACMILLAN is the global academic imprint of the Palgrave Macmillan division of St. Martin's Press, LLC and of Palgrave Macmillan Ltd. Macmillan® is a registered trademark in the United States, United Kingdom and other countries. Palgrave is a registered trademark in the European Union and other countries.

ISBN-13: 978-0-230-60457-5
ISBN-10: 0-230-60457-9

Library of Congress Cataloging-in-Publication Data

Struett, Michael J.
  The politics of constructing the international criminal court: NGOs, discourse, and agency/by Michael J. Struett.
      p. cm.
  Includes bibliographical references and index.
  ISBN 0-230-60457-9
  1. International Criminal Court—History. 2. Non-governmental organizations—Political activity. 3. Human rights advocacy. I. Title.
  KZ6311.S77 2008
  345'.01—dc22

2007045683

A catalogue record for this book is available from the British Library.

Design by Macmillan India Ltd.

First edition: May 2008

10 9 8 7 6 5 4 3 2 1

Printed in the United States of America.

For
Ekaterina,
Sebastian, Alexandra, and Samantha

Table of Contents

List of Figures	ix
List of Tables	xi
Acknowledgments	xiii
List of Abbreviations	xv
1 The Meaning of the International Criminal Court	1
2 Norm Contestation in World Politics: Civil Society, States, and Discourse	13
3 Discursive Limits: The Failure to Establish an International Criminal Court; 1946–1954	49
4 Context: An Opening for an International Criminal Court; 1989–1994	67
5 Negotiations: NGOs Shape the Terms of the ICC Debate; 1995–1998	83
6 Building the Rome Statute: 1998	109
7 Principled Discourse and the Drive for Ratification: 1998–2002	131
8 The Legitimacy of the International Criminal Court	151
Postscript: Construction Continues	179
Notes	183
Bibliography	201
Index	213

Figures

7.1	State signatories to the ICC by July 17, 1999	135
7.2	State signatories to the ICC by December 31, 2000	136
7.3	States ratifying the ICC by December 31, 2000	138
7.4	States ratifying the ICC by April 11, 2002	138
7.5	States ratifying the ICC by July 17, 2007	139

Tables

| 5.1 | Selected NGO and expert papers circulated during the ICC negotiations | 87 |
| 5.2 | Timeline of the ICC negotiations | 88 |

Acknowledgments

When I first proposed this project, in 2000, I found it necessary to reassure skeptics that even if the International Criminal Court (ICC) never came into being, it would still be important to tell the political story of how the Rome Statute was negotiated and why states ultimately chose not to ratify it in sufficient numbers to bring it into being. Today, the ICC still has many detractors, and there are a wide range of views on the extent to which the establishment of the ICC has fundamentally changed world politics. But there can be little doubt that the ICC is an institutional force that now plays an important role on the world stage. I am thankful that I have had the opportunity to think and write about the political forces that led to this development.

So many gracious people have contributed to the completion of this project, in ways that range from the small to the very large, that it is simply impossible to name them all. I want to thank many of you by name, but I am grateful to many more of you than I can list here.

First, I want to thank the community of experts and activists in the fields of international humanitarian law and human rights law, many of whom I have now had the pleasure to meet in person, and many more of whom I know only through their written remarks and speeches. It really is a unique sort of personality and talent that dedicates so much hard work to the development of institutions of international justice. Everyone who is involved in this community knows of the unique camaraderie that binds it together. Among this group I can name only a few of the many who have been so generous with their assistance. I want to thank Benjamin Ferencz for his personal encouragement and for being an example to so many scholars and activists who follow in his footsteps. I am grateful to everyone who agreed to be interviewed for this project; everyone I spoke with was generous with their time and as forthcoming as their professional commitments allowed. In general, these people are named below in the text, but especially I want to thank Adrian Bos, who was a gracious host in addition to being tremendously informative; and Herman von Hebel, who, in addition to taking time out of his own schedule, also was enormously helpful in helping to put me in touch with many of his colleagues. Finally, I want to thank my dear friend Heather Hamilton, who listened and responded to many of the ideas presented here during the first ICC Assembly of State Parties meeting in September 2002.

I thank Timothy Canova for the invitation to present some of this work at an excellent conference at Chapman Law School. An earlier version of part of the argument in Chapter 8 was first published in 2005 in *Chapman Law Review*. I also thank Anne Heiber at *Peace Review*, where a preliminary version of part of the argument in Chapter 1 was published. We thank both publications for permission to reproduce that work in the present volume.

Funding for this research came primarily from the Institute on Global Conflict and Cooperation, based at the University of California, San Diego. Additional support was received from the William Podlich Fellowship Award and the Department of Political Science and School of Social Sciences at the University of California, Irvine. The School of Public and International Affairs at North Carolina State University provided funds to aid in the preparation of the final manuscript. I also want to thank my graduate research assistants, Andrei Iovu, Justin Moody, and Tanisha Gill, for their work editing several chapters and preparing the manuscript for publication.

Parts of this work have been presented to others and critiqued in a wide variety of places from formal conferences to simple discussions of ideas over meals and beverages, much to the benefit of the final product. In particular I want to briefly thank Wouter Woerner, Ige Dekker, Diane Amann, Antonio Franceshet, Mervyn Frost, Eric Leonard, Molly Cochran, Ned Lebow, Dorie Solinger, Pat Morgan, Bernie Grofman, Claire Cutler, Mark Petracca, Monica Nalepa, Marek Kaminski, Anne Clunan, Cara Robertson, Gretchen Helmke, Barry O'Neil, Terry Bowers, David Scheffer, Greg Fox, Leila Sadat, Khoi Ta, Diane Orentlicher, Sean Butler, Steve Roach, Brent Steele, Jaque Amoureux, and Juan Guzman. Nicholas Onuf took the time to respond with formal written comments to an earlier version of my argument many years ago.

I cannot fail to mention some of my colleagues and friends, who have been a tremendous source of intellectual stimulation and personal support. Again, at the risk of naming some but not everyone, I want to thank Brian Adams, Molly Patterson, Ryane Straus, Sharon Lean, Celine Jacquemin, Michael Jensen, Michael Latner, Bruce Hemmer, Leah Fraser, David Harrison, Alix Van Sickle, Catherine Corrigal-Brown, Natalie Masuoka, Madeline Baer, Brian Fisher, Fabrice Paracuellos, Andy Drummond, Susan Kupperstein, Lara Nettlefield, Bill Boettcher, Mike Cobb, Charlie Coe, Richard Clerkin, Steve Greene, Erik Faleski, and Steve Weldon. I especially want to thank Alison Renteln and Etel Solingen, who both saw potential in this project when it was still little more than a formative idea. I am grateful to Alison Brysk, Wayne Sandholtz, and Joseph DiMento for their numerous readings of versions of this project. Each provided ideas and insights that have significantly influenced the final text. I am especially fortunate to have had the opportunity to work under the supervision of Cecelia Lynch. Last, I want to thank the late Ernst B. Haas, who first encouraged me to continue thinking for myself.

I have the support of a tremendously wonderful extended family in California, Chile, and elsewhere, without whom I could not have succeeded in this endeavor. I especially want to thank my aunt and uncle Janice and Jim Southworth, who have done so much over the years, not least of which was donating the laptop on which much of this book was initially written. I want to thank my parents, John and Judy Struett. Finally, I want to thank my wife, Ekaterina, whose support and understanding made this book possible. This is dedicated to her and our children, Sebastian, Alexandra, and Samantha.

Abbreviations

ABA	American Bar Association
AI	Amnesty International
CICC	Coalition for the International Criminal Court
ECOSOC	Economic and Social Council
FAO	Food and Agriculture Organization
FIDH	Fédération Internationale des Ligues des Droits de l'Homme (International Federation for Human Rights)
GA	General Assembly
HRW	Human Rights Watch
ICC	International Criminal Court
ICCPR	International Covenant on Civil and Political Rights
ICESCR	International Covenant on Economic, Social and Cultural Rights
ICJ	International Court of Justice
ICTR	International Criminal Tribunal for Rwanda
ICTY	International Criminal Tribunal for the former Yugoslavia
IGO	Intergovernmental Organization
IHD	Insan Haklari Dernegi (Human Rights Association [of Turkey])
ILC	International Law Commission
IMF	International Monetary Fund
IMTFE	International Military Tribunal for the Far East
INGO	International Nongovernmental Organization
IR	International Relations
LRA	Lord's Resistance Army
NATO	North Atlantic Treaty Organization
NGO	Nongovernmental Organization
NPWJ	No Peace Without Justice
OECD	Organisation for Economic Co-operation and Development
TAN	Transnational Advocacy Network
TIHV	Türkiye Insan Haklari Vakfi (Human Rights Foundation of Turkey)
UK	United Kingdom
UN	United Nations
U.S.	United States

1

The Meaning of the International Criminal Court

> Innumerable treaties, conventions, and conferences, and the charters of the League of Nations and the UN, have made all the provision for world peace that language can describe, but the failure to establish authoritative bodies to interpret and to enforce that language has turned the laws against war into a graveyard of good words. There is, as always, no shortage of rules: endless, overlapping, repetitive formulae devised by delegates in the expensive comfort of Geneva hotels, later to be signed and ratified by states secure in the knowledge that should any question arise about their meaning or application, they will be judges in their own cause.
>
> —Geoffrey Robertson, *Crimes against Humanity*[1]

Introduction

The International Criminal Court (ICC) is now operational. What is the meaning of this innovation in global governance? Most concretely, the ICC will mean prosecution and jail time for some individuals who commit war crimes, crimes against humanity, or genocide, as defined in international law. In a larger sense, though, what role will this institution play in bringing to bear the rule of law in the context of war? The answer depends not just on the details and limitations of the first few cases that will be heard by the new court, but on the long-term institutionalization of this supranational institution with the power to punish some of the world's most abhorrent crimes.

By ratifying the Rome Statute for the ICC, states created a strong, independent, and potentially effective institution for ensuring punishment for the worst crimes under international law. At its inception, the ICC has jurisdiction over three categories of crimes: war crimes, crimes against humanity, and genocide. As such, the ICC is an institution with significant powers to regulate the ways that states or other groups use force and to punish individuals who violate these international laws. This introductory chapter describes the main features of the ICC and offers an assessment of the meaning of this new court for global governance.

It is a preliminary step toward answering the central question of this book: How did it come to pass that so many states were willing to cede such substantial authority to an international tribunal?

My claim is that nongovernmental organizations (NGOs) played a crucial role in shaping the Rome Statute for the ICC and in securing its entry into force less than four years after it opened for signatures. This observation leads to a series of further questions that have become focal points in the broader discussion of global governance in the last decade. How is it that NGOs were able to play such a decisive role? What are the implications for the structure and legitimacy of emerging forms of global governance? I claim that NGOs were persuasive, and ultimately effective, because of their reliance on communicatively rational arguments that can be justified to a (potentially) universal audience. Beyond merely establishing the nature and extent of NGO influence on the process of establishing the ICC, I account for it through an analysis of NGOs' discursive practices.

In December 2003, Uganda, a party to the ICC statute, referred a situation taking place within its borders to the ICC prosecutor, thereby triggering the jurisdiction of the new court for the first time. The prosecutor subsequently determined that there was sufficient evidence that five leaders of the Lord's Resistance Army (LRA), a rebel group in Uganda, bore criminal responsibility for a number of counts of war crimes and crimes against humanity. A pretrial chamber of ICC judges subsequently concurred with that finding and issued warrants for these leaders' arrest.[2] The LRA leadership has been accused of large-scale crimes against civilians, including summary executions, torture, child abductions, rape, slavery, enslavement, forcible displacement, and the destruction of property. The prosecutor and the three judges of the pretrial chamber also satisfied themselves that the case met all the jurisdictional requirements of the ICC, including that the accused were among those "most responsible" for the crimes and that Uganda's government was not able at that time to bring these perpetrators to justice in Ugandan courts.[3] The ICC prosecutor, Luis Moreno Ocampo, also has indicated that if other parties in the region have committed ICC crimes, he will investigate those parties as well. Presumably, this would include any crimes committed by government forces. The ICC statute allows states only to refer "situations" to the court. It is up to the prosecutor to determine which individuals are charged with committing crimes. This rule of the ICC statute is intended to promote impartiality, since in a conflict situation both government and oppositional military forces can commit international law crimes.

Since the Bush administration chose to withdraw the signature of the United States from the ICC statute, many commentators have wondered aloud whether international humanitarian law can be enforced impartially. The invasion of Iraq in 2003, arguably in violation of the international law ban on aggressive war, only magnified those concerns. Further abuses in the Abu Ghraib prison and the apparent execution of wounded combatants in Iraq also have tested the willingness of the United States to prosecute its own personnel and leadership for violations of international law. The ICC is powerless to consider violations of the laws of war by American or Iraqi forces in Iraq. The court's jurisdiction is limited to those states that have ratified it. Does this mean that the ICC is a meaningless paper court? Is the effect of the ICC simply to create one standard of international humanitarian law enforcement for the developing world, one that will not apply to the developed world?

The answers to these questions are complex. The ICC will not be able to punish every violation of the laws of war. Still, the establishment of the ICC is a watershed development in the history of international humanitarian law. Because the ICC is a supranational institution with the permanent authority to punish war crimes, crimes against humanity, genocide, and potentially aggression, it fundamentally alters the relationship between the laws of war and state authority. The ICC does exist in a global context characterized by sharp inequalities in power and resources. The court cannot fully escape the implications of those global inequalities, but it can work in ways that minimize rather than exacerbate them. The importance of the ICC is that it establishes a permanent institution responsible for ending the culture of impunity that has historically protected the individuals responsible for the most atrocious mass violence in human history. That permanence offers an opportunity to build a global culture of balanced enforcement of law.

Ending Individual Impunity

One of the primary purposes of the state is to monopolize the use of force and, in so doing, to provide security for its inhabitants. That much has been understood since Thomas Hobbes wrote *Leviathan* in the 17th century.[4] Indeed, the state has proved to be such a successful form of political organization that we now live in a world that is dominated by states. The violence witnessed in failed or weak states, like Somalia, Rwanda, or Colombia, should remind us that the security function of the modern state is still a valuable one. But the security provided by states has also come at a terrible price. Violence committed in the name of states has proved horrifically destructive.

There is an old piece of wisdom that says if you murder one person, you are likely to go to jail; but if you murder thousands (or millions) you are likely to be recognized as an important political leader. For too long now, the world has lived with this terrible irony of the state system of political organization. Leaders such as Stalin, Hitler, and Pol Pot were effectively immune from accountability for their crimes. State authority limits the resort to violence by other actors, but violence perpetrated by state authority, or by groups seeking to gain control over a state, has been difficult to control through rule of law mechanisms. The fiction of state corporate responsibility historically shielded political leaders from accountability for violent crimes carried out *in the name of a state*. The individuals responsible for many instances of mass violence escaped accountability because they acted on behalf of states. States could punish other states through war or other sanctions, but particular individuals who acted in the name of the state routinely escaped criminal punishment.

International humanitarian law, the Convention on the Prevention and Punishment of the Crime of Genocide of 1948, the Convention Against Torture and other Cruel, Inhuman or Degrading Treatment or Punishment of 1984, and other law-building achievements of the 20th century represent an effort to reign in the worst excesses of state-sponsored violence. However, the fact that leaders of states must ultimately punish themselves or their subordinates limits the effectiveness of these treaties. States have been too unwilling, for a variety of political reasons, to ensure that these developing rules of the international community are consistently enforced.

Temporary international criminal tribunals have been established in the past on a few occasions. The tribunals at Nuremberg and Tokyo created the precedent that international criminal law can be enforced by states against the leadership of other states. However, these courts have only been established in fairly unique circumstances, when powerful outsiders have perceived an immediate interest in bringing individuals to justice (Bass 2000). During the Cold War, the limits of that formula became obvious. War crimes committed by the powerful went unchallenged. On the other hand, the international community frequently ignored international crimes committed in the world's periphery, especially when the victims were not the citizens of powerful states. The ad hoc tribunals for the former Yugoslavia and Rwanda reinvigorated the mechanism of international criminal justice, but because their jurisdiction was limited to the conflicts in these two areas, they could not deal with future crimes in other parts of the world.

If a criminal norm is widely recognized, it is valid even if not always enforced. But ad hoc tribunals are too inconsistent to persuade doubters that the norms are really universal principles and not just propaganda of the powerful punishing the defeated. The claim that the enforcement of international criminal law is the implementation of universal principles *is inherently suspect* when courts are imposed on conflict-torn societies by powerful outsiders.

If the ICC is cautious and judicious in handling its first several cases, there is every reason to believe it will result in the successful punishment of at least some of the worst violators of international criminal law. Over time, there is reason to expect that this will lead to a transformational change in the importance of the laws of war. Instead of the laws of war being a discourse entered into by warmaking states to justify their own actions and condemn those of their enemies, international humanitarian law has the potential to become a regularly enforced criminal standard. The crucial advantage of the ICC is its permanence. As a standing judicial institution, it does not require the tremendous initial investment of political resources that ad hoc courts require before they can deal with each situation. Moreover, as a standing institution, the ICC promises a permanent commitment to punish these crimes consistently, at least among the large group of states that have agreed to ratify the Rome Statute.

The idea of a supranational criminal court with the power to hold individuals responsible for war crimes, genocide, crimes against humanity, or other violations of international criminal law is an idea about how to modify the organization and conduct of international politics. The court's establishment represents a powerful change in the rules of state sovereignty because it creates a supranational judicial authority with the power to rule whether or not particular uses of force by state officials are criminal and sanctionable violations of international law. Since the establishment of the sovereign state system in Europe over 500 years ago, the rules of sovereignty have undergone more or less constant change. The establishment of the ICC represents another significant change in those sovereignty rules for the states that have agreed to ratify it.[5]

The notion that individuals can be held responsible for violations of international law challenges predominant conceptions of state sovereignty in international law and world politics. International law is generated by states, and is primarily a set of rules about how states are to interact with one another. Sovereign states, though, are an abstraction, ultimately composed of individual human beings. The concept of an international criminal court brings into full relief the debate about who is obligated under international law norms.

By creating an individual standard of accountability for violations of the laws of war, the ICC potentially places meaningful restrictions on the way states can employ organized violence. The four classes of crimes over which the ICC will have jurisdiction all involve international norms that restrict the way in which states can exercise the use of force. Holding individual state officials responsible for these crimes challenges the sovereign state's right to choose for itself when it will use force, unencumbered by outside political authorities. Historically, this fact was viewed as the major political hurdle to the establishment of a permanent ICC.

The establishment of the ICC places restrictions on states' ability to determine for themselves whether or not particular acts qualify as war crimes, crimes against humanity, or genocide. At times the absence of a clearly specified international criminal code has been seen as the major stumbling block to the very idea of trying international crimes in a court of law. There is no legislative body in the international system with the authority to define crimes. Both customary and treaty-based international law criminalize specific acts, but whether or not those crimes are sufficiently well specified so as to make them enforceable in a court of law was a recurring issue in discussions of the ICC before its establishment. States have traditionally exercised a great deal of control over the content of international law, including the ability to determine in large part through custom what is considered a war crime and what is not. Aside from the few extraordinary ad hoc war crimes trials of the 20th century, enforcement of the criminal provisions of international humanitarian law was almost always carried out by national legal systems, in the rare cases when it happened at all.

Because the Rome Statute created a strong court that can avoid political interference in its work, it also constituted a significant judicial power to decide what counts as a "war crime" with only minimal and indirect supervision from sovereign states. Accordingly, the ICC weakens the sovereign state's hold on the process of determining the content of customary international law. The judges and prosecutor of the new court will have a role in defining the law they enforce as they begin to hear cases. The ICC is a permanent standing court, and the prosecutor, with the permission of judges of the pretrial chamber, is legally empowered to bring charges on his own authority.[6] This procedural independence means that decisions to prosecute are at least partially isolated from the political pressures of interstate politics.[7] Additionally, the drafting of the ICC statute and the specification of the Elements of Crimes after the adoption of the Rome Statute resulted in considerable elaboration of the particular kinds of acts that can constitute war crimes, crimes against humanity, and genocide. Accordingly, the ICC will play a role in giving practical meaning to the vague normative statements in international custom and treaty law that regulate the use of force.

Thus, the ICC reduces in significant ways the authority of the top officials of state governments. Making individuals the legal subjects of international law reduces the ability of state officials to hide their acts behind the state's corporate persona. Effective sanctions for violating international law norms may ultimately restrict state officials' ability and willingness to use force. Creating a judicial authority with the ability to interpret international law definitively reduces the ability of state officials to shape that law.

Why, then, did the leaders of over nearly 100 states agree to give up so much authority over the use of force and ratify their ICC statute? One crucial reason was pressure from the nonstate actors that now constitute an embryonic transnational civil society. As the subsequent analysis demonstrates, NGOs made communicatively rational arguments in favor of a strong effective court that ultimately were persuasive for the negotiators of the statute and the state decision makers who chose to sign and ratify the Rome Statute. It is perhaps not surprising that state officials would only pursue the ICC project under compelling pressure from this transnational civil society. Otherwise, the interests of state officials would appear to run strongly against the creation of a supranational criminal court. A crucial context for the effectiveness of these persuasive efforts was the repeated experience of peoples around the world with the excesses of state-sponsored violence in the 20th century. People and their leaders in Latin America, Africa, Asia, and across Eastern Europe are far too familiar with the forced disappearances, summary executions, and targeting of civilian populations that make up the crimes covered by the ICC's jurisdiction. It was this historical context, the reality of the repeated experience with these crimes, that gave the NGOs arguments in favor of a strong ICC resonance.

Many violent acts that history has witnessed in the last 150 years are so morally abhorrent that states ultimately made the choice at Rome to establish a strong court that could deal with them in the hope that it would serve as a deterrent. Michael Perry cites accounts of some particularly terrible cases of man's inhumanity to his fellow beings to dispel the argument that standards of what is morally acceptable are hopelessly relative (Perry 1998, pp. 61–4). Mass atrocities occur that are so barbaric that no broad-based cultural tradition, legal system, or religious code would characterize them as being socially acceptable.[8] Importantly for the establishment of the ICC, such horrific acts have motivated the vast majority of states to accept the modification of their own sovereignty that is inherent in an ICC. Joining the ICC means states give to a new international institution the prospective power to punish international law crimes. This is not a power states would readily have created if the need to deal with the problem of impunity were not real. Of course, there are moral and normative disagreements around the world about the importance of particular elements at the margins of the definitions of war crimes or crimes against humanity. Still, with respect to the core acts that the ICC can punish, such as violent attacks on civilian populations, executions or torture of captured and wounded soldiers, and rape as a tool to terrorize civilian populations, there is a broad-based global consensus that such actions are highly reprehensible and should be punished vigorously.

The ICC statute was drafted and ratified with substantial input from NGOs. Their participation contributed to a statute that embodies a set of rules that are fair and potentially effective. They developed their own arguments about the legal details of how a court should be created and whom it should prosecute. Because their discourse was oriented toward creating a court that would be a truly universal institution, without making any compromises to protect the interests of powerful states, their arguments were ultimately persuasive and compelling for the vast number of national delegations. Many of those national delegations representing minor powers and developing countries had little time to study all the issues and get up to speed on the tactical moves being pursued by the powerful states. But because smaller states had access to the NGOs' legal analysis, the arguments presented by the NGO coalition carried the day.

I argue that the NGOs were successful because of the nature of their normative discourse. That discourse was oriented toward finding a normative solution to the problem of individual impunity in the Westphalian state system that could be universally justified. As analysts, we must be careful not to overstate, nor to understate, the role of NGOs as agents in this case or others like it. The leaders of the NGO coalition for an ICC self-consciously sought to bring about fundamental change in some of the most enduring institutions of international politics, including the traditional rules of sovereignty, which allow states to use force to maintain their internal control over territory and their external independence from other political authorities. Such long-standing institutional practices cannot easily be modified.

After a long period of scholarly neglect, the phenomenon of discursive persuasion based on reasons in world politics has received increased attention in recent years (N. Crawford 2002; Hawkins 2004).[9] Crawford has written a comprehensive book on the subject, laying the theoretical groundwork for analyzing the role of ethical argument in world politics through an exhaustive study of the key role played by ethical argument in the global processes of abolition and decolonization. Hawkins's contribution focuses on the idea that arguments that draw on widely accepted norms can be persuasive, as they were in the case of debates about the adoption of the UN Convention against Torture. Typically, most political analysis assumes that power resources and material interests drive outcomes. Those factors were not absent from the negotiations on the establishment of the ICC, but the persuasive campaign by pro-ICC NGOs influenced the drafting of the statute and ratification process in many states. By studying another case where the substance of discursive arguments had a decisive impact on the outcome, this study builds on our understanding of the circumstances where persuasive argument matters and also expands our knowledge of the dynamics of influential arguments.

In the balance of this introduction, I describe the major features of the ICC that was established on July 1, 2002, following the ratification of over 60 states. Then I will outline the plan of the book.

Features of the ICC

The International Criminal Court was established by a multilateral treaty negotiated by the representatives of sovereign states.[10] As such, it is not an organ of the UN,[11] nor is it functionally a part of any other international organization, although the court does give particular privileges to various UN organs. The treaty, normally referred to as the Rome Statute for the International Criminal Court, like any treaty, is only binding on those states that have formally ratified it. The Rome Statute establishes the court and gives it jurisdiction over persons "for the most serious crimes of international concern" as provided for in the terms of the treaty (Article 1). It also gives the court international legal personality (Article 4).

The Rome Statute gives the court jurisdiction over the crimes of genocide, crimes against humanity, and war crimes, and it specifically defines those crimes (Articles 5–8). It also gives the ICC jurisdiction over the crime of aggression, but only if and when states agree to a definition of that crime via an amendment to the ICC statute (Article 5). Such an amendment would need to be ratified or accepted by seven-eighths of the states that are ICC members before it would come into effect, and cannot be formally considered until July 2009 (Articles 121 and 123). This procedure could also be used to add additional crimes to the jurisdiction of the court in the future.

Part IV of the Rome Statute (Articles 34–52) provides for the election of 18 judges, a prosecutor, and a deputy prosecutor by the Assembly of States Parties to the ICC. The Registrar of the court is elected by the judges (Article 43). The Assembly of States Parties is composed of a representative from each of the states that ratified the Rome Statute. The Assembly's organization and administrative powers over the other organs of the court are described in Part 11 of the statute (Articles 112–118).

The jurisdiction of the court is complementary to the jurisdiction of national courts, which also presumably have the authority to prosecute the international law crimes covered by the Rome Statute (Preamble, Article 1). This concept for the jurisdiction of the court was labeled "complementarity" during the ICC negotiations. Complementarity means simply that the court's jurisdiction overlaps with that of national courts, without allowing the supranational court to act as an appellate court for domestic criminal trials. In general, a case is inadmissible before the ICC if it is being investigated or prosecuted by a state with jurisdiction, "unless the State is unwilling or unable genuinely to carry out the investigation or prosecution (Article 17)." In other words, the ICC normally must defer to trials by states in their domestic legal systems. The ICC is limited to handling cases that national courts fail to prosecute. The ICC statute adopts the traditional legal norm against double jeopardy; therefore the ICC will not hear cases in which a domestic court has already rendered a not guilty verdict, unless it can be shown that the domestic trial was a show trial intended to shield the accused (Articles 17 and 20). The statute does give the ICC judges the authority to determine whether or not a state is genuinely willing and able to prosecute and, therefore, whether or not the ICC prosecutor can investigate any particular case (Articles 18 and 19). This relationship between national courts and the ICC was critical to the willingness of states to establish a permanent ICC, and the exact specification of this relationship was a central issue in the negotiations. Later on we will focus on the politics of this arrangement in more detail.

The court can exercise its jurisdiction over the core crimes whenever they take place on the territory of a state that has ratified the statute or when the perpetrator carries the nationality of a state that has ratified the statute. Additionally, the court's statute allows the Security Council of the UN to refer cases when they take place anywhere in the world, using its powers to regulate international peace and security under Chapter 7 of the UN Charter. Significantly, the Rome Statute does not grant the ICC universal jurisdiction over genocide or any of the other crimes, even though the 1948 Genocide Convention does give state courts the authority to prosecute that crime regardless of where in the world it occurs. The ICC can only exercise its jurisdiction if a state party refers a situation where crimes have allegedly occurred to the prosecutor, the Security Council makes such a referral, or the prosecutor has information indicating that crimes within the jurisdiction of the court have been committed and he receives authorization from the pretrial chamber of judges to open an investigation (Articles 13, 14, and 15).

The ICC only has jurisdiction over crimes that were committed after the Rome Statute entered into force on July 1, 2002 (Article 11).

The foregoing are some of the major features of the ICC. Overall, it must be said that the ICC statute grants considerable authority to the supranational court it creates. During the ICC negotiations, many widely different proposals were considered. Much of the analysis that follows is directed toward understanding why the court was established with these provisions and not others that some participants would have favored.

Plan of the Book

To understand the politics of the construction of the International Criminal Court we must account for the success of nongovernmental organizations in securing support for a strong, independent court. I document the process through which NGOs' discursive practices shaped the content of the Rome Statute by analyzing the arguments surrounding the treaty negotiations and ratification process. The central finding is that NGOs' use of principled discourse appealing to notions of fundamental fairness was persuasive during the ICC negotiations. The ICC was established with a strong independent prosecutor and jurisdiction that states cannot refuse on a case-by-case basis, features that few observers expected states to accept before 1998. This project makes a significant contribution to our understanding of processes of norm change and institution formation in world politics and the role of nonstate actors in those processes. Methodologically, I adopt a constructivist approach employing process tracing and discourse analysis rooted in the theory of communicative action.

This introductory chapter described the main features of the ICC and offered an assessment of the meaning of this new court for global governance. The ICC is a significant modification of state sovereignty norms. For the first time, states granted permanent authority to a supranational institution to determine when individuals have violated international humanitarian law. Additionally, this chapter identified the major controversial issues inherent in establishing such a supranational court and considered the many reasons why state leaders were initially reluctant to pursue such a project.

This introduction is a preliminary step toward answering the initial question that motivated this research: How did it happen that so many states were willing to cede such substantial authority to an international tribunal?

Chapter 2 outlines the theoretical, ontological, and methodological approaches employed in the research. Consistent with the constructivist methods employed, this work also adopts a constructivist ontological understanding of world politics: the social world is constituted by the use of language and the elaboration of intersubjective beliefs. I also situate my approach with respect to other understandings of the development and change of international institutions, including regime theory, neoliberal institutionalist approaches, sociological institutionalism, and critical theory. In particular I review the use of the concepts of norms and institutions in the international relations (IR) literature. Finally I discuss my approach to actor agency, which is rooted in the theory of communicative action as developed by Jürgen Habermas (1984; 1996) and Robert Alexy (1989), and as applied to world politics by Friedrich Kratochwil (1989) and Thomas Risse (2000). Communicative action is distinguished from strategic action as a strategy for human action oriented toward reaching shared understandings.

The method applied to analyzing discourse about the ICC involves establishing criteria for distinguishing between discursive moves that are forms of action oriented toward reaching mutual understandings as opposed to discursive practices focused on achieving strategic objectives. The project contributes to the literature on the foundations of international cooperation by demonstrating the role that nonstate actors can play in the discursive development of shared norms, which in this case served as the principled foundations for a new international institution. Continued resistance to the ICC by the United States and others shows the limits of such principled consensus but does not negate the cooperative achievement attained by the ICC member states and the success of pro-ICC actors in institutionalizing their normative preferences.

Chapter 3 analyzes the discourse about establishing a permanent international criminal tribunal from the time of the Nuremberg trials through the International Law Commission's (ILC's) decision in 1953 to suspend further discussion of the issue. The objections raised to ICC proposals in this early debate highlight the difficulties that would be faced by ICC negotiators again in the 1990s. In the context of the early Cold War, states were simply unwilling to contemplate binding, third-party decision making at the international level regarding whether or not particular acts were war crimes, acts of aggression, or genocide.

Chapter 4 begins with a discussion of the political context in which the ICC debate was reborn. The ILC produced a conservative draft charter for an ICC in 1993 that envisioned a court with fewer powers than the one ultimately established in 2002. I also analyze the various pathways toward establishing an ICC that were discussed by ICC interlocutors at the time. This serves as a baseline for Chapter 5, which analyzes the discursive practices of NGOs in terms of the criteria of communicative and strategic action. I show that certain *topoi*, or "seats of arguments," became foundational assumptions that were ultimately shared by most of the ICC debate participants in the four years before the Rome conference. Often these topoi were advanced first in policy papers by international NGOs. These principles became the foundation for an ICC debate that closely approximated the ideal type of a communicatively rational discourse. I identify NGO proposals on particular features of the ICC and show how these proposals shaped the direction of the interstate negotiations prior to the Rome conference in 1998.

Chapter 6 focuses on the negotiations in the crucial year when the final text of the ICC statute was negotiated and opened for signature. In the months prior to the Rome conference, held in June and July 1998, the ICC negotiations took on a sense of increased urgency and gained increased attention. I describe particular discursive moves by states and NGOs during this period and categorize them as being forms of communicative or strategic action. I show that the communicatively rational arguments advanced by NGOs and some states were increasingly persuasive to those involved in the ICC debates. In contrast, strategically oriented discursive moves that rejected the principled topoi established in the earlier phase of the discourse tended to be rejected by most participants in the negotiations. Often it was powerful states such as the United States, France, and China that made such strategic moves. The result was tremendously broad support for a strong ICC that embraced nearly all of the pro-ICC NGOs' principled goals. The final ICC statute made very few concessions to powerful states, even when these states claimed the new court threatened their strategic interests. This chapter also assesses the conditions that contributed to the success of communicatively rational discursive strategies that were most frequently employed by NGOs. In so doing it contributes to our understanding of the mechanisms through which NGOs impact world politics.

Chapter 7 analyzes NGOs' role in the campaign for prompt ratification of the ICC statute from a global perspective. Since delegates to the Rome conference adopted a strong treaty with far-reaching authority, many observers anticipated that it would languish with few ratifications for decades or more. Instead it achieved the necessary 60 ratifications in less than four years and entered into force on July 1, 2002. The continued use of principled arguments by NGOs during ratification debates in capitals around the world contributed to this outcome. This chapter provides examples of such communicatively rational discursive moves by NGOs and shows how they shaped ratification debates in parliaments and governments in several illustrative cases.

In Chapter 8 I discuss the normative legitimacy of the ICC in light of its major features and the processes that brought it into existence. Because international organizations are composed of state governments, they often are not responsive to nonstate actors such as human rights groups. The effectiveness of NGOs during the ICC negotiations suggests the possibility that at least under some circumstances, NGO voices can ameliorate the legitimacy crisis of the institutions of global governance.

Ad hoc efforts to enforce international criminal law in the wake of mass killings have by definition occurred only irregularly and consequently have struggled to establish the legitimacy of the normative order they seek to enforce. The ICC stands in a considerably stronger position to gain worldwide respect and legitimacy. Partly this is because it is a permanent court. Like all courts, if it successfully settles outstanding disputes, it will add to its own authority (Stone Sweet 1999). But most importantly, the rules, procedures, and crimes embodied in the ICC statute are the result of a broadly consensual, rational, communicative discourse. As a result, those norms are deserving of rational assent as norms that ought to be enforced and defended. This is the strength of the ICC.

The final chapter brings together the major conclusions from this research. The ICC represents the most substantial effort in human history to institutionalize individual criminal responsibilities for atrocities committed by state leaders during interstate warfare or civil conflicts. This is a step that state governments only took under normative pressure from global civil society actors. The analysis in this book demonstrates the potential for NGOs to contribute to the establishment of strengthened institutions for global governance. Creating institutions that promote the rule of law at the global level will only succeed in building peace if those institutions are widely perceived as legitimate, and the broad inclusion of NGOs in interstate negotiations is one pathway toward developing that global legitimacy.

Formally, states created the ICC. The Rome Statute of the ICC is a multilateral treaty negotiated by the representatives of states. Administratively, the ICC's governing body is the Assembly of States Parties made up of states that have ratified the ICC treaty (Rome Statute Article 112). Yet NGOs played a crucial role in the discourse surrounding the drafting and negotiating of the ICC statute's text (Benedetti and Washburn 1999; Pace and Thieroff 1999). This book examines the strategies used by NGOs to insert themselves into the process of conceiving, drafting, ratifying, and implementing the ICC statute. In what follows I describe the way that NGOs' discursive strategies shaped the elaboration of the ICC statute and the campaign for the statute's ratification. By accounting for NGO success in this case, I highlight the conditions that allowed nonstate actors to play this role and build inferences about other issue areas where nonstate actors might play a similar role in developing the norms of global governance.

2

Norm Contestation in World Politics: Civil Society, States, and Discourse

And henceforth, the only honorable course will be to stake everything on a formidable gamble: that words are more powerful than munitions.

—Albert Camus, *"Neither Victims nor Executioners"*[1]

Questions

How do the norms of world politics change? How can new norms come to be institutionalized? This book examines the political process of norm contestation and development. Norms are contested both through discourse and through practice. Norms govern virtually every aspect of human behavior, including the conduct of world politics.

Many political scientists now recognize that nongovernmental organizations have entered the norm modification and transformation game through their discursive practices (Keck and Sikkink 1998). What is less well understood is why some NGO discourses are particularly persuasive and effective, whereas others are not. What is the nature of powerful discourse? Under what conditions is discourse powerful? Whose voices are powerful and whose are marginalized? These are crucial questions at the forefront of the constructivist research agenda for understanding the ways that nonstate actors can shape the normative structure of international politics.

My research shows that NGO discursive practices shaped the Rome Statute for the ICC. NGO advocacy also played a crucial role in securing the entry into force of that treaty less than four years after it was negotiated. Through careful analysis using process tracing, this book develops an understanding of the nature of these discursive practices in an effort to account for their surprising influence on the development of the permanent ICC.[2]

The establishment of the ICC is a case where we can see clear and fairly rapid change in the norms for dealing with the perpetrators of mass atrocities in the world political system. It is also a case where NGOs, through their discursive practices, have played a crucial role in shaping the content of emerging norms. Through a thick description of the negotiating history and public debate, I analyze the parameters surrounding the deployment of NGOs' discursive strategies to establish the reasons for NGO effectiveness in this case.[3]

The impact of NGO discourse on the ICC is profoundly significant because it shows that transnationally organized NGOs can play a role in determining what ends states pursue and, consequently, what outcomes are produced in the international system. This raises some major issues for our understandings of world politics. Under what conditions can global civil society play such a decisive role in shaping preferences and, ultimately, outcomes? States remain central actors in the world political system. But to the extent that the ends states pursue can be transformed by a normative consensus developed by actors from global civil society, analysts of world politics would be ill advised to take the perspective that states' interests and actions are the only important drivers of outcomes.

I account for the efficacy of NGOs through an analysis of their discursive practices and the interactions of those discourses with the wider discourse on the ICC. This project adopts a Weberian view of social science epistemology. From that perspective, the task for social science is to understand the historical context and contingent meaning of particular actions (Ruggie 1998, Ch. 1). As Ruggie notes, a crucial aspect of that task is to identify ideational factors that are *reasons for actions* as compared with *causes of actions* (ibid., p. 22; see also Kratochwil 1989, Ch. 1). Accordingly, I utilize a constructivist methodology in conducting this research (Klotz and Lynch 2007). The core advantage of this approach is the explicit recognition that the social world is composed of intersubjectively constituted social facts. The fact of intersubjectivity is particularly important because of the focus in this research on analyzing institutional change. Institutions themselves are intersubjectively constituted and continually renewed (Powell and DiMaggio 1991; Ruggie 1998, pp. 45–6).

Raymond Martin has noted that the way one portrays subjectivity, agency, and meaning "importantly influences the meaning [one] finds in events, [and] even which whats and whys get mentioned in an interpretation" (Martin 1997, p. 13). The goal of an interpretivist historian or social scientist must be focused then on interpretation and meaning and agency and subjectivity in a way that positivist approaches to scientific method born out of the physical sciences cannot be. Accordingly, then, accounting for the emergence of the particular ICC embodied in the Rome Statute that entered into force on July 1, 2002, is really only one side of the project undertaken here. In order to understand the agency of the individuals involved in establishing the ICC, I discuss the meaning of the ICC for these actors and their own self-understandings of the project they undertook.

While constructivists have used a variety of conceptual strategies for attacking the problem of intersubjectivity (Klotz and Lynch 2007), I will focus on an analysis of discourse. This choice follows from Friedrich Kratochwil's claim that an intersubjective grounding for rule systems can be guided by discursive practices that recognize the rationality of "the other" and the universality of metanorms such as "do no harm" (Kratochwil 1989). Kratochwil's efforts to understand the influence of norms in world politics are based on theoretical work by Habermas to understand the legitimacy of norms as arising out of free communication among all of those affected by the norms (Guibentif 1996, pp. 55–9). The founding of legal systems such as the ICC then turns on reaching intersubjective agreement about how such vague metanorms can be applied to specific human circumstances. How did an intersubjective international discourse lead to support for an ICC on the basis of universally recognized norms?

My strategy is to analyze NGO discourses by reconstructing as nearly as possible their meaning in historical context. Analyzing NGOs' discursive practices allows us to account for NGO success in shaping the statute. My central claim is that NGO use of principled discourse appealing to notions of fundamental fairness was persuasive during the ICC negotiations. NGO participation in the ICC dialogue was instrumental in securing a limited but powerful and potentially effective ICC. The court's statute adopts early proposals from the NGO community on a number of issues that were contentious during the ICC debate.

Later on I offer a discussion of the methods I employ in conducting the analysis of the discursive practices of NGOs. Here I offer only a brief illustration of what I mean by the claim that the use of discourse, which appealed to notions of fundamental fairness, was decisive.

NGOs' normative analysis of various proposals for the design of the ICC focused on the likely consequences of particular arrangements for the new court. They insisted that proposals had to be justified in terms of their fairness and effectiveness at achieving justice. The judges and prosecutors of the new ICC have significant powers to determine whether or not particular events can be classified as serious violations of international criminal law. The sovereign rights of states are not decimated by the ICC statute. But they are transformed. States remain primarily responsible for enforcing international criminal law under the complementarity provisions of the ICC statute. But in order to ensure that serious atrocities would not continue to go unpunished because the relevant states were unwilling or unable to act, states accepted that the new international institution should have substantial powers.[4] NGOs were key advocates of these provisions. The ICC is a permanent standing court, and the prosecutor, with the permission of judges of the pretrial chamber, is authorized to bring charges on his or her own authority.[5] This procedural independence means that decisions to prosecute are at least partially isolated from the short-term political pressures of interstate politics.[6] States' behaviors in constructing an ICC with these powers can only be understood in the context of NGO discourse.

The outcome of the Rome ICC treaty conference was driven by a discourse that was oriented toward creating the widest possible normative consensus to support the new court. The relatively disinterested nature of NGOs allowed them to shape and contribute to this discourse in a way that was morally resonant; consequently, they were influential. Of course, the leaders and members of NGOs may have private interests, such as increasing group membership and funding, individual career motivations, or personal friendships that motivate particular courses of action. Still, NGOs do not decide public policies on their own accord, in national or international fora. This simple fact means that in order for NGOs to be effective, they must persuade other decision makers, and consequently, they are uniquely disposed toward giving reasons that logically support their preferred outcomes.[7]

Pro-ICC NGOs oriented their discursive practices toward a universal audience by promoting a court that corresponded with notions of fundamental fairness. In contrast, state governments often are constrained from taking such a universal stance by the need to be responsive to particular interest groups in their national political contexts. During the debate on the Rome Statute, many participants understood that they were creating a judicial institution that could potentially endure for generations. In that context, the NGOs' choice of a rational, universally oriented discursive strategy was particularly successful.[8]

Antonio Franceschet has noted that the responsiveness of international organizations to the justice claims of nonstate actors is frequently poor, since those organizations are nearly always based on statist organizing principles (Franceshet 2002). The effectiveness of NGOs during the ICC negotiations suggests the possibility that at least under some circumstances, NGO voices can ameliorate the legitimacy crisis of the institutions of global governance. But caution is warranted; the circumstances that led to successful NGO input into the drafting of the Rome Statute were somewhat unique and may be difficult to replicate in other issue areas. For example, in the technically complex policy area of global climate change, Gupta (2004) notes that sometimes the cacophony of NGO commentaries on the official statements of governments during multilateral negotiations may lead to information overload rather than clarity.[9] I do suggest, however, that the successful work of NGOs in shaping the Rome Statute for the ICC provides a model for a way that NGOs might attempt to play a similar role in other international issue areas, thereby increasing the range of voices that are heard during interstate negotiations. Accordingly, one of the goals of this project is to describe and analyze as completely as possible the conditions that led to the success of NGO discourse in this case so that we can identify other situations in which a similarly principled discourse might be effective.

Limits of the Neoliberal Model

Neoliberal models of international cooperation focus on explaining the reasons why states with partially complementary interests sometimes create international regimes (Baldwin 1993). The Rome Statute cannot be accounted for with these models. Such state interests are normally assumed to be stable, self-evident, and exogenous to the political process of building cooperation. However, there are limitations to such an approach (Ruggie 1998, pp. 13–4). In order to understand why an ICC was created and supported by over 100 states in the late 1990s, even though states had rejected the idea previously, we have to account for the change in states' preferences. Since both neorealist and neoliberal approaches either assume state preferences[10] or identify them tautologically as "revealed preferences," those models cannot account for the shift in the way that states viewed international humanitarian law that led to the Rome Treaty conference.

Moreover, the ICC, as it is embodied in the 1998 Rome Statute, cannot be understood as a conventional intergovernmental organization. Instead, it creates a permanent supranational judicial institution with the power to enforce international criminal law. Predominant views of international politics assume that international rules and norms will be particularly ineffectual in the domain of regulating the use of force by states, given the anarchical nature of relations between states. If one assumes that international politics is fundamentally about often violent relations between sovereign states (Morgenthau 1948), then the construction of an ICC is a puzzling anomaly. Only by breaking with a statist ontology and examining the agency of individual actors is it possible to account for the emergence of an ICC.

State of the Art on Understanding Norms

This book develops an understanding of the processes through which norms of global governance become institutionalized in world politics. Social norms interpenetrate every aspect of social life, and world politics is no exception (Giddens 1984; Searle 1995). IR scholarship now broadly recognizes that the anarchical pattern of relations between states does not mean that norms are unimportant in world affairs (Bull 1977; Buzan 2004; Falk, Kratochwil, and Mendlovitz 1985, pp. 45–6). Norms shape the behavior of all types of actors, and simultaneously, some actors consciously promote certain understandings of what behaviors are socially acceptable with a view toward promoting political goals. In recent years scholars have paid greater attention to the role of norms in world politics. But conceptualizing norms and their role in social life has proved to be exceptionally complex. The role of norms has been studied at various levels of analysis. As scholars have attempted to understand the emerging patterns in global governance, a series of vital questions have emerged about how norms impact political outcomes. These questions include how and when norms influence actor behavior, and how "norm entrepreneurs" promote norm change with varying degrees of success (Keck and Sikkink 1998; Risse-Kappen, Ropp, and Sikkink 1999). It is of critical importance that scholars understand what norms are shaping world politics today, how competing norms interact, and which actors are influential in shaping normative standards.

Ontology

In order to analyze norm change in world politics, we need to begin with an understanding of the ontological foundations of social life. Social collectivities such as states, universities, and corporations are an undeniable element of our lives. Such collectivities are composed of individual human beings, and yet they seem to take on a life that goes beyond that of their individual component members. Even though we know that such structures or social institutions could not exist without the actions of individuals, from the perspective of any single individual (even governors, chancellors, and CEOs), such institutions appear to exist independently and largely beyond our control. These structures of social life both enable and constrain human agency, and simultaneously they only exist as they are re-created through human agency (Giddens, 1984, pp. 1–29). This is the famous agent-structure problem in the social sciences. People are agents in the always ongoing reconstruction of the social world around them, but their agency and autonomy are also always constrained in important ways by existing social structures.

John Searle, the philosopher of language and mind, has developed the concept of social facts first elaborated by Emile Durkheim. Social facts are beliefs about the nature of the world that are shared by two or more people. This property of intersubjectivity gives an aspect of concreteness to people's otherwise subjective beliefs (Searle 1995, pp. 1–29). If a number of people believe something to be true, that fact will have real social consequences for other individuals, *notwithstanding the fact that those beliefs are simply "beliefs" inside the heads of other individuals.*[11]

Searle develops a subclass of social facts that he defines as "institutional facts," which exist when human beings assign status functions or constitutive rules to some phenomena in a way that goes beyond the physicality of the phenomena themselves (Searle, 1995, pp. 31 57). Thus, institutional facts have a deontic status, meaning they create "rights, responsibilities, obligations, duties, privileges, entitlements, penalities, authorizations, permissions, and other such deontic phenomena" (Searle 1995, p. 100).

The deontic status of institutional facts provides reasons for action that are independent of our individual inclinations. The rights and obligations created by institutional facts only exist if people believe they exist, and they function as reasons only if people accept them as reasons (Searle 1995, pp. 62–3). Norms of world politics are exactly this sort of institutional fact. And the norms institutionalized as the ICC are particularly significant as emergent institutional facts because they constitute roles for prosecutors and judges to punish violations of the relevant norms of international criminal law.

By understanding norms in this way, I am deliberately taking sides in a now long-standing debate about the nature of international regimes and the most appropriate way of studying them (Krasner 1983). I am persuaded by Ruggie's argument that the most satisfactory understandings of the origins and functions of international institutions in world politics will take as a starting point the intersubjective nature of these phenomena. Importantly, once one accepts that ontology, the most appropriate epistemological approach is interpretive rather than positivist (Ruggie 1998, pp. 85–101).

Norms have been defined in a variety of ways. A frequently employed definition says norms "describe collective expectations for the proper behavior of actors with a given identity" (Katzenstein 1996, p. 5; Keck and Sikkink 1998, p. 3; see also Klotz 1995, p. 14).

Norms can be analyzed at a variety of different levels of abstraction. Specific norms are grounded in more general norms, which in turn are grounded in appeals to metanorms, such as "equality," "justice," or "liberty." New norms, progressive or otherwise, modify or replace existing norms; they are not created from nothing. The strongest conceptualizations of norms recognize that norm change involves competition between different normative frames that are advocated by competing actors (N. Crawford 2002).

International legal norms are a formal subset of all the norms that influence world politics. This study is concerned with the development and change of both international legal norms and the broader set of informal norms that exist outside of international law. In international politics, there are a series of procedures for formally codifying norms through treaties, informal agreements to cooperate, the resolutions of international organizations, and judicial decisions. These practices give some norms an explicitly legal character. But just as important, there are less formal expectations for behavior in the international realm that also shape the nature of world politics. One way that norms become embedded is when institutional structures are put in place that create officials who then have to engage in enforcing norms as part of their formal duties. This is one important aspect of the institutionalization of the international criminal law embodied in the ICC.

Why do some prospective norms resonate in the context of a rational discourse, while others do not? Kratochwil has noted that norms fulfill three interdependent functions in society. Norms "'rul[e]-out' certain methods of individual goal seeking" (1989, p. 70) by prohibiting some kinds of conduct, thereby bounding conflict. Second, they create rule systems for the individual or joint use of scarce resources. Third, norms enable parties with conflicting goals to engage in a discourse on their grievance in order to negotiate a settlement or submit the conflict to third-party resolution based on principles and rules (Kratochwil 1989, p. 70).

The ICC is an effort to develop all three types of rules. The treaty codifies forbearances against some of the most heinous acts of violence in world politics—genocide, war crimes, and crimes against humanity—in ways that are consistent with existing international criminal law. The ICC is a scheme for managing the limited resources that the international community is willing to spend on international tribunals in the wake of the experience with the United Nations ad hoc tribunals for Rwanda and the former Yugoslavia.[12] Finally, the ICC also codifies a set of procedures for prosecuting individual offenders in a way that is designed to limit and regulate future disagreements between states about whether or not particular individual prosecutions should be allowed to go forward and which court should exercise jurisdiction.

Criminalizing certain kinds of violent acts at the level of global politics is constitutive of global society. Kratochwil observed that norms against lying, norms against violence, norms against breaking promises, and norms governing property rights have been viewed historically as "natural law" by thinkers like Pufendorf. Other theorists, such as Hume, or more recently, Hedley Bull, have seen these norms as minimum conditions for social life (Kratochwil 1989, p. 71). Of course, norms protecting the lives and freedom of diplomatic representatives have existed for a long time. These norms have offered a degree of protection to the society of international diplomats. But the group of persons protected by the prohibitions against genocide, crimes against humanity, and war crimes is far broader, protecting all of the world's people from certain kinds of political violence. Thus, the ICC is indicative of a larger transformation in world politics, a broadening from an "international society" of diplomats to a truly global society of the world's citizens.[13]

Political scientists sometimes try to explain the existence of norms in purely utilitarian terms. This is inadequate, as Habermas and Kratochwil note. As Durkheim first began to describe, in modern societies, the prescriptive force of norms is justified as a claim to legitimacy that can be redeemed discursively (Kratochwil 1989, p. 97). Kratochwil's analysis demonstrates persuasively that the prescriptive force of norms depends on the degree to which those norms can be justified through rational argument (1989, Ch. 4). The theory of communicative action developed by Habermas and others provides a framework for understanding such discursive practices and the grounds for considering that some normative claims are more valid than others.

Of course, it is also possible to develop a system of rules in which the required conduct is compelled through an appeal to force, and rules are simply imposed on people who are subject to those rules. But in such a case, no justification can be made for the legitimacy of the imposed rule set. In the messy universe of world politics, international rules and norms, to the extent they are enforced at all, are implemented through a mixture of appeals to normative legitimacy and the imposition of superior brute force. In the discussion about establishing a new permanent international tribunal to enforce international criminal law, a core set of actors deliberately chose to pursue the establishment of a court that could be justified to the greatest possible extent on rational grounds and not primarily on an appeal to force. In that context, negotiations over particular treaty provisions had to be grounded in principled normative reasons.

Why should this be the case? I review Kratochwil's understanding of the conditions that permit normative discourses on grievances between human beings in order to show what is meant by the notion of advancing "principled arguments" about the development of the international criminal legal system. His analysis demonstrates that in order to have a discourse about grievances, the participants must first accept the universalization of their claims (Kratochwil 1989, p. 142). If I claim the right not to be treated in a certain way, there is an implicit promise that I will not in the future treat others in the same way. But this universalization is not in and of itself sufficient; some substantive content must be added. The parties in the dispute must have sufficient equality of status to allow them to plead their cases on their merits rather than via an imposition of force or other superior resources. Finally, the participants in the discourse must share some substantive moral values at the start, which the simple rule of the categorical imperative cannot by itself provide. This is in effect the Habermasian notion of a "lifeworld" that provides the background conditions for a communicatively rational discussion of facts *or* values. Kratochwil suggests some of the principles identified by Pufendorf as "laws of nature."[14] These include that (1) no one should hurt another, (2) people should treat each other as equals, and (3) people should offer help to others when they are reasonably able to do so (Kratochwil 1989, pp. 140–1). These criteria provide grounds on which is possible to have a discourse about the validity of norms. They *do not* lead to preordained outcomes but do suggest rules that permit some discourses to be marked out as rational, and Kratochwil shows that in practice these are necessary minimal conditions for a discourse on grievances.

In everyday social practice, people frequently discuss the validity of social norms. This is particularly true of legal norms, but arguments are also made to justify moral norms and informal norms. In practice it is possible to give reasons that are understood to justify or challenge the conclusion that a particular norm is valid in some society. In everyday experience people justify normative claims all the time. Consider the norm "it is justified to kill in self-defense if one's own life is threatened." In practical, everyday discourse it makes sense to assert that this is a "valid" norm and to give reasons for that claim.

For my purposes, namely, analyzing the discourse surrounding the negotiation and ratification of the Rome Statute for the ICC, the Habermasian framework is useful because it provides us with a theoretically well-grounded basis for evaluating the rationality of normative arguments. In the Method section beginning on page 30 I elaborate in more detail the methodological approach I will use to conduct the analysis of the ICC discourse in this book. At this point, the conceptualization of norms and normative discourse I will employ should be clear. Now we turn to the question of human agency and norm change.

Agency and Norm Change

Norms are sometimes maintained through habit or routine or unintended consequences of social organization. More often than it might appear at first glance, however, norm change and maintenance are the result of deliberate political action. I will pay particular attention to the role of agency in creating, sustaining, and reproducing norms. Different types of actors, including states, intergovernmental organizations, NGOs, media outlets, academics, religious leaders, and corporations sometimes play roles as norm entrepreneurs in world politics. Actors of each type experience widely varied degrees of success in norm promotion from one issue to another. Also, actors vary in the impact specific norms have on their behavior. Traditionally, the IR literature has tended to focus on norms that regulate state behavior. It has also focused on states as the primary promoters of norms (Bull 1977; Wendt 1999). Here I argue that this is a limiting perspective on the ontology of norms in world politics and make a case for a focus on individuals as the primary promoters of norms.[15] Looking beyond the issue of the ICC, such an ontology provides a better conception of the role of norms in world politics because it enhances our ability to empirically determine whether or not we have merely a society of states as described by Bull (1977) or if in fact a cosmopolitan global civil society is emerging (Wapner 2000). Recognizing that norms are ultimately created by and have an impact on individual people also opens up the possibility that political scientists can draw more directly on the insights of the social psychology literature on the role of norms in social life (Terry and Hogg 2000). Because the ICC involves holding individuals responsible for crimes under the law of nations, it is a particularly appropriate place to analyze the relationship between individuals and norms in world politics.

Why are NGOs powerful? What allows a small group of individuals representing organizations with only very modest budgets and small, often poorly compensated staffs to play such a definitive role in world politics? I argue that their power is a function of the fact that NGOs as corporate entities are primarily oriented to communicative action rather than strategic action (Habermas 1984). Habermas's conceptual apparatus is useful because it captures the unique orientation of NGOs. Habermas has noted that in modern secular society social integration depends on communicative action oriented toward a rational justification for normative rules; however, strategic actors paradoxically are inhibited in their ability to pursue such a normative dialogue oriented to reaching understanding because of their constant tendency to perceive situations in terms of their strategic preferences (Habermas 1996, pp. 25–7). The NGO community that has advocated an ICC is oriented toward producing a normative system that can be justified as having universal validity. This has allowed NGOs to fulfill a role in generating a dialogue oriented toward reaching a universally justifiable understanding about the best way to enforce norms in international law, fulfilling a discursive need of modernity that Habermas identifies, namely, producing normatively acceptable consensuses.

According to Habermas, the legitimacy of modern legal systems hinges on two factors, as Guibentif summarizes:

> What is likely to produce legitimation on a macro-social level is the fact that public procedures are run on two distinct levels: through "legally constituted political will-formation" procedures, on the one hand, and in the "communicative flows of autonomous public spheres" on the other.
>
> (Guibentif 1996, p. 57)

Of course, in the international legal system, the "legally constituted political will-formation procedures" consist of the well-known sources of international law, including the negotiation and ratification of international treaties by the duly appointed representatives of sovereign states. The ICC was established through those legal procedures. My focus in this work is to examine the other side of the legitimation process that Habermas identifies as theoretically necessary social acceptance of legal norms, namely, "the communicative flows of autonomous public spheres." My claim is that those communicative flows in fact had a decisive impact on the outcome of the formal legal decision-making procedures.

Following a similar line of reasoning to that of Habermas, Boli and Thomas (1999) conceptualize the power of NGOs in terms of the authority carried in the emerging world society by volunteer experts who put forward rational arguments to advance their solutions to global political problems. They have begun to define the empirical terrain where scholars can begin to assess the role that NGOs are playing in world politics through the use of discursive power. Thomas and Boli state:

> The rational voluntaristic authority of [international] NGOs is demonstrably effective in some domains in some periods, but at this point we can say little about the factors that condition its effectiveness.
>
> (1999, p. 47)

Through a detailed examination of the NGOs' role in writing the Rome Statute, we can draw out the factors that mattered in enabling NGO success in this case.

The Construction of an International Criminal Court

How can we understand why a statute for a permanent International Criminal Court was drafted and adopted for ratification in 1998? I argue that a crucial factor leading to the adoption of the Rome Statute was the development of a normative discourse between nongovernmental organizations, lawyers, academics, international civil servants, and states. In many respects it was the NGOs, and not state governments, that predominantly shaped the content of the Rome Statute. The outcome of the Rome ICC Treaty Conference was driven by a discourse that was oriented toward creating the widest possible normative consensus recognizing the legitimacy of the new court's powers to enforce international criminal law. The relatively disinterested nature of NGOs allowed them to contribute to this discourse in a way that was morally resonant; consequently they were influential.

I view the construction of the ICC as an effort to design and institutionalize a set of new procedures for enforcing international criminal law. In other words, the creation of the ICC represents an effort to institutionalize a particular set of norms for punishing individual violators of international criminal law. Because the ICC is a shift from the traditional view of state sovereign responsibility for individual culpability, the ICC represents a major change in the norms for dealing with some kinds of mass violence perpetrated by states.

Contesting the Norms for Dealing with Atrocities

Prior to the twentieth century, managing violence in world affairs was seen as the task of states. Through warfare, states could defend their own territory and conquer new lands. Through their police power, states could limit the use of private violence.[16] The only path to security was to reduce the capability of another state to wage war on your own. Responsibility for the waging of aggressive wars was generally viewed as the responsibility of corporate entities, usually nations or states. The particular individuals involved mattered very little. Now there is a shift toward individual responsibility. In world politics there are norms that govern the way that states, and now supranational courts established by states, should go about enforcing violations of international law. The ICC as constituted is one of many possible mechanisms for making individuals accountable under international law. A variety of other practices have been tried by states in the last century, with varying degrees of success, including the possibility of ignoring individual culpability. Each of these different "options" for enforcing international criminal law (or not) constitutes an actual or potential norm in this domain of world politics. Over time, the extent to which each of those norms was accepted has risen and fallen.

Until this century, the predominant norm was that states could prosecute their own nationals for violations of the law of war. Prisoners of war could not be tried as individuals for their actions and needed to be treated with dignity and ultimately released once hostilities ceased, if not before; if they were guilty of actual war crimes, only the state where they were citizens could try them criminally. A second option was an ad hoc court constituted multilaterally to dispense justice against the perpetrators of international law crimes in particular conflicts. The Nuremberg tribunal established after the Second World War was the first successful effort to impose such justice on vanquished aggressors. In the 1990's the United Nations Security Council created two such courts to deal with crimes committed in the former Yugoslavia and in Rwanda, under the explicit authority of Chapter 7 of the United Nations Charter. Another option pursued in recent years is the notion that international law crimes should be prosecuted by national courts, even when the crime did not take place within the court's normal territorial jurisdiction. The U.S. federal courts claimed the authority to do this, at least to impose civil penalties, with the 1980 *Fligarta v. Pena-Irala* case (630 F2d 876). Other examples of the use of domestic courts include the Spanish prosecution of Augusto Pinochet (Roht-Arriaza 2005) and the U.S. prosecution of Manuel Noriega (Albert 1993). In the aftermath of the U.S. invasion of Afghanistan, the Bush administration sought to revive the rather anachronistic procedure whereby military tribunals under the authority of military forces in the field can undertake criminal prosecutions of enemy belligerents. The national courts of many states have recognized during the twentieth century that states have universal jurisdiction to prosecute some international law crimes, including war crimes (Paust 2000, pp. 157–65).

Each of these alternatives is a different potential mechanism for enforcing international criminal law. To the extent that any of these is widely perceived as legitimate, it would be a norm of international politics. The ICC, however, will likely achieve a degree of institutionalization (Stone Sweet 1999) that none of these other norms has achieved. That is because the ICC is a permanent supranational entity, with sitting judges and prosecutors.

The particular set of norms embodied by the permanent ICC has been developed by the deliberate action of a set of actors in world politics. Those norms are inconsistent with some of the past practices for enforcing (or ignoring) violations of international law. Since 139 states signed the ICC statute and over 100 have ratified it, this set of norms is well on the way to being established as the primary mechanism through which the world community enforces international criminal law. A wide variety of actors have voiced their support for these norms around the world.

A number of the most powerful states in world politics opposed the normative approach adopted in the ICC statute at the time, and a few continue to do so, including China, India, and the United States. For instance, the U.S. administration of George W. Bush continues to oppose the ICC. They instead offer competing visions of the appropriate norms that apply to the punishment of international law crimes, including ad hoc enforcement.

It is puzzling from the perspective of realist understandings of international politics that the drafting of a major international agreement would take a direction that was opposed by the most powerful states in the international community. During the negotiations themselves, a much wider range of approaches to constructing a permanent ICC was considered, with vastly different approaches to the powers, jurisdiction, and role of the new court. So, the basic empirical task to be undertaken in this book is to explain how and why the particular set of norms embodied in the ICC treaty has become so widely accepted. I argue that the ability of the NGO Coalition for an ICC (CICC) to offer rational justifications, grounded in what would be most just, fair, and effective, led to the widespread support for their preferred outcome on foundational ICC issues. Demonstrating this empirically involves determining the reasons that the actors involved gave to explain their own actions in the ICC process. Further, it involves analysis of the logical structure of reasons given for and against particular normative claims in the process of negotiating the provisions of the ICC statute and its implementation.

To be clear, it is not my contention that NGO discourse was the single factor that led to the creation of the ICC. NGOs entered into a discourse about an international criminal court in the 1950's, and a very few continued to do so in the 1980's. So it would be ludicrous to claim that NGO discourse alone has the power to create international criminal courts or any other norm change in world politics. Indeed, as I have suggested earlier, causation is an elusive phenomenon in the social sciences. We are not in a position to "rerun" history or to change particular variables in order to establish definitively the independent impact of each factor. What we can do is document the impressions that key decision makers had regarding the importance of NGO communications about the ICC. We also can analyze the way NGO arguments cast particular meanings on proposals advanced by states and other actors. Finally, we can attempt to identify the crucial conditions in this case that allowed NGO arguments to resonate so effectively. This last task is important because it speaks to the potential generality of the pattern found here.

This is a single case study, and as such, it is not sufficient support for a general claim that broad participation by NGOs in developing and designing international institutions contributes to the establishment of such institutions and the perception of their legitimacy. However, if carefully designed, a single case study like this one can be suggestive of the conditions that were important to the outcome in this case. In this way this project lays the groundwork for future comparisons with other cases of NGO participation in the design of policy and institutions for global governance. The advantage of case study work is that it is more likely to uncover the mechanisms that produced the particular outcome in this case as opposed to a larger N study (a study that looks at many independent cases of the phenomena being examined) such as the work by Boli and Thomas (1999), which suggests a correlation between the founding of international non-governmental organizations (INGOs) and intergovernmental organizations (IGOs) but offers a less detailed examination of mechanisms. As has been suggested by various methodologists, case study–oriented research and large N studies directed at the same general problems complement each other's strengths (George and Bennett 2005; Gerring 2004).

The existence of a unique set of circumstances in world politics was an important condition that facilitated the success of NGO efforts at discursive persuasion. The end of the Cold War, the tragic developments in the former Yugoslavia and the creation of the International Criminal Tribunal for the former Yugoslavia (ICTY), the International Criminal Tribunal for Rwanda (ICTR), and the election of Tony Blair as British Prime Minister, among countless other local and global factors, were all crucial developments that facilitated the prompt establishment of an ICC. The end of the Cold War removed the tendency to view every international conflict in terms of its implications for the categorical struggle between the West and the East. This allowed for the possibility of an international criminal court based on universal norms that could apply to all individuals. The experience with the ICTY demonstrated that prosecution was possible. The Blair election brought to power a government in control of a permanent Security Council seat with a proactive human rights agenda that was willing to endorse the concept of a permanent and universal ICC. Each of these changes contributed to the political climate that led to the ICC statute's adoption. Still, it is difficult to imagine that an ICC like the one now constituted in The Hague would have come into existence without the work by NGOs on this issue.

It is my contention that the NGOs' discursive efforts substantially shaped the ultimate form of the ICC statute, and that in the counterfactual absence of those voices in the discourse, a very different ICC might have emerged, most likely over a much longer time frame, or no court would have gained sufficient support to be established at all.

Assessing the Influence of Nonstate Actors

A variety of scholars have now engaged in studies that attempt to assess the influence of nonstate actors in world politics. In what follows, some of the lessons from those efforts are distilled in relation to the method of discourse analysis proposed here, with reference to the particular effort to assess NGO influence on the process of establishing the ICC.

One paradigm for assessing the influence of nonstate actors is the sociological institutionalism associated with John Meyer that was first brought to the attention of IR scholars by Martha Finnemore (1996). This body of work understands broad changes in the world political system as having originated in the extension of Western rationality as a cultural norm around the world, embodied in part in the adoption of the modern state around the world on the European model (Meyer et al. 1987). Finnemore distinguishes sociological institutionalism from constructivism in IR, and in their origins they were separate intellectual developments. She notes in particular that constructivists have focused on particular norms or norm areas, while the sociological institutionalists ground their claims in a wider understanding of the evolution of a global culture based on a particular conceptualization of rationality and individualism. However, constructivism and sociological institutionalism also share much in common. "World polity" theory (as the sociological institutionalism approach is sometimes called) is important because it suggests that "the rise and diffusion of a large number of norms" is linked to the proliferation of intergovernmental organizations and international nongovernmental organizations in the state system (Keck and Sikkink 1998, 210).[17] It is also particularly relevant here because it suggests that NGO authority hinges on the commitment to a particular version of rational discussion of public policy problems in the world political system.

One issue that remains difficult to understand is how small vocal minorities are able to delegitimize dominant understandings of international politics. Keck and Sikkink echo Finnemore's call for further analysis of the politics of the cusp, where norms are transformed from radical ideas into conventional wisdom. If a commitment by nonstate actors to communicative rationality is related to NGO efficacy in contexts that are hospitable to communicative action, then the method developed here should shed light on the difficult problem of understanding how norm change begins to "cascade" at the tipping point.

The drafting and ratification of the ICC is a case study of just such a phenomenon of normative tipping. In the late 1940s and early 1950s, states and nonstate actors advanced serious proposals for establishing a permanent ICC. Those proposals lost momentum in the context of the early Cold War. Over these decades, ICC proposals faced a difficult conceptual hurdle because they required that international criminal law be developed to a point where that law could be fairly enforced (Ferencz 1980). In the mid-1990s, the debate about the ICC accelerated again, and NGO arguments found interested listeners.

A crucial concern in my study is to identify the reasons for NGO success on the ICC issue, since we know that discursive power is often employed to little or no effect in other cases. Keck and Sikkink identify five criteria for deciding what counts as an effective transnational action network (TAN) in different stages of TAN development (Keck and Sikkink 1998, p. 25):

1. Framing debates and getting issues on the agenda.
2. Encouraging discursive commitments from states and other policy actors.
3. Causing procedural change at the international and domestic levels.
4. Affecting policy of states or other important actors.
5. Influencing behavior changes in target actors.

Though developed with respect to other issues, these elements can be seen in the case of NGO activism on the ICC issue. The Coalition for an ICC is an umbrella organization that brought together many pro-ICC NGOs. This group was successful on the first two items. They played a large role in framing the issues surrounding the establishment of an ICC, and sought public commitments from states to support scheduling a diplomatic conference charged with drafting an ICC statute and to support particular proposals that NGOs thought were best for the design of the court. With respect to the third type of activity, I would also argue that NGOs "caused" the procedural changes in enforcing international criminal law embodied in the Rome Statute, so we can say they were successful in creating procedural change at the domestic and international levels as well. NGOs shaped many states' policies with regard to negotiating positions on the issues during the debate, and they also arguably changed the ways states behaved in the negotiating process. Of course ultimately, the real NGO goal is to change the behavior of "would-be" war criminals, if such a category of persons can be imagined to exist. It will be many decades before we can create any systematic account of the NGOs' success on this question.

These are legitimate dimensions for evaluating network success or failure, but they do not do much to help us account for those successes and failures. Of course, to some extent, norm change in the world political system is indeterminate because it depends on the interlocking choices of thousands (or more) individual human beings. Even after major normative changes, such as the abolishment of slavery, a few holdouts may continue to contest the new norms for decades or even centuries. Given the dramatic increase in the number of international criminal investigations and trials since the early 1990s and the sharp increase in public debate and discussion of war crimes, war criminals, and war crimes tribunals, it is fairly clear that dramatic changes in norms have occurred in this area at the level of the international community. So it is clear that a transnationally organized network made principled arguments about changing the enforcement norms for severe violations of international criminal law, with increased discursive activity beginning in the early 1990s. It is also clear that norms for enforcing international criminal law have changed significantly over the same time period. The balance of this study aims to highlight the substantial body of evidence that the discursive activity of NGOs was decisive in bringing about that norm change.

One reason to describe characteristics of the discourse employed by the NGOs who successfully advocated for an ICC is to suggest that emulating those discursive practices could lead to successful norm change on other issues as well.

Keck and Sikkink suggest characteristics of the issues and characteristics of the actors (both the networks and the targets) that can help us account for success. In discussing the characteristics of the issues, they mention three different things, in my reading. First, they suggest that TANs develop on issues where states would be unlikely to act on their own according to neoliberal theory or theorists of collective action. This is either because social problems in other states are easily ignored by many states or because even if collective goods can be identified (such as a healthy environment), the costs associated with achieving it are very high, as are the temptations for free riding (Keck and Sikkink 1998).

I would account for this observation from a slightly different perspective. TANs develop on issues where for whatever reason, the existing political structure of state-centered global politics has failed to address real political issues. Naturally it is in areas of perceived policy failure where TANs are motivated to get involved. That these correspond with areas where neoliberal institutionalist IR theory predicts policy failures (or a failure to provide public goods) is not surprising (Axelrod and Keohane 1993). The need for an ICC, for instance, is driven by a structural failure of the Westphalian system, namely, the fact that the state system historically institutionalized state-to-state violence and offered impunity to individuals who carried out that state-sponsored violence against their own populations or in warfare against other states. It is perhaps possible to think of this culture of individual impunity as a failure to provide a collective good (perhaps we could call it human security), but it stretches the bounds of the neoliberal paradigm.

A second characteristic, according to Keck and Sikkink, is that "*in their general form* they are issues around which mass mobilization is unlikely" (Keck and Sikkink 1998, p. 204, emphasis in original). They note that all of these networks face a problem of figuring out how to transform a diffuse agreement to "protect the environment" or to "defend human rights" into specific concrete actions. Keck and Sikkink note that this may be why TANs pursue advocacy pressure tactics on existing elites rather than pursuing mass mobilization strategies for the most part.

Keck and Sikkink note that Amnesty International, with its letter-writing campaigns, is an important exception to this general rule. During its campaign for an ICC, Amnesty pursued both elite persuasion and mass mobilization strategies in conjunction. The elite persuasion element was the most effective, but it was effective particularly in Britain and other Western European societies where it was *presumed* by state elites and the Amnesty leadership alike that it could mobilize the public on ICC-related issues if necessary.

All of this suggests that traditional forms of power and influence, such as a group's ability to mobilize voters, play a role in NGO influence in addition to the force of normative argument. Still, Amnesty and the representatives of the British government may take the attitude of communicative rationality toward one another, offering reasons for their claims about which ICC rules will be efficacious in bringing an end to impunity and be normatively fair for all concerned. Indeed, Amnesty's potential (if still unexercised) power to mobilize mass publics on war crimes–related issues hinges on the rational binding quality of their arguments, because it is those rational arguments that they would employ to motivate voters to act on particular issues if necessary.

The third characteristic that Keck and Sikkink mention is the most intriguing. They say:

> New ideas are more likely to be influential if they fit well with existing ideas and ideologies in a particular historical setting. Since networks are carriers of new ideas, they must find ways to frame them to resonate or fit with the larger belief systems and real life contexts within which the debates occur. The ability of TANs to frame issues successfully is especially problematic because, unlike domestic social movements, different parts of advocacy networks need to fit with belief systems, life experiences, and stories, myths, and folk tales in many different countries and cultures. We argue that the two types of issues most characteristic of these networks—issues involving bodily harm to vulnerable individuals, and legal equality of opportunity—speak to aspects of belief systems or life experiences that transcend a specific cultural or political context.[18]

The claim that Keck and Sikkink make here is that there is a class of social values that has cross-cultural resonance and accordingly, TANs form around issues that appeal to those values. They also imply that there is a logical structure to normative argument, and that "new ideas" eventually carry the day. Of course, the new ideas that capture popularity are often old ideas that have been ridiculed as radical or absurd for years. I want to draw attention to the widespread consensus among many observers of NGO efforts to influence world politics that there is something about the logic of the arguments that leads to persuasive power. In the terms of communicative action theory, we can think of these underlying values as topoi, or agreed-upon premises that all parties in a given dialogue accept as a starting point for future discussion (N. Crawford 2002; Kratochwil 1989).

Bas Arts employs three different techniques, labeled the EAC method (Arts, Reinalda, and Noortmann 2001, pp. 195–6), to assess the influence of NGOs.

The first technique is *Ego-perception*, or simply establishing the views of key leaders within the NGO itself about how effective they are at achieving their political goals. Since NGOs will tend to overestimate their effectiveness, Arts rightly suggests they should not be trusted, but they can be used as preliminary criteria for identifying cases. To this observation I would add that some NGOs often engage in quite realistic self-assessments of their effectiveness over time in order to evaluate the usefulness of particular tactical strategies they pursue. Accordingly, internal NGO assessments may be reasonable indicators of *relative* success over time, even if they overstate the NGOs' total effectiveness on average. Of course, these internal assessments may usually not be public but may be made available to researchers.

The second technique Arts calls *Alter-perception*. The idea is to confirm NGOs' effectiveness through the assessments of government officials involved in the relevant decision-making processes. Finally Arts refers to *Causal Analysis*, which "covers the reconstruction of negotiating and decision-making processes to detect possible causal links between NGO interventions on the one hand and effects on political outcomes on the other."

I prefer to label this later approach *process tracing*, and I discuss this method in detail in the next section. Arts describes this last technique as difficult, and so emphasizes the importance of *Alter-perception*. In my own work, I consider process tracing the most important technique, and I have used *Alter-perception* as a secondary approach to validate the findings from the process tracing. Specifically, I follow the written discourse in time to see who publicly presented crucial arguments first. Interviews with participants in the negotiations were used to confirm that state representatives who were the targets of NGO efforts at persuasion in fact found those arguments to be influential in the process. Having reviewed some of the lessons from existing attempts to assess NGO efficacy, I turn now to a description of the method of discourse analysis based on communicative action theory that I have developed in my own research.

Method: Analyzing Normative Discourse and Process Tracing

We have seen that once one accepts the intersubjective ontology of institutions in world politics, the most appropriate method for understanding changes in those institutions is an interpretive approach. In my analysis of the political process that led to the establishment of the International Criminal Court, I have relied on two major methodological techniques: discourse analysis and process tracing. In what follows, I elaborate on the methods I employed in my analysis. I begin with a review of the scholarly literature regarding discourse analysis in the study of world politics.

The effectiveness of NGO discourse is important because NGO participation in transnational politics has been hailed as a possible solution to the democratic deficit that characterizes most international decision making. NGO voices offer a counterweight to powerful states' hegemonic influence over the definition and conceptualization of global political problems. However, others see NGO voices as fragmentary, contributing to a cacophony of isolated voices that represent only narrow special interests or the privileged sectors of mass publics. The method of discourse analysis proposed here provides a systematic approach to analyzing these issues by assessing the communicative rationality of NGOs' discursive gambits in their global political contexts. If we can develop a rigorous methodology for assessing the communicative rationality of the discursive practices of NGOs and other actors in world politics, it should allow us to deepen our understanding of the conditions under which the arguments of nonstate actors are influential. If some discursive practices can be systematically identified as communicatively rational, we can assess whether or not communicative rationality is related to successful cases of NGO influence in particular contexts. On the other hand, if speech can be systematically identified as being primarily strategic in intent and not communicative, we can then assess whether such discursive gambits by NGOs are also sometimes effective in achieving the goals of the actors.[19]

Scholars have become increasingly focused in recent years on the role of nonstate actors in world politics. Several lines of analysis have pointed to the discursive practices of such actors as accounting for their authority in international politics (Boli and Thomas 1999; Keck and Sikkink 1998; Korey 1998; Risse-Kappen, Ropp, and Sikkink 1999). What we need is a method for assessing the rationality of the discursive utterances of actors in world politics. The motivation is an understanding that a crucial source of power and influence for nonstate actors is their use of rational discourse (Boli and Thomas 1999). Both empirical claims about how the world is and normative claims about good rules for organizing social life can be characterized as being more or less rational (Kratochwil 1989). Ethical arguments are important because they sometimes have an impact on outcomes in world politics, as Crawford has impressively demonstrated in the cases of the decline of slavery and the process of decolonization (N. Crawford 2002).

My claim is not that discursive power moves the world. Indeed, sometimes material factors, including the distribution of power, shape outcomes. Over time though, discursive gambits can change actors' conceptions of their own interests and the meaning or value of their material assets (N. Crawford 2002, pp. 28–37; Klotz 1995; Lynch 1999). Crawford's theory of argument in world politics systematically addresses the issue of the causal importance of argument (N. Crawford 2002, pp. 78–82). Readers who are skeptical about the importance of arguments should look at her analysis. The focus here is on developing my own methodological approach to analyzing discourse in world politics from the foundation of communicative action theory.

Discourse Analysis Today

This section briefly reviews some of the existing literature on discourse analysis and directs interested readers to more comprehensive reviews. The objective is to situate the communicative action approach developed here in relation to other approaches to discourse analysis. As Milliken has noted, "No common understanding has emerged in International Relations about the best ways to study discourse" (Milliken 1999). In presenting my own approach, my intent is to take seriously Milliken's call for more dialogue about what constitutes good research method in the area of discourse analysis.[20]

In *The Theory of Communicative Action*, Habermas lays out a philosophy of the social sciences that insists social scientists must combine the roles of *objective observers of* and *active participants in* social life (Habermas 1984). We as social scientists must constantly alternate between taking the "objective" attitude of an outside observer and the performative attitude of a member of society caught up in the social world. In order to understand the meaning of social facts we must be at least proximally participants in the social world we seek to describe. A truly *social* science must not only observe but also participate in society and consequently cannot avoid taking up normative as well as empirical concerns. A critical blind spot for the social sciences generally, and the field of IR particularly, has been the tendency in positivist approaches to take an objective view while denying the reality that normative claims are necessarily implicitly or explicitly tied up with allegedly objective claims about how the world works (Frost 1996; Smith 2004).

Many world politics scholars who utilize discursive analysis as a research methodology explicitly adopt an interpretive approach that takes as a core goal of the social scientific enterprise a critique of existing relations of power on normative grounds. I share this concern with creating space for explicitly normative critiques of the existing international system (Campbell 1992; Doty 1996; Lynch 1999; Walker 1993). Still I remain committed to the effort to attempt to explain why particular outcomes are produced in world politics.[21] I accept that causation in any social process is an extremely complex phenomenon, and that at the level of world politics any individual analyst faces an almost infinite regress of underlying causes of proximal causes of immediate causes of particular outcomes that have been determined to be of interest. The call for parsimony by Waltz was never likely to lead to particularly deep understandings of causal processes (Waltz 1979). From the perspective of any particular observer, including mine, our explanations will inevitably be partial and incomplete. Still I agree with the critical theory scholars mentioned previously that the project of attempting to understand why things happen the way they do is an important one, even if it is never a value neutral one.

My own approach to discourse analysis emphasizes the agency of speakers and listeners engaged in the discourse. Discursive moves are viewed as deliberate political acts. Of course, discourse can also be viewed as a structural force that constrains the range of actions that are available agents.[22]

The appeal of an approach to discourse analysis based on the theory of communicative action is that Habermas provides a coherent philosophical basis for social scientists to alternate between the roles of detached observation and active participation in social life (Habermas 1996). This is an issue that has divided the constructivist camp. Ted Hopf sees a distinction between "conventional constructivists" and critical theorists on precisely the issue of the relationship between the observer of social phenomena and the nature of the phenomena observed. He says that "critical theorists self-consciously recognize their own participation in the reproduction, constitution, and fixing of the social entities they observe. They realize that the actor and observer can never be separated. Conventional constructivists ignore this injunction, while largely adopting interpretivist understanding of the connectivity of subjects with other subjects in a web of intersubjective meaning" (Hopf 1998). While Hopf's point is well taken, I do think it is reasonable from time to time to temporarily suspend our concern with the researcher's role in reconstituting the social world. I would like to carve out a space where it is possible to suggest that observed identities and beliefs of actors explain actions they undertake, even while accepting that to interpret is in part to construct what is interpreted, and further down the road, analysts' interpretations may have real consequences. I think it is possible from the perspective of the theory of communicative action to suspend critique, at least for the moment, even while we recognize that some future listener may desire to raise the role of the analyst in creating the interpretation. This may be precisely to challenge the power that the analyst has inadvertently (or self-consciously) appropriated to herself in carrying out the analysis. Now I turn to a discussion of recent scholarship that has applied the theory of communicative action to the analysis of discourse in world politics.

Thomas Risse has noted that communicative action is a crucial modality of social action in world politics, which is insufficiently captured by the logic of consequences, the focus of rational choice approaches, or the logic of appropriateness, the focus of (some) constructivist analyses of world politics (Risse 2000, p. 18). Because strategic behavior and reasoned argument are ideal types, the question to ask is not whether actors behave in one way or the other, but which mode captures more of their behavior in a particular situation (Risse 2000, p. 18). The method of discourse analysis developed here seeks to systematically identify discursive practices that approximate the communicative orientation to action.

Risse allows for a relaxation of the requirement for communicative action that all interested speakers be allowed to participate in political discourse (Habermas 1996). Obviously, in world politics, standing to speak is normally quite restricted. Risse uses the example of the United Nations Security Council, where membership is restricted and some voices clearly have more weight than others. He points out that it should be possible, however, to have rational dialogues in such a setting, even though membership is restricted. The limitation here that Risse does not elaborate on is that conclusions about truth claims or value claims reached in such a discourse may not have any rational validity for groups that were not able to exercise voice in the process. To the extent that discourses among official representatives, such as members of a legislature or delegates to the United Nations Security Council, are informed by and responsive to discourses that include a wide range of broadly representative groups from civil society, they can potentially offset the legitimacy crisis that is created by strictly limiting the number of formal representatives in the decision-making body (Risse 2000, p. 18). Of course, the formal representatives are only likely to pay attention to voices in the broader civil society that have influence in selecting them as the official representatives. Consequently, the legitimacy problems remain if many groups are systematically not represented or are underrepresented. Social groups whose members are citizens of the permanent five countries are more likely to see their positions fully reflected in Security Council debates.

Risse points out that the real issue is not whether or not power relations are absent in a discourse but to what extent they can explain the argumentative outcome

(Risse 2000). This is a crucial insight. If arguments are won based on reasons and not appeals to power, then the underlying power relations are less important.

Groups with little or no influence over the selection of governments, and therefore United Nations representatives, may find their voices periodically ignored even if they are based in one of the permanent five states. Amnesty International was listened to during the ICC debate in part because it had the potential to have an impact on Tony Blair's government and reelection prospects. It is less influential in the United States when a coalition like the one that elected George W. Bush is in power.

Democracy deficits remain a problem then, even when government interlocutors listen to some NGOs. However, if actors maintain a communicative orientation to action, the theoretical possibility remains that such communicative rationality will lead to political outcomes with a high degree of legitimacy, even in a situation where not all interested speakers have standing within the formal institutions. Consider the possibility that state representatives in international institutions are prepared to engage in truly communicative action with some NGOs, and NGOs similarly prepare their position statements with a commitment to respond to all other perspectives, even voices not well represented in global civil society. In that case, a commitment to rationally take into account the points of view of all persons who are likely to be affected by particular global decision-making procedures can go a long way toward ameliorating the democracy deficit. The problem of course is that NGOs based primarily in advanced industrial societies must be careful not to try to speak for groups that are not well represented in intergovernmental decision making. So long as NGOs committed to communicative rationality participate in open dialogue with all interested parties, and states similarly interact with those NGOs in communicatively rational terms, it is possible for communicative rationality to produce rules and decisions that enjoy legitimacy because of their appeal to reason. The key is that NGOs with a communicative action orientation must make an extra effort to hear those fainter voices from the marginalized areas of the world political system. The Coalition for an International Criminal Court, particularly in the later years of the ratification campaign and in the first five years of the ICC's operation, has done an effective job of enhancing communication with victims, individuals, and groups in war-torn or otherwise marginalized parts of the world community. The NGO community has also been instrumental in institutionalizing these outreach efforts at the ICC itself.

If we can develop a systematic approach to discourse analysis, we can identify particular discursive moves and entire political debates where communicative rationality is approximated. My suspicion is that NGOs' degree of commitment to communicative rationality may also go a long way toward furthering our understanding of why NGOs are sometimes influential whereas at other times they are not.

Process Tracing

Process tracing has recently received increased attention from social science methodologists (George and Bennett 2005; Gerring 2001; King, Keohane, and

Verba 1994, pp. 85–6; Van Evera 1997). While methodology texts discussed the approach briefly in the 1990s, George and Bennett examine the utility of the method in considerably more detail. Van Evera notes that process tracing can be of particular value in the analysis of causal sequences *between* theorized independent variables and particular outcomes (Van Evera 1997). In this study, I trace the process through which the communicatively rational discursive practices by NGOs led to decisions to design the ICC statute in a particular way. My use of process tracing is a form of "explaining cases," in Van Evera's terminology.

George and Bennett offer a useful metaphor for understanding the value of process tracing. They imagine a series of dominoes, standing in a row, where only the first and the last are visible. If an observer returns after being away and sees that the first and last domino have fallen, only closer examination of the intervening dominoes can help the observer determine whether or not the far left domino set off a chain reaction causing the far right one to fall, or if it was the other way around, or if some other intervening force, like jarring the table, caused both dominoes to fall. Observation of the in-between evidence, in other words process tracing, can likely distinguish between these possible explanations (George and Bennett 2005, pp. 206–7).

I view the evidence presented later on in precisely this way. I link NGOs' discursive practices to steps taken at various points in the ICC negotiations to show that the pattern of available evidence is consistent with my claim that NGO interventions decisively influenced the overall direction of the negotiations.

I view the process that led to the development of the ICC both as a critical juncture and a path-dependent chain.[23] It is a critical juncture in that once the ICC was designed in a particular way with particular powers and rules for its operation, other ways of designing a permanent institution to enforce international humanitarian law were foreclosed. It is path-dependent because particular decisions taken during the negotiations foreclosed other possibilities for the institution's design and made aspects of the final outcome increasingly more likely as time went on. Process tracing within a single case as a methodological approach is particularly strong at uncovering this type of path-dependent causal mechanism (Gerring 2001, p. 164).

Assessing the Communicative Rationality of Discourse through Process Tracing

As noted above, norms can be ranked in terms of their degree of generality. In the context of a rational discourse, it is socially unacceptable to advocate specific norms that violate more general foundational principles (Kratochwil 1989; Habermas 1998; Klotz 1995). Moreover, Habermas and others arguing in the tradition of the theory of communicative action have established that is possible to demonstrate that normative claims can be justified as more or less valid through specific forms of rational argument (Habermas 1984, 1987, 1994; Kratochwil 1989). The key insight from the theory of communicative action is that while it may be impossible to state at the outset which normative claims can be considered "true" or valid, it is possible to identify processes through which norms can be justified discursively as having validity in a given social context.[24] I propose to analyze the discursive arguments made in favor of and against particular proposals for an international criminal court in terms of the rational groundings offered by those presenting the arguments.[25] What I expect to show is that NGOs frequently made arguments that were justified in terms of underlying ethical principles that in practice few speakers in the ICC debate were prepared to challenge. The reasons for some other proposals, such as some arguments advanced by delegates from the United States, were often not grounded to the same extent in such fundamental moral principles.[26] For a variety of reasons, many of which were very specific to the context of establishing a judicial institution for a newly emerging legal system, normative arguments that were grounded in reasons justifiable to the broadest possible audience tended to carry the day. Frequently it was NGOs that made those sorts of arguments first.

During the early phases of the ICC negotiations, beginning in 1995, central actors promoted a view that the negotiations should proceed in a way that sought the broadest possible legitimacy for the court. The court's provisions had to be rationally defensible in a wide variety of cultures. This led to an emphasis on designing the court in a way that its operations would be perceived as transparently fair. In that context, it ultimately proved impossible for the United States to argue rationally that members of its armed forces should be effectively exempted from the jurisdiction of the ICC. Initially, U.S. diplomats avoided making this argument directly, but various mechanisms, such as Security Council oversight over the ICC prosecutor's office, would have had the effect of exempting U.S. citizens from compliance with some international norms.[27] Since this violates the principle that law should apply to all equally on the face, NGOs were very persuasive when they attacked the U.S. position on these grounds. This is offered as a brief illustration of the kinds of debates I analyze in terms of communicative action theory; the analysis will contain considerably more detail.

Sources and Evidence

I examine legal writings, NGO policy statements, General Assembly debates, and government policy statements, and interview some of the individuals involved in the ICC process.[28] What I show is that temporally, some crucial arguments were formulated first by scholars and NGOs, and then picked up by state officials as government policy. The discourse should be understood as a dialogue; U.S. policy is fairly independent of NGO voices, and at times, the NGOs are persuaded by the U.S. or other key states on some issues. Still, frequently it is NGO proposals that were adopted and ultimately accepted in the Rome Statute and the subsequent constitutive documents of the court. On a variety of issues, NGO voices clearly framed the terms of the debate.

I link discursive practices at particular times to political developments that led to the treaty conference and agreement on its specific provisions. Beyond establishing a time line that shows that NGOs often advanced arguments before they were adopted by states and then formally agreed to in the process of the negotiations, I also analyze the logic of the reasons employed by NGOs to justify their positions. What I can show is that NGOs used arguments that gave discursively rational justifications for their normative claims based on widely accepted moral principles.

Process tracing allows me to identify evidence that would support or refute my claim that the discursive practices of NGOs persuaded decision makers to adopt particular provisions for the ICC treaty. If, for example, decision makers who negotiated the final ICC statute, or state delegates who voted to adopt those proposals, were unaware of NGO comments on particular issues, it would suggest that NGO discourse was not important to the outcome. Alternatively, if the key decision makers adopted the same proposals favored by NGOs but gave different reasons for doing so, this would also tend to invalidate my argument. Similarly, if knowledgeable observers of the process believe that key actors were deliberately concealing their true motivations, this would also tend to disconfirm my analysis. To the extent that the decision makers share NGO reasons in their statements about why particular actions were taken, give those reasons in similar terms to the way they were first presented by NGOs, cannot be shown to have taken those positions prior to the release of key NGO statements, and confirm in interviews and/or public statements that they perceived NGO analysis as being influential, such evidence provides substantial support for my overall argument.

Topoi

Moral and legal dilemmas often cannot be readily resolved through reasoned argument if different speakers begin from different premises.[29] If competing claims appeal to different fundamental values, it is sometimes difficult or impossible to rank order the logical force of those different values. Decisions about which values to prioritize instead have to be made socially. They can only be justified with reference to preexisting beliefs that many members of a social community are willing to accept as persuasive for them, intersubjectively and collectively.

Political scientists sometimes try to explain the existence of norms in purely utilitarian terms; rules simply serve the interests of rule makers. This is inadequate.[30] Kratochwil's analysis demonstrates persuasively that the prescriptive force of norms in international politics depends on the degree to which those norms can be justified through rational argument. Norms do not cause behavior in a mechanistic sense, but they do become reasons for actions by actors, particularly when the justification of a norm is viewed as persuasive. The validity of arguments about the rightness of norms depends in turn on intersubjective decisions about the topoi, or relevant premises from which reasoning about norms should begin (Kratochwil 1989, pp. 37–9).

Habermas's discourse principle states "just those action norms are valid to which all possibly affected persons could agree as participants in rational discourses" (Habermas 1996, p. 107). Because the discourse theory sets out to account for the legitimacy of law in postconventional societies, it offers a promising basis for assessing the legitimacy of developments in international law, including the creation of the ICC. The theory leads us to recognize the importance of distinguishing between communicative action and strategic action as types of discursive moves.

Communicative action is characterized by actors who want to reach an understanding with one another about facts or norms, and they are willing to give reasons for validity of their claims if they are challenged by other participants in the discourse. The participants in turn understand that they have the freedom to challenge the validity of other speakers' claims, and indeed an obligation to do so if they do not agree with the validity of what is uttered. The only reasons that count for justifying claims are those kinds of reasons that all the participants together find acceptable. In strategic action, in contrast, actors are not concerned if the reasons that are persuasive for them are not shared by others. Strategic action is characterized by purposive rationality. Actors pursue goals and may try to influence other actors' behaviors, but not by reaching rational agreement about what is the case or what ends ought to be pursued (Habermas 1996, pp. 118–20). Of course, the concepts of communicative action and strategic action are ideal types, but the overall tone of the ICC debate approached the communicative action ideal. When strategic appeals were made, other negotiators often rejected them as illegitimate.[31]

Before a particular dialogue can be characterized as communicatively rational, it must be the case that the participants in such a conversation have some shared premises or starting points.[32] Legal reasoning is in this sense different from strictly deductive reasoning about how the world is in an empirical sense. Kratochwil and Alexy characterize legal reasoning as a form of practical reasoning, or what Aristotle referred to as "dialectical reasoning" in the *Topica*[33] (Kratochwil 1989, pp. 37–42, 215). Topoi are widely shared beliefs that serve as starting points for analyzing legal questions (Alexy 1989, 20–6). Legal reasoning frequently is not deductive but proceeds by analogy. Of crucial importance are the decisions made in a discourse about how to characterize a particular legal question, or in other words, the selection of particular topoi (Kratochwil 1989, pp. 212–48). For example, in a formal legal proceeding it is normally necessary to make a prior determination of which particular rules will be applied in a specific case, that is, to identify the topoi for the particular arguments that will be presented to the judge. Perhaps a mafia boss could be charged with income tax evasion, or alternatively with murder. Which charge is actually filed sets the starting point for all further discussion about what sorts of evidence and arguments will be in order in the courtroom. In legal and practical political reasoning in general, we find that rational arguments begin from widely accepted premises. Debates that are not subject to rational discussion and resolution tend to be precisely those debates in which interlocutors cannot agree about which starting premises should frame a discussion. For instance, we can consider the clash of political values between a right to life and a right to liberty as two different topoi or premises that one might draw upon to support or attack a government policy of secretly monitoring telephone communications in order to prevent terrorism. If you accept the liberty topoi as being paramount, it is possible to justify rationally the policy that the state should not be permitted to use such surveillance of citizens. On the other hand, if the debate centers around the protection of life topoi, it is possible to conclude rationally that the state should have the surveillance power in order to maximize its chance of disrupting an attack on civilian life.

During the debate on establishing an international criminal court, a series of widely shared premises began to emerge in the conversations. Some of these date back at least to the discussions of a draft ICC charter at the International Law Commission in the 1940s and 1950s, as I discuss in Chapter 3. For instance, the premise that international criminal courts of any form should include rules protecting the rights of the accused, including a presumption of innocence, came out of the Nuremberg process and was widely accepted by the late 1940s. Others emerged during the interim period between 1994 and 1997. I analyze these in Chapter 4, where I list them in detail. By the Rome conference in 1998, nearly all of the interlocutors accepted these first principles as being the crucial logical foundation for the adoption of an ICC charter. Once this occurred in the months leading up to the Rome conference in June and July of 1998, much of the debate about how to design an ICC approximated the Habermasian ideal of achieving communicative rationality.

Topoi: *Discursive Rules of the Road*

Because the concept of topoi is crucial to the subsequent analysis of the ICC negotiations, I want to explain in more detail how I conceive of topoi and how they relate to the larger concept of norms in world politics and social life generally. Norms are a broad category of ever-present social phenomena that include rules, institutions, manners, language, and all manner of shared expectations for behavior. It is possible to think of topoi as a very specific type of norm as well. In effect, topoi are shared expectations about what kinds of arguments will be considered generally acceptable in the context of some particular discourse. We can think of topoi as rules of the road for a particular debate or negotiating session.[34] These shared expectations are an emergent property of whatever discourse they regulate. Topoi can be identified by an observer of discourse because arguments based on the topoi will generally be accepted by the interlocutors, while arguments that violate them will be challenged.

Robert Alexy has extended Habermasian theory for the purpose of analyzing the justification of legal argumentation (Alexy 1989). Alexy develops a series of "pragmatic rules" to govern the kinds of statements that can be made and the permissible conduct of speakers to be followed in normative argumentation if the discussion is going to be characterized as "rational." He says that "Observance of these rules certainly does not guarantee the conclusive certainty of all results, but it does nevertheless mark out the results as rational ones" (Alexy 1989, p. 179). One way to assess the rationality of arguments made during the course of the ICC negotiations would be to determine whether or not that discourse satisfies Alexy's rules for "rational practical discourse." This provides the criteria to assess my claim that NGOs' normative discourse was powerful because it was rationally grounded. These rules can be thought of as an effort to delimit more specifically Habermas's conditions for rational communicative action in the establishment of legitimate legal norms and legal systems (1994). Alexy's rules are as follows[35] (1989, pp. 187–208):

> 1.1 No speaker may contradict herself.
> 1.2 Every speaker may only assert what he actually believes.
> 1.3 Every speaker who applies a predicate F to an object *a* must be prepared to apply F to every other object which is like *a* in all relevant respects.
> 1.4 Different speakers may not use the same expression with different meanings.
> 2.1 Everyone who can speak may take part in discourse.
> 2.2 (a) Everyone may problematize any assertion. (b) Everyone may introduce any assertion into the discourse. (c) Everyone may express her attitudes, wishes and needs.
> 2.3 No speaker may be prevented from exercising the rights laid down in 2.1 and 2.2 by any kind of coercion internal or external to the discourse.
> 3.1 Whoever proposes to treat a person A differently from a person B is obliged to provide justification for so doing.
> 3.2 Whoever attacks a statement or norm which is not the subject of the discussion must state a reason for so doing.
> 3.3 Whoever has put forward an argument is only obliged to produce further arguments in the event of counterarguments.
> 3.4 Whoever introduces an assertion or an utterance about his attitudes, wishes, or needs into a discourse, which does not stand as an argument in relation to a prior utterance, must justify this interjection when required to do so.
> 5.1.1 Everyone who makes a normative statement that presupposes a rule with certain consequences for the satisfaction of the interests of other persons must be able to accept these consequences, even in the hypothetical situation where she is in the position of those persons.
> 5.1.2 The consequences of every rule for the satisfaction of the interests of each and every individual must be acceptable to everyone.
> 5.1.3 Every rule must be openly and universally teachable.
> 5.2.1 The moral rules underlying the moral views of a speaker must be able to withstand critical testing in terms of their historical genesis. A moral rule cannot stand up to such testing if: (a) even though originally amenable to rational justification, it has in the meantime lost its justification, or (b) it was not originally amenable to rational justification and no adequate new grounds have been discovered for it in the meantime.
> 5.2.2 The moral rules underlying the moral views of a speaker must be able to withstand critical testing in terms of their individual genesis. A moral rule does not stand up to such testing if it has only been adopted on grounds of some unjustifiable conditions of socialization. (Including conditions of socialization that result in individuals being unable or unwilling to participate in rational discourse.)
> 5.3 The actually given limits of reliability are to be taken into account.

Many of these rules, as Alexy notes, are ideals and in practice compliance with them can only be achieved to a degree and not in any absolute sense. Still they do provided a concrete list of criteria, with strong theoretical foundations, for deciding whether or not particular normative arguments made as part of a larger discourse should count as rational. In my analysis of the discursive moves of participants in the negotiations that led to the establishment of the ICC, I confine myself to evaluating the rationality of particular arguments by employing only these criteria. Still, this is an unwieldy list, and in carrying out my own empirical analysis I have found it useful to summarize Alexy's foregoing criteria into a shorter and more manageable list, which I will lay out in the next paragraph. While some theoretical richness is lost by taking this step, it is necessary as a practical matter in order to make the analysis manageable. I do assert that my shorter list of criteria is theoretically consistent with Alexy's more developed set of criteria as well as with Habermas' general elaboration of the concepts of communicative and strategic action. When nuanced issues arise in conducting the analysis, it is possible to fall back on Alexy's more elaborate list of pragmatic criteria for rational discourse about the validity of norms.

My summary of the criteria for characterizing a discourse about norms as rational are the following.

1. Everyone who is physically able to speak in a discourse may do so, in a way that is free from external coercion.
2. Speakers must be prepared to give reasons for their assertions.
3. Normative claims should be universalizable.
4. Speakers should only assert what they actually believe.

These are understood as procedural standards for labeling the products of a particular discourse as being rational. To say that a particular norm was rationally produced does not mean that the norm is valid with certainty, but nevertheless it provides verifiable criteria for marking out some normative claims as rational ones (Alexy 1989, p. 179).

I want to expand a bit on the discussion of giving reasons for normative assertions drawing on Alexy's discussion of these issues (Alexy 1989, pp. 177–9). If we assert that A lied, and conclude from that observation that A behaved badly, we have presupposed a rule that "to lie is to behave badly." Such a rule can be brought into question in a discussion of norms and justified by giving further reasons. For instance, a speaker called upon to justify the norm that lying is bad behavior might claim that "lying causes avoidable suffering." Such a logical chain could be carried on indefinitely, with normative reasons always requiring further justification. This is precisely the reason why Habermas turns to a procedurally oriented focus on the validation of norms. In practice, in conversations about norms, interlocutors reach a point where everyone involved in the discussion is inclined to accept some normative premise, such as "lying causes avoidable suffering," without requiring further justification for that claim. For Habermas, such unquestioned assumptions are conceptualized as the lifeworld that is a necessary background condition for communicatively rational discourses among people to be carried out. This is the logical underpinning of the criteria 1 and 2 above, requiring open participation in discourses and that speakers be able to justify assertions if they are called upon to do so.

Major Criticisms of Deliberative Discourse Theory

Communicative action theory and its variants have been advanced by theorists of deliberative democracy as a legitimating force for democratic social orders in postconventional societies, both by Habermas and many others (Gutmann and Thompson 2004; Habermas 1996; Olson 2003). While it is not necessary to review that discussion in full here, I would like to address a few of the major criticisms of the deliberative democracy approach that could also easily be extended as critiques of this project. I do not imagine that I can completely anticipate and rebut such critiques; instead this brief passage is intended as an offer to open a dialogue with such other perspectives.

Iris Marion Young has developed two main critiques of standard deliberative democratic theory that posit deliberative discourse as an ideal type by which democracies should be evaluated. The first criticism focuses on the tendency of deliberative theorists to "assume a culturally biased conception of discussion that tends to silence or devalue some people or groups" because of the focus on critical argument as the preferred form of communicative interaction (Young 1996, p. 120).

The center of this critique focuses on ways that power reenters ostensibly discursive forums because of the agonistic nature of debate. Because interlocutors attempt to "win" political debates and achieve their objectives, Young says "speech that is assertive and confrontational is here more valued than speech that is tentative, exploratory, or conciliatory" (Young 1996, p. 123). Also there is a privileged status given to speech that is dispassionate and disembodied, with a tendency to downplay the value of emotional appeals (Young 1996, p. 124).

The negotiations on establishing the ICC certainly favored legalistic forms of formalized speech and actors who presented it wearing particular uniforms of dress and projecting the level of social status that comes with graduating from elite law schools. Undoubtedly, these simple facts of diplomatic protocol weakened access of some potentially interested persons to the ICC debate. However, one of the most effective strategies of NGOs was precisely to translate the emotional appeals of victims of war crimes into the formal legalistic reasoning that characterized the ICC debate. Early Amnesty International papers that took the form of careful legal treatises also included first-hand stories of war crimes victims as sidebars or introductory quotations to the legal analysis. It is precisely in this sense that I argue that NGOs contributed to the general opening of the ICC discourse by increasing the capacity of otherwise marginalized voices to be heard. This contribution of NGO participation helped the discourse approximate communicative rationality, even if of course it still fell far short of the ideal norms of complete participation by all potentially interested speakers, including speakers who would tend to use different forms of communication.

Young's other critique focuses on the tendency of deliberative theorists to "assume that processes of discussion that aim to reach understanding must either begin with shared understanding or take a common good as their goal" (Young 1996, p.125). It is probably the case in today's pluralist societies, or certainly in world politics, that there are very few shared understandings that can be drawn upon. In the case of the ICC debate, I will argue below that certain practices and widely accepted principles of international law helped to provide that starting point for rational debate. Of course, there were significant actors who arguably do start from premises fundamentally different from those accepted by other actors. For example, the People's Republic of China consistently articulates a view of international law that pays utmost deference to an absolutist view of state sovereignty and considers sacrosanct the privileged role of the United Nations Security Council in peace and security issues.

The Nature of the Discourse about an International Criminal Court

To gain historical perspective I compare the discourse leading to the adoption of the Rome Statute with the discourse of the 1950s, when efforts to create an ICC collapsed. This allows a temporally comparative perspective, and the difference in outcomes illuminates the search for the factors that led to the adoption of a statute in the 1990s. Through the empirical analysis of the discourse, I show that in the 1990s a diverse set of actors agreed that a major problem with the Westphalian state system was the fact that individuals who perpetrated violent crimes on a mass scale in the name of a state often escaped punishment. While initially there was little consensus about how a supranational court could be created to address that problem, the moral authority of a discourse led by NGOs ultimately compelled world leaders to adopt an ICC statute that allows for depoliticized prosecutions, is potentially universally applicable, and is arguably just. As discussed above, a variety of alternatives to a permanent ICC were attempted to address the problem of enforcing international criminal law during the last 50 years, with a renewed intensity to the activity after 1989. I examine arguments that gave reasons for undertaking these other projects as well as arguments about the problems and limitations with these temporary measures and relate those debates to the analysis of the convergence on broad consensual support for the permanent ICC.

It is worth describing in some more detail the available written discourse on the establishment of the ICC that will be analyzed for this project. Prior to around 1994, discussions of the idea of a permanent ICC were limited to a fairly narrow legal academic community. Government officials who were knowledgeable about the ICC issue contributed to this literature (Rubin 1994; Scharf 1994). Beginning in 1994, with the ILC draft proposal for the ICC, the conversation widened, but only slightly so. A broader number of governments and NGO officials joined the discourse. Academic writings were still a central mode for the debate, and the number of ICC-related publications in legal journals began to rise. Also, the ongoing discussions under the supervision of the Sixth Committee of the United Nations General Assembly led to more statements in the context of the meetings or by government officials regarding the progress of the meetings. Official United Nations Summary reports of the negotiations are available. Leading NGO analyses of ICC-related issues are almost invariably published on the worldwide web and simultaneously distributed to government decision makers. The CICC also published a periodic newsletter that summarized the state of the negotiations and NGO views on outstanding issues, beginning in 1996.

Perhaps the most valuable window into the discourse on the nascent ICC was the compilation of information distributed via listserv, on an almost daily basis, by the CICC itself. Beginning in 1995, shortly after the coalition was established, they began the near daily distribution of almost any public statement related to the ICC. Anyone interested in following ICC issues could subscribe to the listserv. Typically, the coalition would publish announcements of ICC-related meetings, detailed summaries of any developments at the negotiations themselves, reprints of published editorials and letters to the editor , and excerpts from speeches by public officials when they mentioned the ICC. As the coalition grew internationally, so too did its ability to report on ICC-related commentaries almost anywhere in the world. The coalition did not hesitate to publish editorials or speeches that critiqued or attacked the idea of the ICC. Often, rebuttals would be distributed, attempting to clarify misinformation when that was necessary. Because the CICC listserv centrally located information on the ICC from a vast number of sources, it is a useful window on the ICC discourse.

There are some potential complications that should be addressed in using the CICC listserv as a source for materials. Initially, the listserv centered almost entirely on English language sources. Therefore more information is available from the United States and Britain but also from the *International Herald Tribune* edited in Paris, and newspapers from India, Australia, South Africa, and other places where English remains an important language for news and policy discussions related to world affairs. In the post-Rome ratification stage, listservs were created by regional offices of the CICC that focused on the Spanish-, French-, and eventually Portuguese-speaking worlds as well. To a more limited extent, I will also make use of sources that were reported via the Spanish-language listserv.

It is also important to note that these listservs worked systematically to broadcast arguments that were consistent with the positions of the CICC members but also presented pieces by those who opposed an ICC altogether or who opposed proposals favored by the NGOs. The CICC saw its listserv as a way to keep its members informed of the broad dynamics of the debate, and all voices were reported. Many of the documents rebroadcast via the listserv were published elsewhere or otherwise were publicly released. In addition to other sources of ICC-related documents, the listserv provides a window into a range of sources that would be difficult to recreate through traditional bibliographic searches.

In order to validate my understanding of the significance of particular arguments and developments in the discussion of the ICC statute, I conducted a series of elite interviews with leading participants in the negotiations.[36] The primary purpose of these interviews was to validate my understanding of the written record from people who participated in the negotiations firsthand. I interviewed people who played key roles in the negotiations, including representatives of states, NGOs, members of the international civil service, and chairpersons and coordinators of crucial aspects of the negotiations. The focus of the interviews was to identify subjects' views on the major dynamics of the negotiations and their assessment of critical moments of persuasion that took place during the negotiations. I asked these individuals to explain their own motivations either in personal terms or in terms of the constituencies they saw themselves as representing. The discussions also focus on crucial compromises and the meaning of those compromises to interested actors as well as potential compromises that were rejected or roads not taken.[37] Many of the interviews focused on interviewees's broad sense of the nature of the negotiations, in terms of their openness to different voices and the relative importance of different kinds of arguments that were presented. While these were semistructured, open-ended interviews, care was taken to avoid leading questions or discussion of the author's research questions before or during the interviews.

Based on a preliminary reading of the available documentary sources, I developed an understanding of the dynamics of the negotiations and the role of NGOs' discursive activities along the lines of what has been described above. The interviews were designed to provide opportunities to find disconfirming evidence for this working understanding of how the negotiations had progressed.[38] In interviews with NGO legal analysts, who produced and distributed many of the crucial documents I focus on, I asked respondents to describe their relationships with key decision makers on the government side. I asked them to describe their target audience for particular legal analyses of prospective ICC provisions and their methods for distributing their writings and following up with target recipients. NGO leaders were also asked to discuss the organization of their efforts within their own organizations and the nature of their cooperation and/or conflict with other NGOs. I also asked them to assess their own degree of influence in the process. In interviews with government officials who participated in the negotiations, I began by asking respondents to identify crucial political issues that were debated in the negotiations and to try to recall the dynamics of important compromises that raised the number of participants who supported the compromise solution. Only gradually did these interviews turn to the role of NGOs. I asked state government officials if they were aware of various NGO analyses at the time of the negotiations and how, if at all, they used those analyses themselves or felt that the points of view raised therein had any impact on the negotiations.

In summary then, the core research methodology employed was an analysis of the documentary discourse surrounding proposals for the establishment of an ICC. At a later point I analyze arguments in terms of the rationality of the normative claims they employ. In-depth interviews with some of the leading participants in the negotiations validated the understanding developed from the analysis of the documentary evidence, and excerpts from those interviews are referenced in the empirical analysis that follows. The analysis in subsequent chapters demonstrates that rational normative arguments that appealed to broad ethical principles were often advanced by NGOs and that these sorts of arguments often carried the day during the ICC negotiations.

Lessons from the Application of this Method

Communicative action theory is at its best in characterizing entire discourses. The method proposed and employed illustratively here has as its hallmark an effort to assess the individual components of a larger discourse and mark out some claims as rational while identifying others as failing the criteria. I find that the criteria laid out by Alexy are reasonably useful in performing this task, at least for the particular discourse I am examining. The task must be undertaken with a degree of flexibility, and debates about "coding" the rationality of certain discursive moves may be inevitable. Still, the criteria provide a grounding on which different observers could have a rational debate about what is communicatively rational and what is not. We must remember, however, that an overall communicative process that can be characterized as rational, or at least as approaching the ideal typical model of rational discourse, may contain within it discursive moves that are manifestly not defensible on rational grounds, including moves by speakers to pursue strategic ends, or to refuse to submit their claims to challenge by other participants in the discourse.

The success of the method employed here is partly a product of the fact that the broader discourse assessed happened as a matter of historical fact to proceed in a broadly communicatively rational pattern. It remains an open question whether or not this method employed would be useful when applied to the assessment of discourse that never approaches communicative rationality. Discourses that are characterized by predominantly strategic exchanges could be interesting in their own right. I doubt that NGOs would be particularly effective actors in such a context. This method does help us account for NGO influence by demonstrating that the successful NGO campaign for a fair and effective ICC relied on communicatively rational discursive practices. It also suggests that identifying communicatively rational discursive environments might be a useful approach to understanding why some NGO campaigns for norm change are successful in other contexts.

The Fact/Value Distinction in the Social Sciences

I seek to contribute to the elaboration of a general understanding of the role of nonstate actors in transforming the norms of world politics through a detailed analysis of the construction of the ICC. However, I will not confine the analysis to the task of empirical description. The claim that a group of civil society actors had a decisive and deliberate impact in creating the ICC as the newest institution of global governance has significant implications for the normative theoretical underpinnings of global governance. The prevailing archeology of knowledge in the field of political science has maintained a sharp distinction between the domain of political theory, which analyzes the requirements of good (democratic) government within the state, and IR, which has focused on the problem of creating order in the context of amoral relations between autonomous states (Walker 1993). As Walker demonstrates, an important consequence of this division of labor has been a failure to adequately grapple with the deficit of democratic procedures at the level of global governance.

Michel Foucault notes that any description of the world has normative implications, and that such descriptions create and sustain relations of power between individuals (1972, p. 33). Analysis of the influence of norms in world politics necessarily takes place at the juncture between empirical description of how the political world is and normative theorizing about how it ought to be. In reflecting on the turn toward the empirical analysis of normative influences in the study of IR, Martha Finnemore and Kathryn Sikkink note that "Understanding where these 'oughtness' claims come from, how they are related to one another, which ones will be powerful, and what their implications are for world politics is vital, but it is an inquiry that can only be undertaken at the nexus of political theory and IR" (1999, p. 276). Consequently, at least some scholars who focus on global governance need to become political theorists themselves in the classical sense of the term. Scholars need to address the questions of what constitutes "good global government."

These concerns raise another. Who is this knowledge produced for, and what political ends might it ultimately serve? Karena Shaw has raised this question for the discipline of IR broadly in her insightful essay (Shaw 2003). Shaw notes that three recent studies of activism in international politics have explicitly focused on the discipline of international politics as the focal point for their own political message by arguing that studies of the role of activists contribute to a better understanding of international politics, but she points out that there may be significant limitations to this orientation.[39] First, an orientation toward a scholarly audience familiar with disciplinary concepts and language is arguably a very small one, and Shaw points out that larger audiences are likely put off by that orientation Furthermore, while Shaw imagines there is feedback between the discipline of IR scholars and the practice of world politics, she is not convinced that the former are particularly influential. Second, Shaw is not convinced that it is wise to strengthen the discipline of international politics by helping it to understand phenomena that were once outside its purview; instead she thinks it might by more useful to take a critical approach that highlights the very limitations of the predominant understandings advanced by IR scholarship. Finally, Shaw worries that even by broadening the boundaries of the discipline of international politics and making the "activists" fit as part of the phenomena the discipline helps to define and reify, IR scholarship may be limiting our understanding of the true radical potential of some of these social movements to reorder politics itself. Finally Shaw observes, in part through her analysis of older, parallel debates in the field of anthropology, that because of the unintended applications and implications of particular constructions of knowledge, it is always partly impossible to know the real political consequences of particular knowledge projects. I argue that in light of this fact, we should try to be conscious of likely political consequences of particular knowledge claims, but we should ultimately be very humble about our capacity to foresee such consequences. Knowledge, however partial and bound by perspective, is better than ignorance, and since we cannot foretell the future, the best we can do is believe in knowledge for knowledge's sake.[40] This means that I am ultimately driven back to the scholarly habit of assuming some present and future universal audience for my knowledge claims, and I trust that readers will be sufficiently critical as to find the errors and limitations inherent in my conceptualization. I remain committed to orienting my knowledge toward the discipline on the principle that the English language academic discourse is at present as likely as any other existing discourse to provide a broadly accurate description of how world politics functions in practice and how it might best be transformed.[41]

In analyzing the ICC, I address some related normative questions. The first of these is whether or not the Rome treaty process is a normatively justifiable procedure for constituting a new judicial institution of global governance. This issue is inherently bound up with my empirical claim that the use of rational moral arguments provided an important catalyst for the success of NGOs in influencing the content of the Rome Statute. To claim that the ICC negotiations were effective because they used rational discursive strategies requires that it be established that the negotiations were structured in a way that approximated an open discourse oriented toward a universal audience. At the same time, the extent to which NGOs contributed to broadening the range of voices engaged in these negotiations is directly connected to the normative value of participatory global governance. The empirical and normative issues are of necessity intertwined.

Additionally, I discuss the normative implications of the move toward the criminalization of some forms of mass violence perpetrated by state leaders. The movement to prosecute gross violations of international criminal law challenges traditional notions of state sovereignty and potentially modifies practices regarding diplomatic immunity. This movement has the potential to increase the physical security of the world's citizens, but it also complicates the day-to-day business of relations between states.

Antonio Franceschet has noted that the fact that the dominant procedures for global governance today are statist in character systematically limits the justice claims of nonstate actors (2002, pp. 19–20). The participation of a significant number of NGOs in the process that led to the adoption of the Rome statute for an ICC is a significant model for ways that nonstate voices can be included in global governance processes via relatively modest reforms.

Of course, these normative issues are at the heart of the contested political issues that have been raised in the process of proposing and advancing the notion of a permanent International Criminal Court.

3

Discursive Limits: The Failure to Establish an International Criminal Court; 1946–1954

> We all have to recognize no matter how great our strength that we must deny ourselves the license to always do as we please. This is the price that each nation will have to pay for world peace.
>
> —Harry S. Truman, *Address in San Francisco*[1]

Discourse on the Judicialization of International Criminal Law

Why did efforts to set up an International Criminal Court in the 1950s fail and then succeed in the late 1990s? In order to account for this difference, I will examine the discursive practices of both states and NGOs with reference to punishing war crimes in the two periods in light of the international political context in each period. A full appreciation of the political and juridical accomplishments embodied in the establishment of the ICC in 2002 requires an understanding of the challenges that this project faced in previous decades. Understanding the reasons why the effort to establish an ICC failed in the 1950s can help us to appreciate the obstacles that were overcome by ICC negotiators in the 1990s. It also helps us to understand the birth pains that the ICC is now experiencing and the structural limitations that the ICC is facing because it is constituted as part of the interstate legal system. This chapter offers an analysis of the breakdown in the 1950s negotiating process and highlights the challenge of enforcing criminal law in the sovereignty-based international legal system.

I begin with an analysis of the discursive positions of states and other actors on the ICC issue in the aftermath of World War II and the Nuremberg trials. As we saw in Chapter 2, however, states' interests are not self-evident given a specific international situation.[2] An adequate understanding of the outcome of debates about the ICC requires that we look at how states' interests get constructed and modified over time. Given the crucial role that international NGOs played in shaping those interests in the 1990s, it becomes important to examine their role and strength in both time periods. Because of the tremendous power of the United States in both periods, this analysis primarily focuses on the U.S. role.

States' preferences on the issue of the ICC are difficult to predict from their position in the international distribution of power or taking into consideration their other existing foreign policy commitments. Indeed, there are significant reasons to think that government officials, particularly heads of state and their immediate subordinates, would have a personal interest in opposing the development of any supranational authority with the ability to hold individuals accountable for violations of international law. This personal interest of state leaders may differ substantially from the public interest or the "national interest" as conceived of in some collective sense. At the same time, leaders in liberal states at times come under pressure from public opinion to pursue war crimes trials that observe the domestic due process norms of liberal states (Bass 2000). Examples include the British demand for a trial of Kaiser Wilhelm II in the election of 1918 (Bass 2000). The constructivist approach adopted in this research allows for an analysis of the political process that leads to the construction of state interests.[3]

I consider policy statements by executives, acts or resolutions of legislatures, and the statements or actions of formally recognized diplomats at international organizations or conferences to be examples of state discourses. In addition to NGO discourses and academic writings, I include statements of individual legislators and those by members of the international civil service who participate formally in their individual capacities as part of the civil society discourse.

Proponents and opponents of a new political institution make arguments for their position by offering hypothetical cases or historical examples that they believe illustrate the advantages or disadvantages of the proposed reform. In the case of the discourse about an ICC, these hypothetical examples were noteworthy for the way that they addressed the critical issues identified in Chapter 1. Rhetorical examples implicitly address the issues of who might be tried and punished for what kinds of crimes, who ought to have the authority to do the judging, and what larger purposes of justice or political retribution might be served by an ICC.

Understanding the development of the discourse on a permanent ICC requires that we focus on how an abstract normative consensus might be formed to answer these questions. As Bass and others have noted, states are quick and ready to call for punishment of the war crimes of their enemies, but a permanent court requires a principled definition of the crimes to be punished and the procedures to be used in initiating and carrying out a trial. Achieving consensus among a diverse set of actors from different cultures around the world about what crimes ought to be punished by a supranational authority requires a more abstract conceptualization of war crimes than a simple agreement that Adolf Hitler and Pol Pot are examples of war criminals. In subsequent chapters, I show that NGOs played a crucial role in forging that abstract consensus in the process of preparing for and conducting the Rome ICC Treaty Conference in 1998. In the 1950s rational arguments were proposed as well about ways to design a permanent international tribunal. However, the discourse could never resolve the tension between the prevailing understanding of state sovereignty in the 1950s and a legal system focused on individual culpability for violations of international law. I argue that the limits of the communication structure of world politics in the

1950s contributed to the failure to resolve the tension between absolutist views of state sovereignty and international criminal law enforcement.

A Brief History of Efforts to Create International Courts

Before we turn to the analysis of the discursive impasse that was reached in the 1950s on the issue of establishing a permanent ICC, I briefly review prior efforts to establish international criminal tribunals. The growth of modern efforts to place limits on the waging of war is best understood as a reaction to the terrible improvement in the technological capability of weapons by the mid-nineteenth century. The Crimean War in Europe and the Civil War in the United States made clear that the capacity for destruction of human life in warfare had grown astronomically (Weiss and Collins 2000, pp. 13–20). Soon after the Crimean War, the Battle of Solferino in 1959 led to the creation of the Red Cross. These events stimulated Fiore's initial proposal for an international court (Ferencz 1980). The American Civil War led Abraham Lincoln to adopt the Lieber Code governing the conduct of U.S. soldiers in the field, the precursor to today's military code of justice and much of international humanitarian law. At The Hague Peace Conferences of 1899 and 1907, diplomats made a great deal of progress in codifying international norms, but they failed to establish a judicial institution with the power to enforce those norms. At the latter conference, an international court was proposed in response to a British suggestion, and when it was drafted as a convention, 39 states signed it. This international court was conceived as an appellate court that would review the decisions of national prize courts making rulings on the seizure of ships and cargos during times of war (Ferencz 1980, vol. 1, pp. 15–20). However, failure to codify the specific law that the court could enforce at the 1907 and 1909 London Naval Conferences led to a refusal of all the signatory states to ratify the convention for an international prize court, and therefore the proposal died.

Shortly after this early failure, some civil society organizations began to promote the idea of an international judicial body. In 1910, the American Society for the Judicial Settlement of International Disputes was formed. Elihu Root, Andrew Carnegie, President William Howard Taft, and Secretary of State Philander Chase Knox all attended the first meeting (Ferencz 1980, vol. 1, p. 20).

After World War I, Winston Churchill, in his capacity as first lord of the admiralty, pressed for war crimes trials for the Germans. He sought to place everyone from U-boat captains to Kaiser Wilhelm II himself before a court of law. In the end, the Dutch government sheltered the Kaiser and lesser officials were tried by German courts. The German courts acquitted those on trial in the vast majority of cases (Bass 2000, pp. 61–92). During World War II, both sides of the war crimes debate used this episode as justification for their cause. Opponents of courts pointed to the dismal failure of the efforts after World War I. Proponents argued that the failure to fix individual blame, opting instead for heavy punishment of the German people by means of large, required, reparations payments, led directly to World War II.

The Permanent Court of International Justice, the forerunner of today's International Court of Justice (ICJ), known as the World Court, was first convened on January 30, 1922 (Meyer 2002, p. 55). This tribunal was designed to adjudicate conflicts between states, and as such, it has no authority to punish individuals. The World Court reflects the historical tradition of viewing states as the primary subjects of international law. For advocates of a permanent ICC, this limitation of the World Court to a focus on resolving disputes between sovereign states is a handicap to the progressive development of international law that could only be overcome by creating a new permanent institution with criminal jurisdiction.

Analyzing the Establishment of Ad Hoc War Crimes Tribunals

Prior to the ICC, a series of international tribunals were established to exercise criminal jurisdiction over specific crimes in particular times and places, known collectively as the ad hoc war crimes tribunals. Gary Bass has written a history of the way that states have dealt with defeated enemies in order to put the current move toward war crimes trials in perspective (Bass 2000). Bass claims that only liberal states have the legal domestic norms that lead them to push for war crimes trials. In most cases this pattern of liberal states organizing tribunals holds; however, Stalin's desire for Nazi trials is a curious exception. While Stalin was a brutal authoritarian leader in his own right, he favored trials to punish the leadership of Germany at the end of World War II. Presumably, Stalin understood the political theater of such trials could be valuable; indeed, at Nuremberg, the Russian participants in the proceedings were generally not too concerned about the role of trials in protecting the rights of the accused.

Next, Bass claims that states are reluctant to risk the lives of their own soldiers in order to provide justice for third-party victims, and conversely, states are most likely to pursue trials when their own suffering has been great and their own nationals were victims. The state-centric assumption here is problematic, which Bass partially acknowledges with his final point that NGOs can sometimes put pressure on states to pursue prosecutions. Bass does not see NGO pressure as a *necessary* condition for creating war crimes tribunals (2000, p. 33).

Bass concludes that the likelihood of pursuing war crimes trials is fairly constrained by the politics of the situation, and that such trials are likely to occur only when they are self-serving for the prosecuting states. This is usually only the case when a large number of victims of a particular war criminal are nationals of the states organizing the prosecution. Bass's framework cannot account for support for the ICC, which can only try crimes that have occured after 2002, when 60 states agreed to ratify the statute. At the time the text was negotiated, no one could have known who the victims would be of the crimes that the ICC would ultimately prosecute.

It is one thing to consider the establishment of war crimes tribunals as discrete comparable cases. It is another issue to step back and consider the evolution of the war crimes trials practice over time. At present, we can observe an emerging normative order favoring enforcement rather than impunity. It is clear from Bass's account that in each case in which war crime trials were contemplated, attempted, or actually carried out during the twentieth century, the leaders involved learned from the mistakes of prior efforts. Since the establishment of the ICTY in 1994, versions of war crimes trials with some international structure have been held with respect to the conflicts in Rwanda, Sierra Leone, the Lockerbie terrorism case, Cambodia, and East Timor. U.S. soldiers have been prosecuted and convicted of war crimes committed in Iraq in 2003 and 2004. These trials have thus far been limited to low-ranking soldiers. Clearly the incidence of trials is on a significant rise. But the sequential development of the institutionalization of international criminal law was not and cannot now be taken as an inevitable process. It depends crucially on the agency of actors, including NGO activists.[4]

1946–1953: Rejection of a Permanent ICC

With World War II still under way, there was a movement toward holding the leaders of the defeated Axis powers individually responsible for their conduct. In 1941, the London International Assembly called for the creation of an international court to try war crimes, and in the Moscow declaration of October 1943, the Allies announced that top officials would be tried by an international court (Marquardt[5] 1995, p. 81). Considerable effort was made to give a legal justification for the punishment that was meted out to the leadership of the Axis powers. However, it was the victorious Allies who were calling the shots. Even though the U.S. prosecutors at Nuremberg specifically drew attention to the universality of the norms that they were enforcing,[6] it was clear at the time that the people who would be punished for war crimes were those who had been on the defeated side in the war. As late as February of 1947, peace treaties signed with Italy, Romania, Bulgaria, Hungary, and Finland required that persons responsible for war crimes or crimes against humanity be turned over for trial (Ferencz 1980, vol. 2, p. 4; see note 8).

The distribution of power in the late 1940s and early 1950s was already predominantly bipolar. The United States was at its strongest politically vis-à-vis the other members of the United Nations in the earliest years of the organization. Western nations dominated the United Nations, while the Soviet Union and its satellite states were an organized minority that grew in strength during the early Cold War period (Holloway 1990, pp. 279–80). Since decolonization was barely under way, there were few nations in the United Nations that did not associate with one of these groups, and its major initiatives were usually carefully crafted compromises between the two superpower blocks (Holloway 1990, p. 280).

The fact that the United States and the Soviet Union reached agreement on a charter for the Nuremberg court on August 8th, 1945, and subsequently cooperated to operate the International Military Tribunal for the Far East (IMTFE) in 1946 (Appleman 1954, p. VIII) suggests that cooperation between these powers on a permanent court might have been possible in the early postwar period. But those tribunals were limited to considering the guilt of the leadership of the Axis powers; consequently neither the Soviets nor the Americans needed to contemplate the possible culpability of their own forces.[7] The Americans and Soviets might have established a permanent criminal court in which the Security Council would have control over the court's jurisdiction, with the de facto result that these powers would have remained immune to future prosecution. But what purpose would such a court serve? The Soviet Union and the United States no longer shared common enemies.

In the late 1940s and early 1950s there were NGOs that were active supporters of the concept of an ICC. If NGOs were so successful at shaping the establishment of the ICC in the 1990s, why were similar organizations unable to accomplish the same task in the 1950s? Some of the organizations active at that time included The International Commission for Penal Reconstruction and Development, the British Grotius Society, and the American Bar Association (ABA). This last organization passed a resolution in favor of an international criminal tribunal in 1943. Other organizations active in the early 1950's include the American Society of International Law and the *Société Française de Droit International* (Ferencz 1980). In October of 1946, jurists from 24 nations met in Paris under the auspices of the *Mouvement National Judiciare Français* and unanimously called for an International Penal Court and a code of crimes against humanity (Ferencz 1980, vol. 2, p. 4).

These organizations were important in placing the issue of the ICC on the agenda of the United Nations General Assembly's Sixth Committee and the ILC. The draft texts debated at the United Nations and the arguments for and against them were often borrowed from these groups. In the 1950s, as in the 1990s, leaders of NGOs were often legal scholars who moved easily between roles in the civil society sector to academia and even to diplomatic service as part of delegations from their respective nations.

Traditional accounts of the establishment of the United Nations and the other multilateral institutions of the postwar era have tended to ignore the contributions of nonstate actors to the struggle over the legitimacy of norms for organizing world political affairs (Lynch 1999, pp. 173–7). The leading institutionalist view of the emergence of these postwar international organizations has focused on the importance of "*American* hegemony" in explaining the emergence of forms of political organization based on principled rules binding the conduct of sovereign states (Ruggie 1993b, pp. 8–13, 31). For John Ruggie it was the fact of liberalism in American domestic political life that shaped its behavior in the postwar era, and consequently the forms of international organization that were established in that period (Ruggie 1993b). Still, this perspective fails to fully consider the role of popular social movements in shaping the ultimate form that the United Nations took, since the United Nations Charter hardly reflects the initial stated preferences of President Franklin D. Roosevelt for a postwar order based on a concert of powers, known as the "four policemen" (Lynch 1999, pp. 177–208). So nonstate actors had real impact on the interwar period and the aftermath of World War II, just as I argue they did again on the ICC issue in the 1990s.

John Boli and George Thomas have undertaken an extensive study of international NGOs. Their results look at long trends in the number of such organizations that have been created since 1875 (Boli and Thomas 1999). While their results are too general to tell us about the strength of the particular NGOs that were active on the ICC issue prior to the 1950s, their observations do provide a useful backdrop for understanding the context in which these groups came into being.

They observe that the rate of foundings of intergovernmental organizations (IGO's) is highly correlated with the founding rate of INGOs per year. For the 119 years ending in 1973, the correlation is 0.83 (Boli and Thomas 1999, pp. 27–30). They suggest that this process is part of deeper historical trends but note that the coevolution of IGOs and INGOs leads to their mutual legitimization. "INGOs gain prestige by winning consultative status with IGOs, while IGOs gain by the involvement of diverse INGOs that lend IGO policies a nonpartisan flavor as reflections of world public opinion or putative technical necessity" (Boli and Thomas 1999, p. 30). They also recognize that INGOs are often involved in the establishment of IGOs (p. 29). The ICC is clearly one specific case of that phenomenon, although the Rome conference happened after the period that Boli and Thomas consider. Interestingly, the annual rates of INGO and IGO foundings peaked in the years after World War II, relative to the whole 1875–1973 period. In some ways then, the ICC debate of the 1950's might be thought to have occurred under conditions that were favorable for the founding of a permanent ICC, as so many other new international organizations were established in this period. Yet this is not what occurred. It is interesting to note that on December 5, 1952, the General Assembly voted in plenary session to postpone consideration of the draft statute for an ICC (United Nations Document A/L.119, A/2275, and Res. 687, VII, 1952, of the General Assembly Plenary). According to Boli and Thomas, by 1953 the rate of IGO foundings had begun to fall considerably (1999, p. 27).

Since the late 1940s and early 1950s were a period of internationalism triumphant, advocates for a court perceived this and sought to push it. But given the international political context, it was difficult for NGOs in favor of an ICC to offer rational arguments grounded in universal norms the way that they did so successfully in the 1990s. As long as the German and the Japanese war leaders (below the Emperor) remained the clear targets of war crimes trials, a kind of "universal" agreement could hold that prosecution was a good idea. But as the ideological and cultural totality of the Cold War conflict began to develop, it seemed less and less plausible that a neutral institution could adjudicate accusations of war crimes, crimes against humanity, or genocide free of interference from one or both of the superpowers. In that context, there was no space for NGOs or legal scholars or anyone else to make the case for international enforcement of international criminal law by appealing to universal norms.

In the balance of this chapter I examine the discursive arguments advanced by proponents and skeptics of an ICC and show how assumptions of the political world in the 1950s that were taken for granted prevented a principled resolution to the problems inherent in establishing an international tribunal with the authority to conduct trials for individuals accused of international law crimes. Primarily, existing understandings of the rights of sovereign states were incompatible with a principled institution for enforcing international criminal law. Participation in leading discourses about the organization of world politics was sufficiently restricted so that no serious challenge to the prevailing understanding of the rights of sovereign states was possible.

Discursive Dilemmas: State Sovereignty and Individual Accountability

In the years following Nuremberg, there was intergovernmental discussion of prosecuting a variety of international crimes. For example, the United States proposed in the Atomic Energy Commission that violations of agreements to control atomic energy should be punished by international trials of the individuals responsible (Ferencz 1980, vol. 2, p. 5). Also, there was general sentiment in the world community in favor of criminalizing genocide in the postwar period.

In 1946, representatives from Cuba, India, Panama, France, the Soviet Union, Uruguay, Colombia, Chile, Saudi Arabia, and Poland all spoke in favor of the idea of making genocide a crime against international law (Ferencz 1980, vol. 2, p. 6). Initially, the task of drafting a convention on genocide was relegated to the Economic and Social Council of the United Nations (ECOSOC), but the General Assembly also constituted a Codification Committee charged with developing an international criminal code to codify all of the crimes recognized at Nuremberg, including genocide (Ferencz 1980, vol. 2, p. 7).

On September 30, 1947, the United States issued formal comments on the Draft Convention on the Crime of Genocide. It argued argued against draft provisions in the convention that would have created an international court to punish violators of the Genocide Convention. The United States argued that "the task of drafting such a convention (to provide for a permanent criminal court) at least equals that of drafting a convention on genocide. That task should be undertaken as a task separate and apart from the drafting of a convention on genocide" (Ferencz 1980, vol. 2, p. 146). The United States argued that ad hoc courts could enforce the genocide convention's provisions until such time as a permanent court was created and suggested that the new ILC take up consideration of the court issue (United Nations Document A\401, 1947, reprinted in Ferencz 1980, vol. 2, pp. 143–149).

One motive for the U.S. government in separating the court issue from the genocide convention was a legitimate fear that the inclusion of the court in the genocide convention would doom both projects to rejection in the ratification stage. Even though the Genocide Convention did not ultimately contain an international court for enforcement, the United States failed to ratify it for 40 years.

Interestingly, the leading advocate of an international law rule criminalizing genocide, Raphael Lemkin, pragmatically anticipated the reluctance of states to establish an international tribunal with jurisdiction over genocide. Lemkin thought the world was "not ready" for such an international court because it would be too much of a challenge to state sovereignty, and so he advocated instead that there should be universal jurisdiction to punish genocide so that any national court could punish the crime regardless of where it occurred (Power 2002, pp. 55–6). The ILC of the United Nations did take up the question of a permanent ICC once it came into being in 1950. The members of the ILC are elected in their individual capacities to provide their own unique expert judgments on the evolution of international law. However, they are nominated by governments, and their own views on international law historically have reflected the views of their governments; often ILC members are former diplomats themselves (Morton 2000)[8]. The ILC, whose task is to develop international law, functions by appointing a special rapporteur from among its membership to study an issue in detail. The report of the rapporteur is then discussed by the full commission and recommendations are made to the General Assembly. Asked in 1950 to draft a code of offenses against the peace and security of mankind, Special Rapporteur Jean Spiropoulos took it as his task to offer a document that might serve as the basis for conversation at an international diplomatic conference that sought to adopt such a code; thus he was guided from the beginning by a concern for what was politically possible given the existing state of international relations (United Nations Document A/CN. 4/25; reprinted in Yearbook of the ILC, April 26, 1950, VII (New York, United Nations, 1957) and in Ferencz 1980 vol. 2; hereinafter Spiropoulos 1950).

The Spiropoulos report indicates the extent to which global civil society influenced the ILC's thinking on the question of international criminal jurisdiction. In addition to the existing international conventions that dealt with the issue, Spiropoulos notes that he was influenced by nonofficial texts, including the "Plan for a World Criminal Code," drafted by the distinguished international scholar, the Romanian V.V. Pella, under the auspices of three NGOs: the International Association of Penal Law, the Inter-Parliamentary Union, and the International Law Association (Spiropoulos 1950, para. 3). Pro-ICC NGOs then, had an impact in the 1950s on shaping the content of discussion among states at an IGO because the ILC text eventually became the subject of General Assembly debate. What was different when we compare the role of NGOs in the 1950s episode with their impact in the 1990s was not their ability to get ideas on the international agenda but instead their ability to convince governments to take action to put those ideas into force via an international treaty. Once the matter moved before states in the General Assembly, there is little evidence that NGOs were able to mount the same kind of sustained lobbying campaign that occurred in the 1990s. Since codification of crimes is inherently linked to the development of a mechanism of enforcement, the discussion of a code led the ILC directly to the subject of a permanent ICC.

According to the Spiropoulos report, the idea of a formal codification of crimes against the peace and security of mankind was first proposed to President Harry Truman on the occasion of the termination of the work of the Nuremberg court by one of its judges, Justice Francis Biddle. Truman, in his reply to the Biddle report, agreed and added that such a codification should be undertaken "by the best legal minds the world over" under the auspices of the United Nations (Spiropoulos 1950, para. 10).[9] Consequently, the United States initiated discussions at the United Nations that resulted in the ILC's consideration of the question beginning in November 1946.[10]

By November of 1950, when the General Assembly's Sixth Committee took up discussion of the first ILC report on the question of an ICC, the world's nations had cooled considerably to the possibility of prosecuting war crimes. Mr. Gilberto Amando, of Brazil, disagreed with the contention of other United Nations delegations that the experience of Nuremberg and the IMTFE demonstrated the practicality of prosecuting war crimes. He argued instead that because of the total victories of the allies, those trials were more like the will of sovereign states imposing law by coercion over territories they physically controlled rather than being true prosecutions under international law (United Nations Document A\1316 in Ferencz, 1980, vol. 2, p. 291). This was the substantial hurdle that diplomats were unable to surpass in the 1950s. It is one thing to impose justice on the defeated. It is another thing for states to accept an institution with universal rules for prosecuting war crimes in advance of knowing who will stand accused. Mr. Lachs, from Poland, noted that "if an international penal tribunal were given competence to punish international crimes, the principle of the sovereignty of States would be violated" (United Nations Document A\1316 in Ferencz 1980, vol. 2, p. 292).

Except for France, the great powers equivocated in their support for an ICC after Nuremberg and the IMTFE. The question was discussed in the ILC and the United Nations General Assembly's Sixth Committee, but there it was allowed to die.

The beginning of the Cold War and particularly the conflict in Korea dramatically changed the conversation about the emergence of international criminal law. A conversation on the editorial pages of *The Times* of London in 1952 illustrates this impact of the changing times. In the July 17, 1952 edition *The Times*, the Tokyo correspondent reported that the Chinese foreign minister, Mr. Chou, had acknowledged that it would provide prisoners of war with the protections guaranteed by the 1949 Geneva Convention; however, "prisoners of war who have been convicted as war criminals according to the principles established by the international military tribunals of Nuremberg and Tokyo shall not be entitled to the benefits of the convention (6)." This comment by the Chinese led to an impassioned debate in the form of letters to the editor of *The Times*. Lord Cork and Orrerey wrote on July 23 that the Chinese comment showed the folly of the Nuremberg precedent. He argued that prior to 1944, international law did not allow for the trial of war criminals except by their own state. Now, he argued, the Chinese would be entitled to use that precedent to charge allied prisoners of war. He went on to say that "When the list defining 'war crimes' is studied, it will be seen how wide is the net in which perfectly innocent men may be caught, for it includes firing on undefended localities, bombardment of privileged buildings (i.e., churches, museums, schools, and hospitals), purposeless destruction, &c—matters upon which the opponents may differ widely. There need be no difficulty in framing a charge" (*The Times*, July 23, 1952, p. 7). Professor Goodhart of Oxford replied to this attack on the notion of trying war crimes in a subsequent letter to the editor. He pointed out that the Chinese would never allow a fair trial, where the allied air men could choose their own counsel and have the trial open to the free press of the world, as was done at Nuremberg (*The Times*, July 28, 1952, p. 7). But another letter on July 31 by Lord Hankey starkly laid out the political problems with the entire war crimes movement. Hankey pointed out that if the Chinese tried allied airmen, they would likely use only "enemy judges (fortunately not victors), with the possible addition of bogus neutral judges from Russia and other Communist countries to give simple folk a fictitious impression of neutrality." He goes on to allege that the Geneva Convention rights of the Axis accused were violated at Nuremberg and Tokyo, and therefore the allied prisoners in China would have little to complain about (*The Times*, July 31, 1952). While the debate over the merits of enforcement of international law norms continued to rage on *The Times*'s editorial pages for three more weeks, the political difficulty of creating neutral international judicial institutions had become apparent in Western political discourse.

International law scholars of the time were extremely concerned with the issue of the fairness and politicization of war crimes trials. One of the central criticisms of Nuremberg was that those trials were simply the victor's justice. Still, there was international support for the outcome, even in Germany. A German law scholar concluded on the pages of the *American Journal of International Law* in 1949 that it would have been preferable if German judges had been part of the trial, but that the Nuremberg court's conclusions were still a positive result for justice (Ehard 1949).

Once the Korean conflict began, and the accusations of victor's justice at Nuremberg were widely heard, Western leaders apparently cooled to the idea of prosecuting war crimes. The inability to create a universal judicial authority clearly was a function of the continued ideological hostilities between the great powers. NGOs articulated a vision for a permanent court with universal jurisdiction, but ultimately their arguments were not persuasive enough in the context of polarized conflict between the superpowers.

Robert K. Woetzel reports that "the Soviet Union [was] opposed to international organs affecting individuals within the Soviet power orbit, because of the great emphasis it place[d] on its sovereignty. Thus the Soviets and their allies opposed the creation of international court for the punishment of genocide" (Stone and Woetzel 1970, p. 92). The Soviets apparently feared that the most likely defendants to appear before a supranational court would be themselves.

Complaints about the proposals for a "code of offenses against the peace and security of mankind" came from both sides of the Cold War divide. The Soviet's actively sought a definition of aggression. The United States and other states opposed this, arguing that any definition would have loopholes that could be exploited by those planning aggression.[11] Another dispute further revealed the extent of the distrust engendered by the Cold War. One provision of the draft code would have criminalized "the preparation of armed forces for use against any state for any purpose other than self-defense or in connection with a United Nations decision."[12] *The New York Times* reported that "Some delegates said that provision probably would be used by the Soviet bloc to charge that the building of bases by the United States outside North America was a violation."[13]

France was the only major power to support the effort to create an ICC at the time (Nanda 1998, p. 414). Their delegate adopted the arguments of Ricardo Alfaro, the ILC rapporteur who favored the creation of a permanent court. In his thorough report, Alfaro cited the arguments of George A. Finch, who, in an address to the American Society of International Law, had argued that breaches of the peace (particularly launching aggressive war) *had* to be labeled as violations of law if there was ever to be a peaceful community of nations (reprinted in Ferencz 1980, vol. 2, pp. 254–255). Agreeing with Finch and others, Alfaro recognized that ex post facto determinations of violations by victors was not as desirable as a preagreed statute that specified the violations. Alfaro also noted that a serious objection to the possibility of an international judicial organ was the fact that such a supranational court would inherently be in conflict with the doctrine of absolute state sovereignty. In rejecting that argument, he noted that there are some crimes that it is not practical for a national government to prosecute, and more directly, that the doctrine of absolute sovereignty was simply no longer compatible with the present organization of the world into mutually interdependent states (Ferencz 1980, vol. 2, p. 256). He concluded that "The community of states is entitled to prevent crimes against the peace and security of mankind and crimes against the dictates of the human conscience, including therein the hideous crime of genocide" (Ferencz 1980, vol. 2, p. 256).

Alfaro's discourse is emblematic of a principled normative claim oriented to a universal audience. He directed his argument toward identifying crimes that all could agree ought to be punished, including crimes against the peace, crimes against humanity, and genocide. Why, of all the powerful states, was only France persuaded? I argue that it is crucial and not incidental to Alfaro's argument that "the doctrine of absolute sovereignty was no longer compatible with [the] present organization of the world into mutually sovereign states." Ultimately, this premise was not widely shared by Alfaro's interlocutors at the time. As I have suggested, such an argument was difficult to sustain in the emerging global political context of the Cold War.

The leading argument against an ICC in the ILC and the General Assembly's Sixth Committee in 1950 was that a court would need a clear code of law, jurisdiction, and enforcement possibilities. One of the first ILC rapporteurs, Mr. Emil Sandström of Sweden, argued that states were unlikely to take all three of these steps at once and that creating a court without all of these things in place could lead to haphazard justice, or worse, the retrograde development of international law. The British delegate to the Sixth Committee, Mr. Fitzmaurice, agreed with Sandström and argued that the ILC had been misled by "assuming the desirability on idealistic ground [of an ICC] . . . and to have brushed aside questions of practical possibility" in a way the United Kingdom thought "unrealistic" (Ferencz 1980, vol. 2, p. 270). But these statements reflect more of a lack of political will to create a workable court than they do principled reasons why such a court should not be undertaken. Britain, the Soviet Union, and ultimately the United States rejected the principled argument being advanced by Alfaro and others because they refused to accept the possibility that universal norms could be impartially enforced against themselves and their enemies. In that context, preserving the legal notion of state sovereign independence was deemed to be of utmost importance.

On December 5, 1952, the General Assembly of the United Nations adopted resolution 697 (seventh session) that established the 1953 Committee on International Criminal Jurisdiction. It met 23 times between July 27 and August 20, and it discussed in some detail the legal challenges associated with creating a permanent ICC as well as a particular proposal for the draft statute of such a court. Sixteen states, then members of the General Assembly's Sixth Committee, were represented (Ferencz 1980, vol. 2, pp. 429–33). The report of that committee summarizes the views of states about the ICC project and highlights the reasoning that ultimately led to the delay of the ICC project for the next 40 years. It said:

> Some members, though considering the establishment of an international criminal court an important and ultimately highly desirable development in world affairs, expressed the conviction that at the present stage any attempt to establish an international criminal jurisdiction would put a strain on international good feeling and co-operation, and would meet with insurmountable obstacles. Present international law was based on relations among States. The Charter of the United Nations was also based on these premises. International criminal jurisdiction over individuals, therefore, did not fit with the present set-up of the United Nations. An international criminal court presupposed an international community with the power necessary to operate the court, and such power did not exist. *A surrender of some present State sovereignty would be the condition for the establishment of the court, and such surrender was highly unlikely.* Therefore, the court would be powerless, and its establishment would be an empty gesture. It would be improper to establish the court before international criminal law had been defined in generally adopted conventions. Moreover, this establishment, it was said by one member, would interfere with the principle of universality in the prosecution of such crimes as piracy and would interfere with existing extradition treaties. For these and other reasons, some members felt that the General Assembly should be advised not to proceed further in this field for the time being.[14]

I highlighted the pivotal sentence in the reasoning. In 1953, diplomats, and the governments they represented, did not believe that most governments would be willing to allow the encroachment on their sovereign rights that would be inherent in the creation of an ICC. This did not stop the delegates from designing a detailed proposal for the statute of such a court on the basis of prior proposals and their own discussions. They proposed resolutions to some of the conflicts that challenged ICC statute negotiators in the 1990s and they avoided other crucial issues. The 1953 draft statute proposed a court that did not specifically enumerate the crimes over which it would have jurisdiction. Instead the drafters proposed simply that "The Court shall apply international law, including international criminal law, and where appropriate, national law."[15] The consent to the jurisdiction regime proposed was much more protective of state sovereignty than the mechanism ultimately adopted in the Rome Statute. The 1953 draft statute said in the article titled "Attribution of Jurisdiction:"

1. Jurisdiction of the court is not to be presumed.

2. A State may confer jurisdiction upon the Court by convention, by special agreement, or by unilateral declaration.

3. Conferment of jurisdiction signifies the right to seize the Court and the duty to accept its jurisdiction subject to such provisions as the State or States have specified.[16]

In the next article, the draft said that persons would only be tried if both the state of the person's nationality and the state where the alleged crimes took place had conferred jurisdiction on the court. Given this restrictive jurisdiction regime, it is difficult to imagine situations in which the court would have been used at all. States were empowered under the draft to withdraw their consent with one year's notice. Moreover, proceedings could only be instituted by a state that had accepted the courts' jurisdiction with respect to the particular crime relevant to the initiated proceeding.[17] Since each state would undoubtedly attach a number of reservations and conditions to its own acceptance of the court's jurisdiction, it seems likely that this proposal would have led to a court with endless disputes about the limits of its own reciprocally recognized jurisdiction, much like the disputes that have hindered the work of the International Court of Justice because of the reciprocal nature of its voluntary jurisdiction regime (Meyer 2002).

Indeed, the unworkable nature of this proposal may have been one of the very reasons for its failure to attract much support. Compared to the rule adopted for the ICC in the Rome Statute of 1998, the 1953 proposal seems much less likely to have led to regular prosecutions. By carefully protecting the sovereignty rights of the potential member states, the 1953 draft proposed a court that would be unlikely to be a significant force in bringing an end to impunity for the perpetrators of serious international law crimes. That is because several states would have had a procedural veto over any particular prosecution under the 1953 draft statute. Thus, the probability that at least one state would be inclined to use that veto in any particular case would be high. Moreover, this has implications for the normative legitimacy of such a jurisdiction regime. As I elaborate in the next section, a jurisdiction system that allows each state to place different conditions on the jurisdiction of the court can easily be accused of applying justice with different standards for different defendants.

Analysis of the 1950s Discourse

We can consider further whether or not the legal regime proposed in 1953 would have complied with Habermasian conditions for justifiable normative rules. I am especially concerned with the requirement in a communicative action–theoretical approach to the legitimacy of law that requires that legal norms should be universal in their application in order to be rationally justifiable. Also, we are interested in the level of participation and the openness of this discourse in the 1950s.

Habermas says that

> The norms passed by the political legislature and the rights recognized by the judiciary prove their "rationality" by the fact that addressees [of the law] are treated as free and equal members of an association of legal subjects. In short, this rationality is proven in the equal treatment of legal persons who at the same time are protected in their integrity. This consequence is juristically expressed in the requirement of equal treatment. Although this includes equality in applying the law, that is, the equality of citizens before the law, it is equivalent to the broader principle of substantive legal equality, which holds that what is equal in all relevant respects should be treated equally, and what is unequal should be treated unequally.
> (Habermas 1996, p. 414)

What is crucial here is the question of whether or not the norms suggested in the 1953 statute can be considered to meet the requirement of equal treatment.

Clearly the drafters of this text sought a legal norm for the exercise of the court's jurisdiction that had reciprocal validity. States could compel the citizens of other states to be brought before the court only to the extent that they accepted the jurisdiction of the court with respect to their own citizens. One potential problem for the rational justification of these proposed norms was that if states placed radically different conditions on their acceptance of the jurisdiction of the court, including what crimes they would allow the court to hear, the court could not ensure the equal application of the law at the level of individual defendants. Whether or not one might be subject to the ICC's jurisdiction under the 1953 draft statute would depend on one's nationality and where the crime was committed, and the terms under which a state that wanted to initiate the prosecution of the accused had accepted the court's jurisdiction. To illustrate the problem consider the following example. Genocide committed by some individuals would be punishable, subject to whatever limitation their own state or the accusing state attached to the court's jurisdiction. But the exact same crime might not be punishable at all if committed by the national of a state that accepted the court's jurisdiction with respect to the crime of aggression, but not genocide.

Even the advocates of the draft statute in the 1953 report recognized that the crux of the issue was precisely the relationship between the legal personality of states and the legal personality of individuals under international criminal law. The report summarized their views as follows:

> Other members, although realizing the rather primitive stage of inter-State relations . . . —emphasized the point that modern international law was beginning to recognize the individual as a subject possessing rights (for instance, in the Universal Declaration of Human Rights), and also possessing duties. In the judgment of Nürnberg, it was decided that those duties transcended even obligations to the national state. The moral obligation of living up to the principles of the post-war judgments, and the undeniable fact of the existence of a common standard of norms to be applied, e.g., the unanimously affirmed principle of Nürnberg, made international criminal jurisdiction desirable, and it should be promoted by establishing the possibility of such international criminal jurisdiction as far as present inter-State relations would permit. Consequently, those members favoured the establishment of a court, the jurisdiction of which would depend on voluntary submission to that jurisdiction by the States willing to so submit. They were aware of the intricacy of the problems involved, and were willing to proceed only with the utmost caution.[18]

This passage shows that even supporters of the ICC in the 1950s saw the tension between existing views on state sovereignty and the necessity for an ICC to treat individuals as legal persons. In 1953, the debate simply did not advance to a point where states would consider more serious alterations of their sovereignty in order to allow for the establishment of an ICC that could claim to provide equal justice for all of the individual defendants and victims who might find themselves with relevant matters before the court. Similar debates raged about legal and practical effects of particular proposals for the design of the court in the 1990s. Those debates, as we will see, reached markedly different conclusions.

In summary, there were important NGOs that advanced arguments in favor of an ICC that ultimately were considered at the United Nations in the 1950s. In the end, however, states who argued that an ICC was impractical carried the day. The ICC was defeated on the grounds that the technical legal minutiae required were impossibly complex. Dissenting voices could not coordinate their complaints via the Internet that was still 40 years away, as would happen in the 1990s. There was nothing particularly rationally compelling about the argument against a court, and the world arguably paid a high price for failing to prosecute war crimes in the Cold War period. But in the context of a world divided into two ideological camps, each of which saw the other as a threat to their very way of life, it was perhaps impossible to expect that a normative argument in favor of institutionalizing the third-party judgment of violations of international criminal law could be persuasive. Still, at least one important power, France, chose to back the court. Perhaps also there was an international fatigue with creating new international institutions after the birth of the United Nations, the International Monetary Fund, and the North Atlantic Treaty Organization in short succession. More important, the superpowers already realized that the Cold War was to be fought by proxies, in Greece, in Korea, and elsewhere. In the West, the construction of the threat of the Communist bloc made it inconceivable that a neutral court could be established. In the Soviet Union, the possibility of Western prosecution of Soviet offenses already seemed too real, given that Soviet responsibility for the Katyn massacre in Poland during World War II had already been raised at Nuremberg (Abarinov 1993). Consequently, there was no ground for a universal consensus about how to enforce international criminal norms.

Ultimately, then, we might say that the effort to establish an ICC in the 1950s lacked two elements that were essential for a successful resolution of the relevant legal issues and the emergence of widespread support for such an institution. First, the dialogue in the 1950s remained fairly restricted.[19] Nearly all the participants in the debate were formal state representatives or state-appointed members of the ILC. In effect, we could conceptualize the failure to establish an ICC as being a failure of the communication structure of world politics in the 1950s. By communication structure of world politics I refer to what Habermas means by this term, not the content or function of everyday speech but the social space generated in communicative action (Habermas 1996, p. 360). If we assume for a moment that a lack of institutionalized international penal jurisdiction was in fact a problem in the world political system of the time, the crucial question is why people were unable to find a resolution to that problem. Consider Habermas's comment on the role of civil society in democracy, in which he says, "From the perspective of democratic theory, the public sphere must, in addition, amplify the pressure of problems, that is, not only detect and identify problems but also convincingly and *influentially* thematize them, furnish them with possible solutions, and dramatize them in such a way that they are taken up and dealt with by parliamentary complexes" (Habermas 1996, p. 359). We cannot say that the institutionalized public discourse at the United Nations failed to problematize the issue. As we have seen, Alfaro and others argued forcefully that some form of ICC was necessary to bring law to bear on international politics. Those advocates spoke from formal positions of authority, (primarily as members of the ILC), but of course they had no decision-making power themselves. When confronted with the claim that the reforms they proposed would undermine existing norms of sovereign state autonomy, they were unable to show the weight of their claim. In effect, the future victims of war crimes, genocide, and crimes against humanity did not have sufficient voice within civil society to bring their views to bear on the decision makers in national governments. It is in this sense the structure of the discourse was truncated in the world political system of the 1950s. This is an intuitive result; indeed, it would not occur to most to analysts to suggest that the world political system of the 1950s approximated the conditions for democracy on the basis of communicative action. The payoff from this line of analysis is instead to highlight the consequences of the extremely finite opportunities for international political dialogue in the 1950s. It highlights the extent to which particular forms of political organization, in this case the sovereign state system organized loosely by the United Nations, limits the possibility for the development of international law on the basis of communicatively rational consensus. But this lack of discourse was tied to the second, and perhaps most fatal failing of the 1950s.

The second element lacking was that the participants in the discourse in the 1950s were insufficiently willing to fully consider the group of relevant actors as consisting of all the individual and free persons living in the world. Indeed, with decolonization only partially complete, such a conceptualization of the international political community was probably impossible (N. Crawford 2002). The delegates that discussed an ICC court in the 1950s continued to assume that the only legal persons relevant to the discussion were the members of the society of states, sovereign states themselves. But to create a court with the capacity to punish individual human beings separately from states they acted on behalf of, it was necessary to conceive of an international legal system that respected the legal rights of individual persons. To have such a legal system that would be rationally justifiable in the sense of communicative action theory, it would have been necessary to conceptualize that system in a way that guaranteed equal protection under the law for all individuals subject to the court's authority. However, any design for such a court that was sufficiently respectful of the sovereign rights of states to meet with approval in the 1950s could not ensure such respect for individual legal equality.

4

Context: An Opening for an International Criminal Court; 1989–1994

> Difficult as these obstacles to [international] criminal jurisdiction may be, there is a solid basis of achievement on which it is possible to build. We do have a body of substantive law, however inadequate, in various accords and conventions as well as customs and practices among states. There is a continued sense of outrage arising from offenses committed against the peoples of the world and having repercussions on relations between states; also, mankind is often affronted by barbarous procedures and penalties, as well as by the fact that often offenders are not subjected to any penalties at all.
>
> —A. N. R. Robinson, *Statement made in 1973*[1]

Context

In order to demonstrate that the discursive practices of nongovernmental organizations had a decisive impact in shaping the Rome Statute for an International Criminal Court, we must begin with a prior task. That is to try to outline, however briefly, the political and discursive context in which NGOs initially presented their arguments. Only with a sense of those background conditions can we show the ways that arguments presented by the NGOs pushed the ICC discourse toward an outcome that seemed very unlikely at the initial stages of the process. To establish this political context empirically, we must examine the widely held beliefs and perceptions held by knowledgeable actors at the time about whether or not an ICC was feasible or desirable, what purposes its establishment might serve, and what substantial political hurdles existed in the effort to build such a court. These are intersubjective beliefs, and the evidence for them are the statements of the relevant actors at the time and subsequently. In the later analysis of the ICC discourse, I draw on the tradition of narrative explanation, which places facts in relationship to one another in an effort to demonstrate the connections between them (Ruggie 1998, p. 94).[2] The goal is to demonstrate that the crucial features of the court that came into existence in 2002 owe their existence to the discursive practices of NGOs at an early stage in the ICC negotiations and throughout the subsequent negotiations. In the Weberian tradition of social science explanation, the evidence presented shows why the ICC is *so* and not *otherwise* (Ruggie 1998, p. 32).

In the early 1990s, the possibility of establishing a permanent ICC seemed remote and fanciful. Still it was perhaps slightly less fanciful than it would have seemed a few years before. In order to assess the impact of NGOs' discursive practices in framing the debate about establishing an ICC, we should first understand the context that existed prior to the ICC discussions. One element of that context was the predominant power position of the United States at the end of the Cold War. Twice before in the twentieth century, the conclusion of a global great power struggle had resulted in efforts led by the United States to build new institutions of global governance: Woodrow Wilson's plan for a League of Nations, and Franklin Roosevelt's design for the UN. Could it happen again with the end of the Cold War? George H. W. Bush spoke of a "A new world order—where diverse nations are drawn together to achieve the universal aspirations of mankind . . ."[3] In 1991, it was not yet clear what the U.S. president had in mind, but the political climate did not seem friendly to new global governance projects.

In particular, U.S. policymakers were not favorably disposed to the use of international courts to resolve international disputes in this time period.[4] In fact, U.S. policy toward the proceedings of the ICJ during two crucial 1980s cases suggested that the United States maintained an entirely strategic attitude toward the only major multilateral international court with near global membership. The United States sought to use that international court as one instrument to obtain its strategic objectives. American foreign policy makers had refused to take seriously the notion that the ICJ could provide neutral third-party decisions that should be respected by both winners and losers in order to achieve the longer-term objective of promoting the settlement of disputes based on law. During the 1980s, the United States was involved in two major cases before the ICJ in The Hague. In the first, the United States was the plaintiff complaining about the Iranian government's complicity in the taking of American hostages during the 1979 overthrow of the shah. While the court was considering the case, the United States attempted a military raid to free the hostages, resulting in a disastrous tactical failure but also showing a severe lack of respect for the judicial process (Meyer 2002, pp. 127–30). A few years later, when it was charged with the illegal use of force in Central America by the Sandinista government in Nicaragua, the Unites States belatedly withdrew itself from the ICJ's jurisdiction and ultimately failed to present a defense.

In a formal statement announcing its refusal to participate in the ICJ hearings, the United States accused the ICJ of being "politicized."[5] Howard Meyer notes that the accusation that this particular court was politicized was odd since the membership of the court had changed very little since the United States had brought its claims in the Tehran hostages case five years earlier. The Tehran case ultimately was decided in favor of the United States, notwithstanding the botched American attempt to resolve the situation through the use of force. American opponents of a permanent ICC often proclaimed during the 1990s that the new court could be politicized and could therefore be dangerous to U.S. interests, echoing this earlier rhetoric about the ICJ. When President Bill Clinton announced that the United States would sign the ICC statute in December 2000, he felt the need to remind listeners that "in the negotiations following the Rome conference, we have worked effectively to develop procedures that limit the likelihood of *politicized* prosecutions."[6] In any case, U.S. interaction with the ICJ in the 1980s left a high hurdle for advocates of a new ICC in the American political context of the 1990s.[7] Another incident in 1980s American foreign policy also showed the limits of the debate about the role of international law in the United States.

A debate that took place in the late 1980s over U.S. ratification of the *Convention on the Prevention and Punishment of the Crime of Genocide*, adopted in 1948,[8] highlighted the challenges for any proposal for a permanent ICC. Opponents of the Genocide Convention, including the John Birch Society and the Liberty Lobby, focused on the possibility that Americans might be held accountable by an international tribunal or other foreign court (Power 2002, pp. 155–6). Their arguments grossly exaggerated the reach of the Genocide Convention, suggesting that Christian missionaries might be tried "on grounds that to convert cannibals in Africa to Christianity is to destroy a culture."[9] These attacks were spread quickly through conservative talk radio and newsletters. Senator Jesse Helms of North Carolina supported such views and gave them added credibility because of his senior status on the Senate Foreign Relations Committee. In contrast, no broad-based constituency existed to advocate forcefully in favor of the convention.[10] Of course, the reality is that if genocide were committed in the United States or by a U.S. citizen abroad, such a crime would almost certainly be prosecuted by the U.S. judicial system regardless of the existence of any international obligation to do so. Still, the United States failed to ratify the Genocide Convention for 40 years.

When the U.S. Senate finally voted to ratify the Genocide Convention in 1986, it would only do so with reservations that sought to eliminate the possibility that Americans might be tried before an international court (Paust 2000, pp. 942–5).[11] In fact, the enforcement mechanisms of the 1948 Genocide Convention are relatively weak. The convention requires that violations be punished either by a court in the state where the crime took place "or by such international penal tribunal as may have jurisdiction with respect to those Contracting Parties which shall have accepted its jurisdiction."[12] Since there was no such international penal tribunal in existence during the entire 40-year period that the United States delayed its ratification, the United States had no justifiable reason to fear an international court. Still, the potential threat of international prosecution of U.S. citizens was the main motivation for opposition to the Genocide Convention.

Advocates of the Genocide Convention in the United States were often tarred as communists or one-worlder internationalists. These labels were effective enough that few politicians (or academics) wanted to be associated with such positions. There were a few exceptions. Senator William Proxmire, the most persistent advocate of the Genocide Convention in the U.S. Senate, noted that the UN ambassador Jeanne Kirkpatrick observed that "It was contrary to our national interest" to delay ratifying the Genocide Convention. Proxmire emphasized that Kirkpatrick was hardly a "one-worlder internationalist" (Power 2002, p. 158).

Discourses delimit who is entitled to speak on a given question (Milliken 1999, p. 229). In this excerpt we see an *advocate* for the rule of law in international affairs accepting the conventional wisdom of the time that constructing an international political system based on the rule of the law remained hopelessly utopian. Proxmire's point was that it was still possible to advocate American support for the Genocide Convention without succumbing to the hopeless utopianism of one-worlder internationalists. Even serious people, like Kirkpatrick (no misguided communist herself), supported the Genocide Convention.

The point of this is to demonstrate the tremendous hurdle that advocates of a permanent ICC still had to overcome in the early 1990s, at least in the U.S. political arena. They had to challenge the conventional wisdom that the neutral application of principles of law at the international level was impossibly utopian, or worse, a (communist) plot by some outside power to convince Westerners to lower their guard. The collapse of communism undoubtedly contributed to an improvement in the political climate within the United States for people interested in building international law. President George H. W. Bush talked about the establishment of a "new world order" and implied that there might be a greater role for the rule of law. For a brief period during and after the first Gulf War, the UN Security Council seemed positioned finally to play its intended role as a place where major international conflicts could be settled through debate rather than military struggle. But the meaning of the new world order very much remained to be determined. The language used even by advocates of internationalism during the genocide debate shows a tendency to belittle speakers as ridiculous if they showed a belief in the real potential of international law.

This discussion has admittedly focused on the political atmosphere in the United States. There are two justifications for that, besides the fact that this author is a U.S. citizen. First, without the support of the United States, or with outright U.S. opposition at an early stage, it is very unlikely that the remaining states of the world would have pursued the idea of multilateral negotiations to create an international court with criminal jurisdiction.[13] Second, many of the sovereignty concerns voiced in the U.S. political context were also serious concerns in other states. The United States historically has been a leading proponent of rule of law mechanisms at the international level. Consequently, reluctance to pursue such an institution in the United States would tend to indicate that other states would be equally or more reluctant to permit law-based supranational supervision of decisions about the use of force.

By 1998, the U.S. position toward the potential ICC left it more strongly opposed to the increased institutionalization of international criminal law than most other states, but that was something of a surprise. It is worth remembering that this is a far different outcome than what many observers expected in the early post–Cold War environment. After all, the United States has historically been the leading promoter of international institutions based on principled rules.[14] For a brief period in the mid-1990s, the United States seemed willing and able to play this role again with respect to the establishment of an ICC. In fact, it is clear that the Clinton administration fully expected the negotiations to produce a court the United States would be willing to support (Scheffer 1997). However, the court that was promoted by the

U.S. government is not the one whose charter was adopted in Rome in 1998. To see why, we must revisit the ICC discourse of the 1990s.

An Opening—Why States and the International Law Commission Reconsidered the Idea of a Permanent ICC

The end of the Cold War reinvigorated the idea of an ICC.[15] By 1990, much to the surprise of many observers, a broad consensus had emerged within the ILC that there should be a supranational body with the power to try at least some sorts of international crimes (Ferencz 1992, p. 390).

In the aftermath of the Cold War, an increasing number of voices began to call for a permanent ICC for a variety of different reasons. Still there was as yet no consensus about what crimes such a court could punish, under what authority it could be constituted, or what powers it should have. Already in 1982 and 1984 the International Law Association adopted and then amended a draft statute for an International Criminal Tribunal.[16] In 1990 and 1991, discussions within the ILC continued to link the establishment of an international criminal tribunal with a decades-old effort to draft a "Code of Crimes against the Peace and Security of Mankind," as those issues had been linked since the late 1940s. In 1991, Germany's foreign minister, Hans-Dietrich Genscher, said to the UN General Assembly: "We call for an international court of justice of the United Nations where crimes against humanity, crimes against peace, genocide, war crimes, and environmental criminality can be prosecuted and punished."[17] Germany ultimately would be a key state in the group of like-minded countries that favored the establishment of a strong ICC. Also that year, the official position of the United States was still to delay the creation of a court by calling for further analysis.[18] The U.S. representative to the General Assembly's legal committee, Robert Rosenstock, said that an ICC was "an enormously complex endeavor, raising profound legal, political and practical questions."[19] Rosenstock also argued that since an ICC's jurisdiction requirements would require the consent of many states, it might never be able to hear cases. This argument, and others about the complexity of creating a workable ICC, were used to support the United States' claim that "further study" was required before a court statute could be drafted.

In 1992, the ILC issued a draft code of crimes that according to one ILC member "was widely considered to be overbroad and unsatisfactory" (J. Crawford 2002). Given this criticism of the ILC's work, a deliberate decision was made by the members of the ILC to separate the establishment of an ICC from the parallel project of developing the substance of international criminal law (J. Crawford 2002).

The draft statute for an ICC that was finally adopted by the ILC in 1994 and referred to the UN General Assembly for further action was in many ways a very conservative document, particularly in comparison to the Rome Statute that emerged four years later. First, as we have just noted, it made no effort to define or develop the existing definitions of crimes under international law. Instead, it relied on existing definitions of international law crimes incorporated by reference to the relevant treaties. Second, the 1994 draft featured stringent procedural rules before the proposed court could exercise its jurisdiction. First, a state would have to file a complaint, and then a state with custody of the accused and the state on whose territory the crime was committed would have to accept the court's jurisdiction. The ILC draft statute also permitted states to accept the court's jurisdictions with respect to some crimes and not others, to accept jurisdiction for a limited period of time, or even to be a member of the court and participate in its operation but not accept the court's jurisdiction over the state's own territory at all.[20]

James Crawford, who was appointed a member of the ILC in 1992, the year the commission took up discussion of the ICC proposal, writes that "so far as the ILC was concerned, the question was whether an international criminal court proposal modest enough to be taken seriously could be formulated consistently with the basic legal principles which should underpin any criminal process . . . " (J. Crawford 2002). His remarks illustrate the profound difficulties still perceived in persuading states to establish a permanent ICC in the early 1990s. Crawford wrote: "If the intrinsic difficulties of an international criminal court were to be associated with the difficulties of further developing the substantive law in these fields, negotiations might never begin. Thus, there were strong reasons for starting with a modest proposal and few reasons to anticipate the eventual dynamic which was to lead to the 1998 Rome Statute"(J. Crawford 2002). In particular, no one anticipated the role that NGOs might play in pushing states to accept a court with considerably more authority than the ILC thought possible.

A further indication of the dramatic progress in the ICC debate between 1994 and 1998 is the very modest proposal put forward by Cherif Bassiouni in 1993. That year he published a "Draft Statute: International Criminal Tribunal."[21] The proposal was extremely conservative compared to what was ultimately adopted in Rome. Bassiouni's draft proposed a complex jurisdiction scheme that in effect would have allowed each state party to decide which international law crimes should come within the international tribunal's original jurisdiction and which should have concurrent jurisdiction. In many cases, it would have limited the international court to settling disputes between states about conflicts over extradition and the interpretation of state obligations under international criminal law without giving it criminal jurisdiction to convict and punish individuals at all. In his commentary he notes that allowing states to "opt-in" on a crime- by-crime basis "is intended to give the State-Parties the flexibility they may need to induce them to them to ratify the Convention" (Bassiouni 1998). Noting states' cost concerns, Bassiouni proposed a court that would share office space (and a library) with the ICJ at the Peace Palace in The Hague, and whose officers would normally exercise their functions from their home states until a trial required them to convene. Other elements of Bassiouni's draft seemed similarly designed to create a court with very limited powers in order to persuade reluctant states to join. Bassiouni is one of the most distinguished and long-term advocates of a permanent ICC (Bassiouni 1991; Bassiouni and Blakesley 1992). The weakness of his draft statute compared to the much more significant authority granted by states to the ICC in the 1998 Rome Statute indicates the tremendous movement in thinking between the early 1990s and 1998 about what was possible.

Events in the world, including, not least of all, the Iraqi invasion of Kuwait and the disintegration of the former Yugoslavia, led the United States to reconsider its policy of opposition to the establishment of an ICC. But before I turn to a description of those events, I want to review my argument about the role of NGOs in the process.

NGOs had already laid a vital foundation by the time the ILC moved to reconsider the issue in the early 1990s. NGOs had analyzed a number of the legal issues involved, and they continued to do so as the process went forward.[22] Their rationalistic perspective allowed them to identify solutions to normative and practical problems that were broadly acceptable. By engaging in dialogue with government officials, NGOs highlighted the problems and ambiguities with the arguments advanced by states that sought to avoid a court altogether or to ensure that any court created would not challenge their sovereign prerogatives. As the ICC initiative progressed from the preliminary ILC discussions of the 1992–1994 period to the Rome Treaty Conference of 1998, NGOs played a crucial role both in keeping the project alive and in shaping the content of the ultimate agreement that was produced.

The predominant view of IR theorists is that IGOs tend to be established in ways that further the interests of powerful states in the international system. The following assertion by Abbott and Snidal is representative: "We argue that powerful states structure such organizations to further their own interests but must do so in a way that induces weaker states to participate" (Abbott and Snidal 1998, pp. 6–7). We will see that in the case of the ICC negotiations, the United States, China, and India all found their own preferences trumped by a coalition of smaller states. Moreover, the ICC as constituted in the Rome Statute has a high degree of autonomy. This, too, contrasts with the conventional wisdom that "IO autonomy remains highly constrained by state interests" (Abbott and Snidal 1998, pp. 6–8).

Many analysts were skeptical, even in the latter half of the 1990s, that the leaders of states would be willing to consent to the jurisdiction of an ICC once they realized that their own actions might one day be called to account by it (Broms 1995, p. 146). The use of force, both internally and externally, is a significant part of what it means to be a state. Often, the bearing of arms by police officials and security forces is benevolent and helps to preserve social order. Government officials are responsible for deciding when force should be used, to quell a protest or mob, or to resist an external threat to security. Why, then, would any state officials be willing to subject their own decisions on when the use of force was appropriate to a review by a supranational authority that could choose to put those same officials in jail? In fact, when the United States chose to "withdraw" its signature from the ICC treaty, the undersecretary of state for political affairs Marc Grossman explained that "the ICC could have a chilling effect on the willingness of States to project power in defense of their moral and security interests."[23] So the chances of states agreeing to an ICC with substantial autonomous authority still were small in the late 1990s.

By the 1990s, the UN General Assembly was numerically dominated by developing states that had achieved independence in the post–World War II period. Most would describe the world system as multipolar in this period, although the combined military, economic, and cultural power of the United States led some to consider it a unipolar force of significance. In terms of the ICC issue, it is difficult to imagine that a diplomatic conference to consider a statute could ever have gone forward if the United States had actively opposed such a move. But the numerical advantage of smaller states and nonaligned states in the UN organization considerably changed the dynamics of the process of moving from a proposal in the ILC, to full debate among UN member states, to a diplomatic conference empowered to create a court. NGOs were most effective by first persuading, and then coordinating, the diplomatic activities of smaller states that otherwise would have lacked the diplomatic and legal expertise to keep up with and intervene successfully in the complex multilateral negotiations to establish the ICC.

In 1989, a group of Caribbean states in the General Assembly initiated the effort to put consideration of an ICC before the ILC once again (Evered 1994, p. 127).[24] The main impetus for this proposal was the desire of these states to create an international body that could try drug traffickers they were too weak to control on their own.[25]

By 1992 and 1993, Western powers, including the United States, had their own reasons for seeking an ICC with jurisdiction over individuals. Throughout the postwar period, the use of force by the United States in the world has been bedeviled by the problem of fighting wars with states when the fundamental problem was really with one or more leaders of a recalcitrant state. Examples include Libya's Muammar Quaddafi, Panama's Manuel Noriega,[26] Iraq's Saddam Hussein,[27] Somalia's Mohammed Aideed, and, of course, Yugoslavia's Slobodan Milošević, all of whom governed in ways that were corrupt, violent, and in violation of international law. In each case, the United States became involved in military conflicts with these states when it likely would have preferred to simply see a regime change and criminal prosecution of these particular individuals. As early as October of 1990, George H. W. Bush actually threatened Hussein with another Nuremberg-style war crimes trial (Bass 2000, p. 210).[28] The point is that for the U.S. government, the idea of international prosecutions under international criminal law had some appeal by the early 1990s.

By 1991, conflict had erupted in Yugoslavia. As the presidential election in the United States got into full swing in 1992, the crisis unfolded in Yugoslavia. The United States, and to a large extent the European powers as well were unwilling to become involved in the crisis. On October 6, 1992, the Security Council finally adopted a resolution creating a "commission of experts" to investigate war crimes in the Yugoslavian conflict, but Britain and France, fearing that such investigations would make a negotiated settlement to the conflict impossible, obstructed the commission's work. Cherif Bassiouni, a member of the commission, was able to expand the commission's documentation of war crimes only by securing outside funds from the Soros and MacArthur foundations and the government of the Netherlands (Scharf 1997a, pp. 59–92; Bass 2000, pp. 211–2).[29]

Nineteen ninety-three was a banner year for advancing the cause of a permanent ICC that had been stalled for so long. In February of 1993, with the urging of the new UN ambassador Madeleine Albright, the Security Council finally agreed to create an International Criminal Tribunal for the former Yugoslavia.[30]

While Albright pushed for a strong court, this ad hoc court would be hampered for years by relatively weak support from the great powers. Richard Goldstone, the first chief prosecutor for the ICTY, credits NGOs with mobilizing public opinion, pressuring governments, and ultimately securing increased funding for the ICTY from the UN General Assembly. Goldstone said, "Without the public attention, the court would have failed early in its life" (Gutman, Rieff, and Anderson 1999, pp. 14–5).

Also, in October of 1993, the United States reversed its official position on the ICC from one of attempting "to prolong without progressing" debate on the ICC to one of committing "actively to resolve the remaining legal and practical issues" with establishing an ICC (Scharf 1994). According to Scharf,[31] two events in the summer of 1993 recommended the concept of an ICC to the still-inexperienced Clinton administration. Libya had rejected a UN Security Council resolution that demanded the extradition of two individuals whom the U.S. Department of Justice had identified as responsible for the downing of a civilian jet liner over Lockerbie, Scotland. However, the Libyan government indicated it would be willing to send the men to an international tribunal, and U.S. leaders wanted to call Libya on what they perceived as a bluff. The Somali warlord Aideed was also plaguing the UN operation in Somalia, and the U.S. wished it had a way to hold him individually responsible (Scharf 1994).

This was the political context in the United States when ILC process moved forward, leading ultimately to the UN General Assembly's decision to schedule a treaty conference. Still, the U.S. position never reached a point where it would accept a court that would have jurisdiction over U.S. nationals without the case-specific consent of the U.S. government. Since such a position is fundamentally incompatible with the notion that criminal law should apply to everyone equally, the United States' position was ultimately rejected by the 120 nations who voted for the Rome Treaty. Understanding why the Rome Statute created a strong court with considerable capacity to resist political pressure and not a more limited court that was favored by the U.S. government requires that we understand the impact of international NGOs on shaping the treaty process in Rome.

For the rationalist, state-centered paradigm in the study of intergovernmental organizations, this outcome is clearly another anomaly that requires an improved explanation.[32] To provide such an explanation it is necessary to move toward an ontology of world politics that privileges individuals as actors and recognizes the potential agency of individuals that act on behalf of states, NGOs, IGOs, and private corporate entities.

Possible Pathways to a Permanent ICC

Of course, in 1993 the obstacles to creating any ICC remained considerable and, most thought, insurmountable. David Krieger noted at about that time that major problems remained to be resolved, including the perennial issues of how such a court could be created and what law it would enforce. So the difficulty of these issues is not lost in hindsight. It is worth noting that Krieger considered four options for creating the court, including the UN Charter reform process, Security

Council actions, General Assembly action under Article 22, and a full treaty conference; the last option was ultimately selected. Interestingly, Krieger concluded after a thorough review of the issues that the treaty conference option was the least desirable because of the possibility that the court's jurisdiction would be considerably limited by the geography of the ratifying states (Krieger in Al-Nauimi and Meese 1995). Today, the Rome ICC Statute has received many more ratifications than anyone might have imagined in the early 1990s, but the failure of some states to ratify it does remain a significant challenge to the overall legitimacy of the new institution. Amnesty International initially strongly favored establishing an ICC as an organ of the UN through the process of UN Charter amendment. While they recognized that this procedure would be difficult, as it requires the approval of two thirds of the UN members and all five of the permanent members of the Security Council, they still favored it. Most importantly, Amnesty argued that UN Charter amendment was the only way to ensure that the court's jurisdiction would be truly universal, because UN Charter amendments are binding on all UN members. They recognized that the ICC would necessarily be dealing with many situations that also involved the Security Council, the General Assembly, and/or other UN agencies (Amnesty International 1994a). Finally, Amnesty was concerned about securing adequate financial and administrative support for the ICC and felt that making use of existing UN budget mechanisms and the UN Secretariat was the best way to ensure the success of such a measure.

Amnesty suggested that if states in the UN General Assembly's sixth committee decided to use a new multilateral treaty to create the court, the court could still rely on the UN Secretariat and should still be funded out of the regular UN budget. They argued that a relatively small number of ratifications should be required before the ICC treaty would be put into effect, as was the case with the Convention on Torture. Finally Amnesty argued that no reservations should be allowed to the treaty, agreeing with the recommendation of the ILC working group (Amnesty International 1994a, pp. 21–2).

In the end of course, states represented on the UN General Assembly's Sixth Committee decided to go forward with a treaty conference and establish the ICC as an independent treaty organization.[33] The next section reviews how the discussion progressed toward that point. Some of the funding problems that Amnesty anticipated were ameliorated by making provisions in the ICC statute for voluntary contributions to the ICC, a suggestion that later was advocated by several NGOs. By raising these issues at an early stage in the process, NGOs, like Amnesty, were already beginning to help to ensure a successful outcome.

NGO Campaign for the Early Establishment of an International Criminal Tribunal

The NGO community was able to capitalize on the political opening created by the end of the Cold War and conduct a worldwide campaign to generate support for a strong court in the years between 1994 and 1998. I argue that the key to their influence was the nature of the discourse that these nonstate actors both participated in and helped to stimulate. To a remarkable extent the negotiations prior to and during the Rome conference approximated the ideal type of a communicatively rational discourse described by communicative action theory. That tendency was partly a consequence of broad-based NGO participation in the drafting and discussion of specific proposals for elements of the ICC.

I proceed with a description of the activities that NGO staff members engaged in. The CICC engaged in deliberate organizational and communicative strategies that shaped the nature of the dialogue that encompassed the ICC negotiations. These strategies contributed to the evolution of a discourse during the ICC negotiations that closely approximated the ideal type of communicative rationality. After laying out the general features of the NGO strategies, I turn to the analysis of the discourse itself.

Then, we reexamine the role of NGOs at key points in the process of scheduling and preparing for the Rome Treaty Conference. In the next chapter I examine the process of the Rome conference and highlight the way that NGO positions on key issues were translated into the final text of the Rome Statute.

In the early 1990s, only a handful of groups and individuals both inside and outside governments were actively working on the ICC issue.[34] M. Cherif Bassiouni was continuing to analyze many of the legal issues involved with international criminal law both as Professor at DePaul College of Law and through his affiliations with the International Association of Penal Law and the International Institute of Higher Studies in Criminal Sciences, even while he worked on the initial UN war crimes investigation in Bosnia. In July of 1992, Human Rights Watch (HRW) called for an international tribunal to punish the perpetrators of war crimes and genocide (Bass 2000, p. 210). The World Federalist Association in the United States and its international umbrella group, World Federalist Movement, decided around this time that they would actively advocate a permanent ICC as their priority issue.

In 1993 and 1994, William Pace was working on a number of projects, including making a list of contacts of people in the NGO community who might be able to interest their organizations in the movement afoot at the United Nations to push the long stagnated proposal for an ICC out of the General Assembly's Sixth Committee, the standing committee for legal affairs, and toward the creation of an actual court. In 1993, Pace attended the World Conference on Human Rights held in Vienna. Over 3000 participants from 1500 NGOs attended this meeting (Keck and Sikkink 1998, p. 187). This meeting led to the strengthening of network ties between different NGOs, and Pace used the occasion to identify allies that would work on the ICC issue.

A year later, Pace was instrumental in organizing the process that led to the establishment of the CICC. On March 23, 1994 a conference call was organized under the sponsorship of the World Federalist Movement that briefed other NGOs on the status of the ILC proposal that was about to be presented to the General Assembly. The conference call also began discussions on NGO strategies with regard to the crime of aggression, human rights violations, and transborder crime. During the call it was agreed that NGOs should coordinate their efforts when the General Assembly's Sixth Committee took up consideration of the ILC draft criminal court statute in the fall of 1994 (Pace and Schense 2002). During those Sixth Committee discussions in New York, William Pace organized a meeting with representatives from Amnesty International, Parliamentarians for Global Action, Lawyers Committee for Human Rights, and Lawyers for Nuclear Policy for the express purpose of coordinating strategies to ensure progress toward the establishment of a permanent ICC. For its part, the Sixth Committee decided to create an ad hoc committee on the establishment of an ICC. Some member states in the Sixth Committee advocated scheduling a diplomatic conference right away as the ILC had recommended, but France, the United Kingdom, and the United States strenuously objected and the ad hoc committee was proposed as a compromise.

Discussions between Pace and the leadership of Amnesty International about the mandate and working methods of the new NGO coalition culminated in the founding meeting on February 25, 1995, just prior to the initial sessions of the ad hoc committee. Pace says of this process: "Above all, the interest was to avoid the tensions which so often led to the break-up of NGO coalitions by keeping the mandate of the coalition as simple as possible (Pace and Schense 2002). In addition to the groups involved in the Fall 1994 meeting, the *Fédération International des Ligues des Droits de l'Homme,* HRW, the International Commission of Jurists, and No Peace Without Justice (NPWJ) also were founding members of the CICC; these organizations frequently served on the CICC's informal steering committee between 1995 and 2004.

The central activity of the CICC was, as it still is, to serve as a clearinghouse for information, proposals, and arguments about the ICC. The member NGOs all favored some form of an international criminal court. The complexity of the issues involved with specific technical proposals for provisions of the ICC statute made it difficult for many national governments to become aware of the process under way at the UN, let alone understand the implications of the decisions for their national positions. The CICC engaged in direct lobbying efforts, produced position papers, and published media editorials in a coordinated effort to inform states and the media on these issues. The NGO coalition used the various resources of its different member groups in a loosely coordinated way. While some groups had excellent legal expertise, others, such as HRW, made use of their media savvy to spread NGO positions to the widest possible audience.

The NGO coalition for an ICC self-consciously sought to shape the negotiations on the permanent ICC in a way that would lead to their openness. The convenor of the NGO coalition, William Pace, described their role as follows:

> Non-state actors, such as humanitarian, parliamentary, women's, and religious associations are developing an increasingly powerful role in the development of new international laws. Theirs is not a negotiating, but rather a consultative role. NGOs do not represent global civil society, but reflect its many voices and sectors.[35]

There were substantive issues that divided different member organizations within the CICC. Although members in the organization did not always agree on specific proposals about how the court should be constituted and what crimes it should prosecute, they all agreed that some sort of international criminal court was the best way to deal with the impunity that perpetrators of international law crimes have historically enjoyed. In order to facilitate the CICC's work, member organizations agreed to emphasize consensus building. Pace said "We agree on so much we shouldn't concentrate on what we don't agree on."[36]

What is striking about this passage is its modesty. Pace does not see the CICC as an interest group whose "bottom line" must be met by states in the negotiations in order to win the support of these groups. Instead, he focuses on the NGOs' role in ensuring that a variety of different positions are reflected in the input to the debate. This approach was institutionalized in the action strategies of the NGO coalition. Those activities included:

1. Convening meetings of CICC members and working groups,
2. Disseminating information on the ICC via Internet postings and e-mail listserv,
3. Facilitating meetings between government delegations and NGO representatives,
4. Promoting education and awareness of the ICC, and
5. Producing the ICC newsletter and other publications.[37]

A crucial element of the NGO strategy was a willingness to disseminate arguments that attacked the idea of a court as well as those that supported one, and to present multiple points of view on particular proposals for the court's design. The net result was that any group or government interested in following the ICC debate had broad access to the arguments that were presented by actors with a range of views. This is one way that NGO participation helped the ICC debate to approximate the conditions for communicative rationality—by ensuring that interested persons or groups or states without the resources to attend all of the meetings, or who might have been excluded from key negotiations, could still follow the key developments in the negotiations. Of course, this is not the same as meeting Alexy's (1999) exacting standard that the legitimacy of norms requires that all interested persons be allowed to participate. However, by making it possible for interested persons who were not present when particular ideas were proposed and discussed to remain apprised of developments, it gave those individuals the opportunity to attempt to express their views in a subsequent round of negotiations. Since the negotiating process went on from 1995 to 1998, this allowed for a far wider degree of participation than is typical of interstate negotiations.

An important reason for the NGO coalition's ultimate success was this orientation toward expanding the number of NGOs that took an interest in the ICC issue. For example, in October of 1997, HRW issued an action alert addressed to other NGOs with the basics about the ICC process under way at the UN, preparations for the Rome conference, and HRW's reasons for supporting the ICC. The alert concluded with a specific set of tasks that other groups could undertake to raise awareness of the ICC and offered strategy guidelines for creating national coalitions of interested organizations. There was a tremendous response to these outreach efforts.

The CICC grew from its initial 30 member organizations in 1994 to hundreds in the run-up to the Rome conference and thousands after the statute was adopted and the campaign turned toward focusing on ratification efforts.

The CICC included a variety of different types of organizations, including human rights groups, women's rights groups, associations of parliamentarians, professional legal groups, and religious and ecumenical groups. Sometimes, member groups of the CICC found it useful to create smaller subgroupings to focus on particular approaches to ICC advocacy that were not necessarily embraced by all of the organizations of the larger Coalition. For example, in 1997 a number of groups formed the Faith-Based Caucus for an International Criminal Court. The founding participating organizations were the Commission of the Churches on International Affairs (CCIA)/World Council of Churches, the General Board of Church and Society of the United Methodist Church, the World Conference on Religion and Peace, the Quaker UN Office, the Unitarian Universalists Office, the Lutheran Office for World Community, the Presbyterian UN Office, the International Association for Religious Freedom, the Mennonite Central Committee, the Franciscans International, the Bahai International Community, and B'nai B'rith International. Their mission statement says:

> The Faith-Based Caucus for an International Criminal Court is a coalition of religious and interfaith NGOs that examine the moral, ethical and religious considerations surrounding the Court. Religious organizations have a special role to play in raising awareness at the grassroots level and helping to shape the ICC. The Caucus promotes the ICC by disseminating information about the Court to respective religious and ecumenical communities. To inform others about some of the moral, ethical and religious considerations involved in the International Criminal Court, the Caucus holds frequent group meetings and plans events which will bring these issues to the attention of a wider audience.[38]

Thus, the strategies employed by faith-based groups matched those employed by other NGOs. They were somewhat unique in their focus on the "moral, ethical, and religious" implications of the ICC. However, they shared the general goal of all the pro-ICC NGOs to work toward bringing an end to impunity for the perpetrators of mass violence. Their mission statement mentioned a number of focal issues to be discussed by meetings sponsored by the group, including the "moral and ethical dimensions of impunity" and the "relationship between confession, repentance, compensation and forgiveness."[39]

Their target audience was the membership of their particular religious communities, and only indirectly specific policymakers. Still, they held informational meetings that were intended to provide interested parties with information about the ICC issue and its design.

The authority of a state delegate involved in international negotiations turns on her claim to be the official representative of a particular set of interests: a government and its people. NGOs enjoy no such assumption of representative legitimacy. Their arguments only carry the day if they can be justified as rational to all relevant listeners. It turned out that in the context of trying to develop a charter for a new institution that would punish individuals for egregious violations of international criminal law, the type of rational persuasive legitimacy claimed by NGOs was as important and influential as the representative legitimacy enjoyed by delegates representing states.

It is important to realize that the claim here is not that NGOs are neutral actors. They have their own interests and issue preferences that shape the positions these organizations take on particular issues. What is significant is that in the context of negotiations to draft a treaty in international law, NGOs' primary source of power is the persuasive force of their arguments. NGOs do not have any decision-making authority. Their influence during the ICC negotiations rested on their expertise in the area of international criminal law and in their political ability to analyze and quickly disseminate their views about the logical problems with particular mechanisms that were proposed for the court's operation. When states sought complex jurisdictional mechanisms that could limit the effectiveness of the court, NGO legal analysis quickly made transparent to other delegations what might otherwise have remained obscure. Given the complexity of the moral, legal, and practical issues involved, this timely analysis was essential for helping the representatives of governments to build consensus on viable alternatives to resolve difficult issues.

Because so many NGOs were represented and they spoke effectively on many detailed issues, their cumulative effect was to transform the nature of the negotiations toward communicative rather than strategic action.[40] Instead of a situation in which a few states with large cadres of diplomats could shape the discussion to focus on a few proposals that interested them, negotiations were characterized by many delegates from states and nonstate organizations raising a wide variety of issues. Delegates from developing states with relatively small negotiating teams were able to stay educated on proposals being circulated by reading NGO analyses and by discussing their questions and concerns with knowledgeable NGO representatives. The extensive NGO participation meant that every proposal tabled was subject to extensive criticism and discussion.

5

Negotiations: NGOs Shape the Terms of the ICC Debate; 1995–1998

The importance of topoi, i.e., "commonplaces" for practical reasoning, become obvious. Commonplaces are not only helpful in the discovery of the starting-points for practical arguments, an issue with which the classical teaching about "invention" deal. Topoi, as "seats of arguments," are also decisive for attaining assent to choices based on a series of practical judgments. For example, the topos that "more is better than less" is very persuasive as soon as the desirability of a practical matter has been established. The argument utilizing this commonplace becomes controlling by displacing other considerations which could provide grounds for competing evaluations, for example, qualitative distinctions such as in the topos "quality first."

—Friedrich V. Kratochwil, *Rules, Norms, and Decisions*[1]

NGOs Shape the Topoi for the ICC Treaty Conference

Part of my argument about the nongovernmental organizations' role is that NGOs' discursive practices in some cases helped to establish which topoi or shared premises became beginning points for the ICC negotiations. In Chapter 2, I explained the concept of topoi and their importance in the approach to discourse analysis undertaken in this study. By using and repeating arguments that drew on particular topoi, the discursive practices of NGOs helped to cement the place of these topoi in the wider discourse on the International Criminal Court. As anyone who has ever tried to trace a history of the evolution of ideas knows, it is extremely difficult to identify who presents a particular argument first in time. My claim about NGO discourse and use of these topoi is generally more modest. NGOs were not always the first to use these topoi in their arguments, but they did repeat them with frequency and regularity at early stages. Moreover, through process-tracing analysis, I show that these NGO arguments frequently were picked up by other speakers, including state delegates. Once these topoi gained broad acceptance, only arguments that were based on these premises were accepted by most negotiators as rational possibilities. Additionally, the delegates negotiating the ICC on behalf of states all accepted that the legitimacy of their project would ultimately depend on appeals to reason rather than force or other power resources. Delegates generally were not prepared to create an ICC that would be forcibly imposed on societies unwilling to subject themselves to the new international court's authority. Consequently the negotiations themselves took on a communicatively rational tone, and efforts at persuasion based on strategic calculations tended to be ignored by other participants. Arguments that ignored these widely accepted first premises and instead emphasized other values were rejected by the majority of participants in the negotiations and accompanying debates. NGOs frequently made communicatively rational arguments on the basis of these topoi. After examining a great number of statements by state delegates to these meetings, NGO papers, newspaper editorials, and other documents that were part of the conversation surrounding the ICC negotiations, it is possible to identify the most important of these relevant premises or topoi that characterized the ICC debate. Later on I will discuss representative selections from the discourse that highlight the development of these themes. First, I simply identify in summary form the topoi that characterized the ICC debate.[2]

1. The ICC should ensure an end to the culture of impunity that state leaders have historically enjoyed for illegal acts of violence carried out in the name of the state.[3]
2. The ICC should provide equal justice under the law for individuals. In other words, if particular criminal violations of international law are going to be punished in some times and places, they should, in principle, be subject to punishment in all times and places.
3. The statute of the ICC itself should be grounded in existing international law. Therefore, it should not create new international criminal law but should instead take jurisdiction over the most atrocious crimes that are already widely recognized by states as part of international law.
4. Any ICC must have procedures to protect the basic rights of the accused, including a presumption of innocence.

The NGOs' discursive practices particularly emphasized arguments relying on premises 1 and 2, the goal of ending impunity and maintaining the norm that the law should apply equally to all. NGOs' discursive practices were particularly responsible for the emergence of these first two themes as topoi in the final rounds of the negotiations. NGOs also emphasized the importance of focusing on international law norms that already had widespread acceptance, or premise 3. At the Rome conference, each of these premises gained such widespread support that proposals that could not be justified in terms of these goals, or that tended to weaken the prospects for achieving these goals, came to be seen as unacceptable. On the basis of these premises, NGOs advanced communicatively rational arguments (in the Habermasian sense) about which proposals for the ICC should be adopted and which should be abandoned. Arguments that were logical and based on these first principles tended to gain widespread acceptance.

It is worth commenting briefly about the extent to which the topoi pushed by the NGOs rested in turn on an existing consensus that existed in the field of international law more generally. Indeed, the existence of international law serves as the background knowledge that facilitated the use of communicatively rational discussion in the case of the ICC negotiations. In 1994, one Russian legal scholar wrote, marking the 50th anniversary of the Nuremberg and Tokyo tribunals, that the fundamental significance of these charters was establishing "the individual criminal responsibility of heads of states under international law for acts of aggression" (Lukashuk 1994). But he went on to note that notwithstanding this legal development, states and particularly state leaders had been reluctant to enforce the rules during the Cold War period, concluding that "the higher the political significance of the case, the greater the role played by politics in the denouement" (Lukashuk 1994). Thus the problem of impunity from prosecution was widely understood among scholars of international law with expertise on the rules of international criminal law. Although law prohibiting specific conduct was well established, mechanisms of enforcement were wanting. The innovation of the NGOs was to make addressing that pattern of impunity an urgent political issue. In this way, international law functioned as the lifeworld set of background conditions that made possible communicatively rational discourse about the establishment of the ICC. The NGOs drew on that legal understanding to advance their political cause.

We should also consider in more detail the consequences of the premise I labeled topos 2, namely, that if conduct is illegal, its punishment should be consistent across different cases. It is important to note that this principle is in constant tension with the political willingness of states to subject themselves to an ICC's jurisdiction. Recall that this fact was the insurmountable barrier to the ICC negotiations in the 1950s. Any rule of the ICC Statute that makes prosecution more likely in certain kinds of states or situations would violate this principle. By relying on treaty ratification to define the ICC's jurisdiction, the Rome Statute partially compromises on this principle. Still, at least for those states that do ratify the treaty, no such compromise is allowed on a permanent basis. This is very different from the ILC's proposed statute, which would have allowed states to be members of the ICC even while refusing its jurisdiction over particular crimes on the territory of that state, thereby creating multiple standards of international justice that would apply unevenly in different parts of the ICC's jurisdiction.

Topos 4, the norm that international trials should protect the rights of the accused, existed even in the ILC debates dating back to the 1950s and really emerged out of the debates about organizing the Allied war crimes tribunal at Nuremberg. Secretary of War Henry L. Stimson argued with Henri Morgenthau Jr. about whether or not it would be sensible to prosecute the leaders of Germany's National Socialist party or simply to execute them (Smith 1982). There was little debate during the ICC negotiations that the rights of the accused should be guaranteed. There were, however, differences of opinion about how best to ensure that this principle would be implemented in practice.

NGOs Enter the Discourse

The most authoritative way to analyze the arguments put forward by NGOs in the early stages of the ICC negotiations is to examine their formal policy recommendation papers, which are generally publicly available today as they were at the time of their initial distribution. Of course, NGO lobbying also consisted of countless instances of verbal lobbying with delegates to the various negotiations and other government officials at all relevant levels. It was sometimes the authors of the NGO papers themselves that conducted such verbal lobbying, and when it was not, other NGO lobbyists relied heavily on repetition of the printed arguments. Therefore I conclude at least as a first approximation that the reasoning in verbal arguments for and against the court did not differ substantially from what is available in the written record.[4]

Table 5.1 is a list of some of the most important policy papers issued by NGOs between 1994 and the beginning of the Rome conference in June 1998. The list focuses primarily on papers that were produced by the core member organizations of the CICC.

In 1994 Amnesty International issued its first briefing paper focused on the issue of establishing a permanent ICC (Amnesty International 1994b, p. 28). The occasion for this paper was the completion of the ILC draft ICC statute in 1994 and its presentation to the UN General Assembly. This is an interesting example of one strategy that NGOs have consistently employed to insert themselves into the ICC debate. By commenting directly on an ongoing intergovernmental process, NGOs such as Amnesty were timing their commentaries to build on the existing state-to-state discourse.[5]

This raised the probability that officials involved in the process would actually look at the documents the NGOs produced. Official UN delegations had to determine their state's policy on the proposal emerging from the ILC process. NGOs understood they had an opportunity to get their voices heard because government officials immediately involved in the policy development process needed sources of useful analysis. This paper was initially targeted at the members of the ILC themselves, but it was also issued publicly (Amnesty International 1994b). An updated version was released to UN representatives on the eve of the discussions in the General Assembly's Sixth Committee meeting about how to proceed with the ILC draft ICC charter (Amnesty International 1994a). This paper was very comprehensive and defined many of the serious issues that would remain with the ICC debate through July 2002. Because they were thorough and well documented, the papers issued by Amnesty were useful and quickly became a part of the literature that government officials used in developing their own policies. Senior negotiators representing states in Rome confirm that the legal provisions of the NGO papers were both authoritative and influential during the negotiating process.[6]

This paper also used language that suggests its authors were aware of the desirability of promoting openness in the ICC negotiation dialogue. On p. 5, Amnesty says: "The following memorandum is designed to assist members of the general public and governments during the forthcoming debates in the Sixth

Table 5.1 Selected NGO and expert papers circulated during the ICC negotiations

Author	Date	Title
Amnesty International	Oct 1994	Establishing a Just, Fair, and Effective International Criminal Court
Equality Now	April 1995	Recommendations for the Draft Statute for an ICC
Amnesty International	July 1995	@ The Quest for International Justice
Human Rights Watch	March 1996	Commentary for the Preparatory Committee on the Establishment of an ICC
President Antonio Cassesse; ICTY	22 March 1996	Definition of Crimes and General Principles of Criminal Law as Reflected in the the International Tribunal's Jurisprudence
World Federalist Movement	25 March 1996	Views of the World Federalist Movement on the Establishment of a Permanent International Criminal Court
Pax Romana, Josep M. Garcia, Diana Martnez, Javier Darriba	28 March 1996	Commentaries to the Draft Statute of the International Permanent Criminal Court (IPCC)
International Commission of Jurists	1996	The International Criminal Court
Human Rights Watch	August 1996	Commentary for the Preparatory Committee on the Establishment of an ICC (August 1996 session)
Lawyer's Committee for Human Rights—Jelena Pejic	August 1996 updated	Major Unresolved Issues in the Draft Statute
World Federalist Movement—Institute for Global Policy, Daniel MacSweeny	August 1996	Prospects for the Financing of an International Criminal Court
International Committee of the Red Cross	13 February 1997	War Crimes—Working Paper Prepared by the ICRC for the Preparatory Committee for the Establishment of an International Criminal Court
Amnesty International	January 1997	Making the Right Choices: Defining the Crimes and Permissible Defences and Initiating a Prosecution
Lawyer's Committee for Human Rights	July 1997	The ICC Trigger Mechanism and the Need for an Independent Prosecutor
Amnesty International	July 1997	Making the Right Choices—Part II: Organizing the Court and Guaranteeing a Fair Trial
International Peace Bureau	July 1997	A Briefing Paper: An Analysis of Issues and Recommendations for Actions

Committee of the General Assembly and any working group or international conference established to discuss the draft Statute" (Amnesty International 1994a). It is significant that Amnesty mentions first the general public and second the governments that will be most directly responsible for making decisions about whether or not and how to establish an ICC. Amnesty clearly envisioned a fully public dialogue about the merits of an ICC. They sought the complete implementation of Woodrow Wilson's idea for "open covenants, openly arrived at." Amnesty apparently recognized that open dialogue about the design of the court was their best opportunity to influence the outcome. In any case, this passage demonstrates their commitment to a communicatively rational strategy. Yet it remained an open question in 1995 whether or not states would allow such a process or whether they would prefer to negotiate some aspects of the court's creation in private.

Table 5.2 outlines the timing of the major ICC treaty-negotiating steps in order to set the NGO papers in context. Comparing this timeline to the publication dates of NGO papers shows how the release of each paper was timed to influence the course of the negotiating sessions.

It is important to note that the early negotiations on the ICC statute took place simultaneously with the early work of the ICTY and the ICTR. Developments and problems and the ad hoc tribunals provided an important background context for all of the ICC negotiations. The first hearing regarding the ICTY's first defendant, Duško Tadić, was held in The Hague on November 8, 1994. Tadić was formally indicted on February 13, 1995, but his trial did not begin until May 7, 1996 because of delays by Germany in transferring him to the custody of the ICTY and a series of pretrial rulings on the legality and jurisdiction of the ICTY itself (Scharf 1997a, pp. 98–111). Tadić, while clearly guilty

Table 5.2 Timeline of the ICC negotiations

Date	Major Event or Meeting
April and August 1995	Two sessions of the Ad Hoc Committee on the Establishment of an ICC
11 December 1995	UN General Assembly votes to establish a Preparatory Committee on the Establishment of an ICC[7]
25 March to 12 April 1996	First meeting of Preparatory Committee[8]
12 to 30 August 1996	Second meeting of Preparatory Committee
17 December 1996	UN General Assembly votes to extend the mandate of the Preparatory Committee[9]
11 to 21 February 1997	Third meeting of Preparatory Committee
4 to 15 August 1997	Fourth meeting of Preparatory Committee
1 to 12 December 1997	Fifth meeting of Preparatory Committee
15 December 1997	UN General Assembly votes to schedule UN Diplomatic Conference of Plenipotentiaries on the Establishment of an ICC in 1998[10]
16 March to 3 April 1998	Sixth meeting of Preparatory Committee
15 June to 17 July 1998	UN Diplomatic Conference of Plenipotentiaries on the Establishment of an ICC meets in Rome
17 July 1998	Rome Statute for the ICC adopted for signature

of atrocities in Bosnia, was hardly someone who had command responsibility, much less was he a political organizer, and his selection as the ICTY's first defendant was widely criticized (Scharf 1997b). During this period, the ongoing trial of Tadić seemed to demonstrate the weakness of international criminal tribunals because leaders like Slobodan Milošević remained beyond the UN tribunal's reach (Hagan 2003, pp. 71–92). The existence of the ad hoc tribunals demonstrated that international criminal tribunals with authority over serious international law crimes could be designed and could function. The Rwanda tribunal was established in part to forestall criticism that the UN Security Council members were only concerned about war crimes when they occurred in Europe but not in Africa. Thus the development of the ad hoc tribunals themselves contributed to a human rights dialogue that insisted that international criminal norms should be universally punished. This conversation created a space for NGOs to argue that only a permanent tribunal could ensure effectively that international law prosecutions would be applied universally.

A Human Rights Watch paper issued in advance of the first Preparatory Committee meeting in 1996 illustrates the early use of the topoi that became the foundation for the ICC debate. The paper begins by observing: "The upcoming Preparatory Committee meeting presents the first opportunity for States to negotiate and draft the text of a statute for a permanent International Criminal Court (ICC)" (Human Rights Watch 1996). The paper continues by asserting that "progress is essential" in the upcoming negotiations toward drafting a statute. To support this claim, HRW notes: "Underlying the urgency for demonstrable progress during the upcoming Preparatory Committee session is the need to limit impunity for the most egregious human rights crimes—genocide, serious violations of the laws and customs applied in armed conflicts, and crimes against humanity—that have proliferated in the last several years" (Human Rights Watch 1996). At this point in the negotiations, no definitive date had yet been set for a diplomatic conference of plenipotentiaries. The NGO strategy here was to invoke a sense of urgency by reminding state delegates that the atrocious crimes under consideration were recurring problems in the contemporary world. This introductory paragraph also is illustrative of the NGOs' invocation of the topos I labeled as 1, the premise that the central purpose of an ICC is to bring an end to impunity for leaders responsible for mass violence. This is illustrative of the way that NGOs used these topoi to frame their arguments. As the negotiations proceeded, these topoi gained wider and wider acceptance, and eventually nearly all the states in the negotiations accepted the premise that the reason for an ICC was to end the culture of impunity for these serious human rights crimes, and that there was an urgent need to do so in the international community.

The policy recommendations in the paper build logically on these premises laid out in the introduction. The report notes that the upcoming sessions will deal with the subject matter jurisdiction of the court, the complementarity regime, and the mechanisms for the court to exercise jurisdiction. Each of these is among the essential policy choices made in the Rome Statute, where I claim NGOs had a serious impact.

In the balance of this chapter, I analyze the discursive moves of states and NGOs with respect to several of these major issues. I follow the arguments as they developed in time to highlight the influence of NGO arguments at crucial junctures. For ease of understanding and presentation, the analysis is organized around each issue area. The crucial issues I focus on are

1. The list and definition of crimes to be included in the jurisdiction of the court,
2. Defining complementarity, or the relationship between the proposed ICC and national legal systems,
3. The trigger mechanism for activating the jurisdiction of the court, and
4. The pace of progress in the negotiations.

However, it is important to remember that each of these issues is linked and that the overall success of the ICC negotiations depended on resolving each of these questions in a way that was acceptable to most actors. Sometimes, the division into different issue areas is a bit arbitrary, as particular proposals would have implications for more than one area.

Defining the Crimes

As we saw in the discussion of historical efforts to create an ICC in Chapter 3, the lack of a specified international criminal code has been a major stumbling block to the very idea of trying international crimes (Ferencz 1980, vol. 2, p. 41). Of course, there is no recognized legislative body in the international system. Both customary and treaty-based international laws criminalize specific acts, but whether or not those crimes are sufficiently well specified so as to make them enforceable in a court of law has been a recurrent issue in discussions of the ICC idea (Paust 2000; Ratner and Abrams 2001).

Recall that the ILC's draft for an ICC statute, produced in 1994, imagined a court where states would be able to join and then choose selectively whether or not to grant the court jurisdiction with respect to specific crimes.[11] At the time, the ILC favored such a solution because they thought it was the only realistic way that a large number of states would be willing to participate in an ICC at all. Of course, a court that adopted the ILC's proposal would inherently violate the criteria for rational justification of a rule system because it would require the court to treat the same violations of international law differently, depending on where in the world they took place and who committed the crime.

In fact, one of the most difficult issues throughout the negotiations was determining which crimes to include under the court's jurisdiction. Some states felt that including drug trafficking, the use of nuclear weapons, and terrorism as international law crimes under the new ICC's jurisdiction was essential, but each of those proposals met with strong resistance from other states. This issue would remain contentious until the last day of the Rome Treaty Conference, but early NGO statements on the issue shaped the direction of the final outcome.

One of the crucial issues dealt with in Amnesty's 1994 paper was the list of crimes to be included in the jurisdiction of any future court (Amnesty International 1994a). Amnesty advocated the inclusion of serious international law crimes, *even if* they occurred during *internal* armed conflict. Amnesty's arguments can be tested for rationality against the criteria for communicatively rational discourse.

Amnesty argued that:

> It would be unthinkable for any permanent international criminal court to omit these crimes under international law. Failure to include crimes in Common Article 3 or Protocol II [of the Geneva conventions] would mean that perpetrators of breaches of humanitarian law occurring in internal armed conflict—the most common form of armed conflict today—might go unpunished
> (Amnesty International 1994, p. 8).

The normative logic of this statement hinges on the claim that atrocities carried out during internal armed conflict should be treated the same as violations of international law that occur during warfare between two or more states. In general terms, this claim satisfies the criteria for communicative rationality that normative claims should be universalizable. More specifically we observe that this argument falls in line with Alexy's rule 1.3, that like things ought to be treated alike (see Chapter 2).

Amnesty gave detailed reasoning about the status of particular crimes under existing international law, drawing on the complex provisions of the various Geneva Conventions on the laws of war to demonstrate that a number of particular acts were already well established as war crimes or crimes against humanity under existing international law. Amnesty gives reasons for each of its claims and conclusions, just as would be expected in a legal brief (Amnesty International 1994a, pp. 8–12). Amnesty also argued that the acts in question, such as murder, torture, degrading treatment, the taking of hostages, or summary execution, were already recognized as criminal acts under various international treaties with broad acceptance in the international community, even in a purely domestic armed conflict.[12] This appeal to existing provisions of international law is another tactic repeatedly and successfully used by NGOs during the ICC debate. As the negotiations progressed, this grounding for arguments that the ICC rules should be based in existing international law became a generally accepted background consensus point on which basis the negotiations proceeded. Notice that this argument also satisfies Alexy's criteria 5.2.2 for rational discourse, namely, that moral rules should be able to withstand critical testing in terms of their historical genesis (see Chapter 2). In other words, Amnesty International is not attempting to create a new rule of international criminal justice for the international community; it is simply calling for enforcement of existing provisions on an equitable basis. In this sense, its discursive practices can be marked out as communicatively rational. It is prepared to give rationally justified reasons for its positions.

Another crucial element of Amnesty's argument was to demonstrate that because war crimes, crimes against humanity, and genocide were already widely recognized as crimes that generated individual criminal liability under existing international law, it would be unreasonable for states to "opt in" selectively to the jurisdiction of the court with respect to particular crimes.[13] Recall from the discussion above that the 1994 ILC draft statute for an ICC proposed a court where some members might accept the court's jurisdiction with respect to war crimes but not with respect to the crime of genocide or aggression.[14]

Notice that the implicit argument in favor of a court where states would opt in voluntarily to jurisdiction over particular crimes requires a system in which the rule does not apply equally to all individuals. Consequently it is difficult to defend on logically rational grounds, unless one is prepared to make the argument that it is somehow desirable or justifiable to treat the citizens of some states differently from the citizens of other states under international law. The United States defended the ILC's opt-in formula and opposed the notion of "inherent" jurisdiction. Jamison Borak, speaking for the United States, said that "the proposal endorsed by some governments but never proposed by the International Law Commission, that the court have "inherent jurisdiction" over violations of humanitarian law (other than possibly the crime of genocide) is ill-conceived in our view and will not achieve the broad support necessary for a viable court."[15] Notice that this is an example of a strategic form of argument that the United States would use repeatedly during the negotiations, to little effect in the end. Essentially, the United States says the proposal is ill conceived but does not give any reasons to support that claim. Instead, the United States implies that it and other states will not cooperate with a court that has such a provision, and so other delegations must move toward the United States' position if they desire its support for the court.

Amnesty International argued as early as 1994 that the ICC should have jurisdiction over a broad range of crimes and "that all states submitting to the jurisdiction of the Court should agree that the jurisdiction will include a common core of crimes" (Amnesty International 1994a, p. 5). At this stage, this was a radical reconceptualization of the nature of the ICC that was to be created, but it was one that was consistent with the general topos Amnesty and other NGOs advanced, that the entire purpose of an ICC was to ensure an end to impunity for these types of crimes. Gradually, more and more states accepted Amnesty's premise, and once they did, it was difficult to avoid the logical conclusion that all state parties to the ICC should accept the ICC's jurisdiction with respect to these crimes in advance and without reservation.

As the negotiations progressed, the representatives of governments made countless statements about their positions on ICC issues and particular proposals for the court's design. Each year, the UN General Assembly's Sixth Committee had a more general debate on the status of the ICC negotiations, and at that time states made statements about their general views on the crucial issues in the negotiations. I focus on those statements to show how the debate evolved over time, for the most part in ways that were consistent with the initiative taken by NGOs in their policy papers.

In general, different states favored including different and widely ranging crimes under the court's jurisdiction, in large part because of their varied expectations about the purposes the court would serve. Many Latin American and Caribbean states (as well as some others) wanted the court to prosecute international drug trafficking crimes. Many states favored punishing individuals for the use of nuclear weapons or terrorism.[16] But fearing the loss of state sovereignty, there were nearly as many states that opposed having a court with an expansive criminal jurisdiction. The statement by Malaysia's delegate in 1995 reflected this general concern of many states.[17] Malaysia argued that the constituent elements of all crimes should be narrowly defined to promote the rights of defendants. It also said that crimes against humanity and war crimes should be narrowly defined and crimes against humanity should be linked to times of war, perhaps fearing their own government leadership could be indicted for repressing internal dissent. Malaysia also argued that *treaty crimes* should only be enforced against the citizens of states that had ratified the relevant treaty.[18]

One crucial issue was whether or not aggression should be included as a crime, and many argued that it should be treated as a "core crime" in part because of the history of this crime's enforcement by the Nuremberg and Tokyo tribunals.[19] Aggression is unique among international law crimes because almost by definition it is committed by the highest-ranking political and military officials. It is also an inherently political crime. The UN Security Council also has unique responsibilities under international law for identifying that state-to-state aggression has occurred and in authorizing a collective response. Accordingly, if the ICC were to exercise jurisdiction over aggression, some relationship would have to be found between the Security Council's authority to determine whether or not aggression has occurred and the court's authority to determine whether or not particular individuals are guilty of the crime of aggression.

The comments of various states reflected the tension over this issue. Australia stated diplomatically that "only the most serious crimes of concern to the international community" should fall under the jurisdiction of the court, but they recognized that there was debate over which crimes that phrase included.[20] Egypt's delegation, perhaps reflecting the input of the noted international criminal law scholar Cherif Bassiouni, who sometimes participated as a member of Egypt's diplomatic delegation on war crimes issues, said the jurisdiction of the ICC should be limited to the four major crimes of aggression, genocide, crimes against humanity, and serious war crimes.[21] This also reflected the view of many smaller states in the international community that felt they were more likely to be the victims of the crime of aggression than they were to participate in a war in which they might be accused of aggression. The United Kingdom's representative finessed the issue of aggression by saying he observed a growing consensus about limiting the court's jurisdiction to the "three or four" most serious categories of crimes and stating that the United Kingdom favored such a restriction.[22] The three crimes would of course be genocide, war crimes, and crimes against humanity. The question the British delegate was leaving open was whether or not aggression should be on the list. Mexico's delegation aptly summarized the reasoning behind the consensus for focusing on a few core crimes when their delegate said, "Toward the end of promoting a wide acceptance of the court by states, it is necessary that the court's competence be limited to the most serious crimes."[23] The U. S. delegate stated, perhaps optimistically, that he heard consensus on limiting the court's jurisdiction to war crimes, crimes against humanity, and genocide. He thought there was not sufficient support for including aggression, drug crimes, terrorism, or violations of the Convention against Apartheid.[24]

By 1997, there was increased consensus about the need for the court to have jurisdiction over the core crimes, and the debate had intensified about whether or not that included aggression. More important, the argument first advanced by Amnesty International that the Court would have "inherent" jurisdiction of one kind or another, where all states' parties would accept the Court's jurisdiction with respect to all the covered crimes, had grown in strength. Ireland, speaking on behalf of a group of countries known as the "like-minded group" that had begun to work closely with the CICC, spoke in terms that echoed the language of previous NGO policy briefs. Ireland said:

> *My delegation is strongly in favor of the court having jurisdiction to consider . . . the "core crimes," i.e., genocide, war crimes, crimes against humanity and the crime of aggression. In view of the exceptionally grave nature of the crimes involved, my delegation has great difficulty understanding how any state becoming a party to the convention should be in a position to select or choose ("opt-in" or "opt-out" of) the core crimes for which individuals would be answerable to the court. If there is no agreement about including treaty crimes, such as drug trafficking or crimes against UN personnel, "there could be a mechanism to allow the international community to review and add to the list of crimes which would fall within the jurisdiction of the court from time to time."*[25]

Several permanent members of the Security Council, including France, China, and the United States, opposed giving the court jurisdiction over the crime of aggression, noting the specifically that the Security Council was the only appropriate body to determine whether or not aggression had occurred.[26] Trinidad and Tobago, speaking on behalf of all the Caribbean Community and Common Market (CARICOM) states, supported including the three core crimes, noted the problems with the Security Council role and defining aggression, but also continued to insist on the importance of including treaty crimes such as, among others, drug trafficking, terrorism, and attacks on UN personnel.[27] The fact that many states still favored the inclusion of other crimes shows the importance of the compromise advanced by several NGOs and articulated by Ireland and other like-minded states that it would be important to include a mechanism for adding crimes to the court's jurisdiction in the future.

At the December 1997 Preparatory Committee session in New York negotiations were marked by a strong disagreement about the range of war crimes that the court would be empowered to prosecute during internal armed conflicts. HRW made public note of the fact that a proposal advanced by some states that would have severely restricted the court's jurisdiction over such internal armed conflicts was successfully defeated by a group of delegates from smaller states (Human Rights Watch 1999). This was a very public thank-you on behalf of HRW to the delegations of smaller states that had carried the NGO argument about the definition of war crimes into the state-to-state discourse.

As preparations for the Rome conference began in earnest in early 1998, it was clear that there was broad support for a court that would exercise jurisdiction under some procedures yet to be determined over at least war crimes, crimes against humanity, and genocide. The NGOs certainly had laid the groundwork by showing the necessity of including these so-called core crimes. Many states still had strong and conflicting views about giving the court jurisdiction over aggression, the use of nuclear weapons, terrorism, and drug trafficking.

Defining Complementarity and the Court's Jurisdiction

One of the central issues in the ICC negotiations was establishing the conditions under which the ICC would exercise its jurisdiction. Many states feared having a court that would intrude on the ability of states to use their own national legal systems to decide whether or not particular individuals had committed international law crimes. Other states and many NGOs were concerned that if the ICC deferred too much to national legal systems, the former would be used as a shield to protect state leaders from prosecution. To the extent that proposals tended to take the first approach, NGOs argued logically that such rules would allow for a continuation of impunity for many perpetrators of international law crimes, violating the emerging topos of the negotiations that the purpose of the ICC was to ensure an end to impunity.

Complementarity was the key principle of the ILC's 1994 draft statute for an ICC, which dealt with the sovereignty issue in a way that allowed a majority of states to support the ICC project.[28] Complementarity meant simply that the ICC's jurisdiction would overlap with that of national courts. In this way, a supranational court could be created that would be less of a challenge to states' existing sovereign rights. By the time of the Rome conference, there would be widespread agreement that the ICC was primarily intended to deal with situations where there was no state capable of prosecuting the offenders, or where the state was unwilling to do so, or where a national prosecution might appear partisan. It was recognized that wherever possible, nation-states should continue to have primary jurisdiction over violations of international criminal law and that the ICC should only complement that jurisdiction (Holmes, pp. 48–51, in Lee 1999). At an earlier stage in the debate, there was less agreement about the purpose of an ICC, with some states viewing the court as only operating in situations where there was no available domestic court system at all, as in post-conflict situations.

Amnesty International wrote criticizing the ILC draft that "the requirement that both the states where war crimes or crimes against humanity occurred and state parties to treaties with an obligation to try or extradite must consent before a state party having custody can transfer an accused to the International Criminal Court is likely to limit severely the effectiveness of the Court as a last resort when such states are unwilling or unable to prosecute these cases fairly or effectively" (Amnesty International 1994a, p. 5). This argument drew critical attention to this aspect of the court's jurisdiction mechanism from an early point in the negotiations. It utilizes the topos that the central reason for establishing the court is to ensure an end to the culture of impunity. It is difficult to challenge Amnesty's claim on rational grounds without challenging that premise. In other words, to argue with Amnesty, you would have to directly argue that sovereign states should have the right to block the prosecution of their citizens or crimes that occurred on their territory whenever they felt it was in the national interests of such a state to do so. This is a norm that has historically had some weight in international law, but in this context of ensuring a valid, universally accepted judicial system, such an argument was a nonstarter.

The text of the Rome Treaty reflects the input of NGOs on the central issues of complementarity and the court's jurisdiction. The following illustrations from the position papers produced by the CICC and some of its member organizations illustrate the impact that their arguments had on both the course of the negotiations and the final outcome.

An article in the first issue of the CICC's newspaper, *The ICC Monitor*, by Steve Gerber directly addressed the issue of complementarity, including some misgivings about what that principle might mean in actual practice and how it ought to be implemented. Gerber, of the World Federalist Association, noted that the United States sought to use the concept of complementarity to strictly limit the ICC's jurisdiction. The U.S. government argued that as long as a state has an operating judicial system that makes an effort to investigate and prosecute any alleged violations of international criminal law, the ICC should not interfere. Gerber also highlighted the fact that some states disagreed with the United States' position on this issue, complaining that this interpretation of complementarity could tilt the balance of authority too far away from the ICC in favor of national authorities, resulting in a weak court. Gerber concluded his piece by making clear the danger. "[Complementarity] is the argument states are using to protect their sovereignty and to avoid the international scrutiny of the ICC" (Gerber 1996).

Gerber's article was a report and commentary on the results of the first Preparatory Committee session that was held in March and April 1996. At the time of that meeting, both states and NGOs had revealed their initial positions on complementarity-related issues in some depth.[29] Even prior to that, in the Sixth Committee meeting in late 1995, some states had presented their initial positions. We can see in the comments by states at that point that they are already reacting to Amnesty's call for states parties to accept jurisdiction in advance with respect to the "core crimes" (Amnesty International 1994a). China took a particularly clear line, arguing that the ICC had to be designed in such a way that it did not infringe on the sovereignty of member states. Their representative argued that "the ICC should not supplant national courts or become a supranational court or act as [an] appeal[s] court to the national court."[30] They expressed their pleasure with the incorporation of the complementarity idea into the preamble of the draft statute but noted that it was not implemented in practice in later parts of the document. In particular, the Chinese ambassador argued that if the ICC were to be granted inherent jurisdiction over the crime of genocide, this would be a violation of their understanding of the ICC's complementarity concept. China also stated that state consent to the jurisdiction of the court should be required and not be mandatory, even for states that were a part of the court.[31] Of course, after the adoption of the ICC statute, China continued to reject these elements of the ICC's design. In 1995, however, there were many more states that shared China's concern, including some that would ultimately become supporters of the ICC.

Others expressed this concern with limiting the jurisdiction of the court to cases where states had consented. Malaysia supported the proposal in the ILC draft in which states could earn the right to refer cases to the court only if they had also accepted the court's jurisdiction with respect to that particular crime.[32] This was an option that NGOs would later oppose on principled grounds because it risked creating a situation in which the law would apply differently to different perpetrators, depending on where they had committed their crime. Egypt's delegate said, "It should be clear that establishing an ICC does not mean at all that the court shall exercise any supreme role over the National Judicial Systems."[33] Mexico said, "In our conception, the Court should only enter into operation when [national judicial] systems don't exist or when for reasons that we should define, a trial is impossible."[34]

Other states simply expressed skepticism about the idea of inherent or automatic jurisdiction of some kind, without directly opposing it. The Russian Federation's delegate said that inherent jurisdiction "deserves the most careful study," a diplomatic phrase but one that clearly indicated their hesitancy. In 1995 Australia simply noted that states disagreed about whether or not the ICC should have some form of "primary jurisdiction." Australia stated that they took no position on that debate and noted that the discussion was not yet exhausted.[35] This is particularly interesting because four years later Australia played a pivotal role in an advancing a fair and effective ICC as part of the "like-minded" group of states that cooperated with pro-ICC NGOs.

An NGO paper from the group *Pax Romana*, released to coincide with the Preparatory Committee session in early 1996, clearly stated the concerns of many NGOs on the complementarity issue. At the beginning of the discussion the complementarity issue is framed in terms of the need to bring an end to impunity; thus it is another example of an NGO drawing on that topos. The paper reads "We deem essential to clarify the concurrence of the [national and ICC] jurisdictions. The aim of such a relationship is to achieve a complete certainty that the committed crimes will not remain unpunished."[36] The paper goes on to argue that because international crimes are increasingly recognized as offenses that create *jus cogens*[37] rules binding on the entire international community, states must recognize in advance the mandatory jurisdiction of the proposed court over these crimes. To allow states to wait and grant jurisdiction to the court on a case-by-case basis would result in the court becoming "an [i]neffective fiction."[38] This is an example of an NGO argument that draws on existing international law in an innovative way. Because the so-called core crimes are normally considered *jus cogens* rules of international law that trump other conflicting rules, the NGOs argued that it is not rational to put state sovereignty concerns ahead of punishing those *jus cogens* violations, and accordingly, it makes no sense for the ICC to have an opt-in jurisdiction regime. To deny this point, states would have to argue that these crimes are not *jus cogens*, but that premise is well established in international law (Paust 2000).

As the Preparatory Committee negotiations continued, debate on the meaning of complementarity became more complex and sophisticated. The NGOs hammered away at the importance of designing the complementarity jurisdiction in such a way that it would not permit states to shield accused persons for political reasons. For example, the lead recommendation in Amnesty International's briefing paper to governments issued in January 1997 said "the court must be able to act as an effective complement to national courts when they are unable or unwilling to fulfill this duty [to prosecute grave international law crimes]" (Amnesty International 1997b, p. 10). The "unable and unwilling" phrase is exactly the text that was ultimately approved in Article 17 of the Rome Statute. Amnesty continued by stating "The court must have the power to determine whether to exercise its jurisdiction in such cases" (Amnesty International 1997b, p. 10). In order to support this argument, Amnesty and other NGOs pointed out the dismal failure of states to punish many violations of international criminal law between the end of the Nuremberg trials and the establishment of the ICTY. Amnesty continued:

> Neither states where these crimes have occurred nor states where persons suspected of such crimes have taken refuge nor third states which could request extradition have been able or willing to fulfill their responsibility to bring suspects to justice in trials which were neither unfair nor shams designed to shield those responsible.
> (Amnesty International 1997b, p. 12)

For Amnesty, the reality of this historical record was crucial evidence of the need for an ICC. Moreover, not any ICC would do; it should be a court whose rules affirmed states' duty to prosecute these crimes rather than leaving them with the discretion to choose whether or not to do so.

Many states addressed those NGO arguments directly during the course of 1997. Chile's delegate stated in late 1997 that the relationship of the court with national jurisdictions was one of the central remaining problems. "The principle is well enunciated that the ICC should have jurisdiction in the absence of a national court or when such national courts are manifestly ineffective. The problem is to avoid interminable disputes about when that condition is satisfied. We propose developing clear criteria for when national court systems will be deemed ineffective."[39]

Nearly all states accepted by 1997 that the ICC should have jurisdiction when national courts were unable to act, but the more difficult question was determining what to do if national court systems were for whatever reason unwilling to prosecute (Holmes 1999, pp. 46–51). At the August 1997 Preparatory Committee meeting a plausible compromise was hammered out that was unable to generate complete consensus but was widely understood to be acceptable to the vast majority of delegations. It was based on proposals by Germany and Canada, delegations that generally worked closely with the NGO coalition. Other proposals were also presented by Italy, Singapore, and Japan (Holmes 1999, p. 45). From these proposals work was undertaken to find a generally acceptable approach to what became Article 17 in the final statute, the provision on Issues of Admissibility that gives substance to the notion of complementarity. The compromise said the ICC should have jurisdiction when states were unable or unwilling *genuinely* to prosecute. This term of "unwillingness" was defined by specific criteria, including if the proceedings were "for the purpose of shielding the person." Since this could be difficult to prove, a criterion was also included that such unwillingness could be determined by the ICC if there was an "undue delay" that was "inconsistent with an intent to bring the person concerned to justice" (Holmes 1999, p. 50).[40]

Since the normal rule of the Preparatory Committee was to proceed by consensus, a bracketed second alternative was included in the working draft that would have taken a decidedly more conservative approach. The alternative, included as a text box, read:

> An alternative approach, which needs further discussion, is that the Court shall not have the power to intervene when a national decision has been taken in a particular case. That approach could be reflected as follows: The Court has no jurisdiction where the case in question is being investigated or prosecuted, or has been prosecuted, by a State which has jurisdiction over it.
>
> (Holmes 1999)

While this inclusion of an alternative approach to drafting this key clause undermined the sense of consensus, it was supported by only a very few delegations (Holmes 1999). According to the coordinator responsible for negotiating this part of the text, John Holmes, between August of 1997 and July 1998 the number of states preferring this approach declined from several to only two.[41]

At the Rome conference itself, the widespread consensus on the formula governing the statute's complementarity rules was crucial in allowing states to resolve other issues, including the role of the prosecutor, and what crimes would be included in the jurisdiction of the court. The CICC and states that favored the compromise would have to work diligently to preserve this consensus and to attempt to persuade the last few doubters. For states that wanted to slow or stop the progress toward the ICC altogether, reopening the discussions on these conditions for admissibility before the ICC cases was one sure means to accomplish this goal.

Of course, as important as it was to determine the relationship between the ICC and national jurisdictions, states were also concerned with the procedures for how any particular case would be brought before the tribunal.

Trigger Mechanism

The procedural rules for the court to begin consideration of a case were a crucial issue in the ICC negotiations because those procedures would delimit the Court's authority. Michael Scharf, a U.S. State Department official, argued that the consent of the state with custody of the alleged war criminal should be required before the ICC's jurisdiction could be exercised in each specific case (Scharf 1994, p. 114). This is one of the issues that the United States sought to use to isolate itself from prosecution. Interestingly, Scharf relies on a report of the ABA to argue that few states would be willing to have an ICC at all without this provision.[42] In fact, only the United States and China ultimately objected to the Rome Statute on these grounds (Lee, 1999, pp. 582–583, 633[43]). Scharf explicitly acknowledged that a provision requiring the consent of the state of the accused might diminish the effectiveness of an ICC but argued that it was better than nothing. In fact, it seems clear that a court that required the state of the alleged criminal's nationality to consent to jurisdiction on a case-by-case basis would have a very constrained docket, much like the current ICJ, which relies on a similar consent to jurisdiction arrangement. The fact that the final statute avoided such a provision can only be explained in light of the rhetorical positions of the pro-ICC NGOs. They argued coherently, in a wide variety of forums, from a stage early on in the negotiating process that any court that required the state of the accused to consent to jurisdiction on a case-by-case basis could not truly dispense justice because it would be inherently politicized. On this issue, as with the other fundamental features of the Rome Statute, the CICC's arguments prevailed because they were oriented toward creating a discourse that could be normatively justified as producing justice for all.

States proposed various designs for controlling the trigger mechanism for the court to take up a case as a way of limiting the challenge to sovereignty inherent in an ICC. The United States used a variety of tactics to attempt to ensure that it could block the prosecution of U.S. nationals or allies if it so desired. One such position was a reliance on the ILC 1994 draft statute's provision that asserted that an ICC would only have jurisdiction over genocide, war crimes, and crimes against humanity when cases were referred to the court by the UN Security Council. Since an affirmative vote of the Council would be required to confer such jurisdiction, the United States (or any other permanent member of the Council) could effectively block any specific prosecution.

In the fall of 1994 the UN General Assembly's Sixth Committee debated the ILC's draft statute. This led to the establishment of the ad hoc committee to discuss the ICC, which began discussions in April 1995 (Suikkari 1995). Most nations were concerned with carefully defining the subject matter jurisdiction of the new court. At the April 1995 meeting, the Russian Federation's delegate doubted a need for the statute to name specific crimes, arguing instead for a body that would rely entirely on existing treaty provisions. Many countries also expressed concern about including the crime of aggression in the absence of agreement on a clear definition (Suikkari 1995, p. 211).

The United States sought at this point to give the Security Council the sole authority to refer cases of war crimes, crimes against humanity, and genocide, arguing that such crimes were inherently threats to international peace and security and therefore properly fell under Security Council authority. Many nations objected that the Security Council was political and should not have such influence over the disposition of individual criminal cases (Suikkari 1995, pp. 213–4).[44]

In the 1995 Sixth Committee deliberations on the ICC, many states explained their views on the relationship between the ICC and the UN Security Council. Permanent Security Council members, including China, the Russian Federation, the United Kingdom, and the United States, all spoke in favor of establishing a court that would only hear cases when the Security Council had referred the situation in question to the ICC by an affirmative vote.[45] Some other states seemed to accept this basic arrangement, while others objected strenuously. Malaysia argued that an arrangement that would allow the Security Council to block particular prosecutions would give permanent member states too much power.[46] Egypt's delegate suggested that the Security Council might be used to refer cases with respect to some crimes (presumably including aggression) but that for other crimes the trigger mechanism might be different. Mexico said vaguely but presumably with reference to the Security Council issue that "in order to guarantee its independence and impartiality, the court should be removed from whatever type of outside influence."[47]

The United States sought to head off directly the argument that a Security Council role in initiating cases would politicize the ICC. The American delegate argued this position, saying:

> We have heard the role of the Security Council criticized as unduly tainting the independence of a judicial body. Ironically, allowing a State unfettered discretion to launch cases against another State, regardless of whether the resulting international prosecution would be necessary or effective, has even greater potential for political misuse. Under the current draft, the initiation of cases would be subject to whatever political agenda a particular State may have, rather than a collective decision by the Council that in fact would be less likely to reflect a political bias than that of an individual State... At the same time, however, it would be for the prosecutor and the court—not the Security Council—to decide which specific cases should be initiated and against whom. As others have noted, the court must be an independent judicial institution, without interference from political bodies. The role of the Security Council thus can be defined so that it in no way undermines the judicial independence of the court, its judges and its prosecutor, but rather strengthens the court in addressing the important cases that would be part of its mandate.[48]

This approach takes the form of a communicatively rational argument. Of course, the premise that the Security Council's decision-making process *is less* likely to inject political bias than a system that allowed only states to initiate cases is one that many observers of Security Council practice might want to challenge, and in the ICC debate, many states and NGOs did precisely that. In a sense, the United States ultimately succeeded in persuading others that either a state-led *or* a Security Council–led referral procedure could be politically biased. Most of the member organizations of the CICC took the position that since both referrals by states and by the UN Security Council could be subject to political influence, the ICC prosecutor should be able to initiate a prosecution on her own authority when there was evidence that a crime had been committed. Coupled with the topos that the purpose of the ICC was to ensure an end to impunity, it seemed logical to include as many mechanisms as possible for bringing legitimate criminal cases to the attention of the court. Another principled argument in the above statement by the United States resonated with the delegates and was ultimately reflected in the final outcome. That is the idea that whatever the political process was for bringing *situations* to the attention of the court, it should ultimately be the prosecutor, in conjunction with the court's judges, who determines whether or not there is sufficient evidence to bring charges against particular individuals. Between 1995 and 1998 both the NGOs, the large delegation from the United States, and delegations from other states worked to ensure that this procedural integrity would exist to protect the rights of the accused, reflecting a principle of international criminal justice that was well established by the legal discourse surrounding the World War II military tribunals and that I have identified as a topos in the ICC discussions generally.

Back in 1995, the United States developed one other argument about why the Security Council should be involved in initiating all ICC prosecutions.

> In any event, the reality of the hard core categories of crimes is that they are in almost all cases relevant to the matters of which the Security Council is likely to be seized, and which are part of the Council's mandate under the Charter of the United Nations to maintain and restore international peace and security. A primary purpose in establishing a permanent international criminal court is to avoid the necessity of the Security Council establishing ad hoc tribunals to deal with crimes arising under international humanitarian law. The statute should recognize the authority of the Security Council to refer situations to the court, and to do so in a way, as the delegation of Canada suggested on Monday, that will ensure that all States must cooperate with the court. [49]

What the United States argued is that in order to have successful international criminal tribunals, it would normally be necessary to bring a preponderance of power through the collective use of force to bear on conflict situations. Since only the Security Council has the authority to authorize such collective use of force, it was necessary for the Security Council to be involved in initiating all ICC proceedings.

Of course, this is a view of international criminal justice that implies it will only ever take place when it is imposed on weaker states by stronger ones, a normative rule that cannot be justified as applying equally to all. The NGOs were quick to raise such criticisms of the view that the Security Council should play a controlling role in international criminal justice. For instance, this passage is from a paper released by the World Federalist Movement and signed by William Pace and Sir Peter Ustinov in March 1996:

> Those governments who want a court only if they can control it may stall progress in the Preparatory Committee. Also unacceptable are proposals by some countries who want the court to be controlled by the Security Council, reducing an ICC to a sham status of a "permanent" ad hoc tribunal; one which would dispense

international criminal justice only to small and weak countries, never to violators in powerful nations.

(Pace and Ustinov 1996, p. 1)

Amnesty's paper in advance of the February 1997 Preparatory Committee meeting explicitly announced Amnesty International's intention to publish further position papers before future sessions of the Preparatory Committee and before the diplomatic conference itself (Amnesty International 1997b, pp. 2–3). In this way, Amnesty International indicated that it expected to be in a dialogue with states about the issues in the negotiations, and that future positions taken by states would be observed by Amnesty and other NGOs and would be commented upon. This Amnesty paper specifically offered the proposal that the prosecutor should be able to initiate cases on her own authority. The relevant core recommendations read:

> The prosecutor should be able to initiate investigations in any case where the court has jurisdiction, even in the absence of a referral by the Security Council or a state complaint, based on information from any source and to submit an indictment to the court.
>
> (Amnesty International 1997b, p. 11)

Amnesty offered a variety of arguments in support of their position that the ICC prosecutor should have the authority to initiate cases. They argued that the principle of prosecutorial independence was already recognized in the international community, citing the work of the Eighth United Nations Congress on the Prevention of Crime and the Treatment of Offenders, from 1990, and a UN General Assembly resolution that supported the same principle that prosecutors should be able to initiate and conduct criminal investigations free from political interference.[50] Amnesty noted that the prosecutors of the UN ad hoc tribunals already had the authority to determine who should be charged and when to apply for an indictment from the judges, limited only by the confines of the temporal and special jurisdictions of those courts (Amnesty International 1997a, p. 92). This is an appeal to the widely accepted topos that the ICC's design and jurisdiction should be based on existing norms of international law. Amnesty concluded their argument by pointing out the weaknesses in an ICC trigger mechanism that relied only on state and Security Council referrals. They noted that many states have been reluctant to use the complaint procedures in existing human rights treaties, often because they feared the diplomatic consequences of criticizing other governments. The Security Council had established ad hoc tribunals in two cases, but in other situations, even since 1993, when the Council found that a threat to international peace and security and international crimes clearly had been committed, they still failed to provide for criminal tribunals. Finally, the Council could restrict the hand of the prosecutor by referring situations that covered some criminal acts but not others. This could lead to effective amnesties for some perpetrators.

At the fourth Preparatory Committee meeting held August 4–15, 1997, the Security Council issue was again debated extensively. The United States and France led the charge for Security Council control over initiating prosecutions, but the vast majority of nations rejected the notion because of the obvious political constraints it would put on the court.[51]

The Singapore Compromise

Singapore proposed the compromise on the Security Council role that was ultimately adopted in the statute at the August 1997 meeting of the Preparatory Committee. Their proposal held that the Security Council could positively postpone any prosecution if it seemed necessary for the exercise of its UN Charter duties but only for 12 months at a time and only with nine affirmative votes, including those of all of the permanent five members[52] (Hall 1998c, pp. 131–33).

The NGOs were immediately involved in the campaign to support the "Singapore compromise." NGO leaders would not know how successful their own campaign had been until the final day of the plenipotentiary conference in Rome.[53]

As the Rome meeting approached it was clear that the issue of the Security Council's role in referring matters to the court's jurisdiction was one of the major outstanding issues before the conference of plenipotentiaries. Christopher Hall's brief article raised the issue explicitly in his conclusion on the pages of the *American Journal of Internationl Law* only weeks before the conference. Hall wrote here in a scholarly format, but he was the lead legal analyst for Amnesty International working on ICC issues.[54] The CICC was vital on a great number of issues, but it particularly worked to remind the national delegations that Security Council oversight of case referrals could lead to a politicized court and would be inherently unfair by protecting the permanent five and their friends. Hall noted after the fifth and sixth Preparatory Committee meetings that the "increasing effectiveness of the coordinated lobbying of the 316 members of the NGO Coalition for an ICC ... was marked" (Hall 1998b, p. 339). Louise Arbour, prosecutor for the ICTY and ICTR, also made an address to the fifth Preparatory Committee that was seen as having a large impact on many delegations. She pointed out that a weak court would be a "retrograde development" because it would be unable "to dispense fair justice" and would "exacerbate the sense of legitimate grievance of the disenfranchised"[55] (Hall 1998b, p. 339).

Progress in the Negotiations

Of course, the most important ICC-related political decision that was taken between 1995 and 1998 was whether or not to hold a diplomatic conference empowered to negotiate the statute of an ICC at all. It was not a foregone conclusion that such a conference would take place even after the ILC presented a draft ICC statute to the UN General Assembly in 1994. The NGOs understood this and worked constantly to create a sense of urgency among state delegations in order to move the process forward.

In 1995, the ad hoc committee on the establishment of an ICC was charged with the task of moving forward from the ILC's draft statute to possible procedures for actually bringing about the establishment of such a court, if sufficient interest in so doing existed among the community of nations. Their final report contains some language that broadly outlines the parameters of the ICC discourse at that point in the discussion. This is not a document that was produced by an NGO, but it nicely illustrates the early parameters of the debate on adopting an ICC treaty and some of the points of consensus that enabled the entire discourse to continue to approximate communicative rationality. It says that there "was broad recognition" that the establishment of an "effective and widely accepted ICC could ensure that the perpetrators of serious international crimes were brought to justice and deter future... crimes" (Bassiouni 1998, p. 618). This consensus point, that many states and nonstate actors recognized a need to bring an end to the impunity historically achieved by the perpetrators of mass human atrocities, provided an ethical starting point, a topos from which debate on an ICC could progress. Of course, NGOs had emphasized this broad goal from early on in their campaign.

Subsequently, speakers who made proposals that contradicted this broad consensus on ending impunity would be challenged by other participants in this discourse as having advanced an illegitimate proposal. For this reason, efforts by the United States or other groups to exempt some classes of persons from potential prosecution for violating the crimes in the ICC statute would be roundly rejected. But the ad hoc committee report also reflects the political constraints in play at the time. An excerpt follows:

> The hope was expressed that an independent court free from political pressure, established on a legal basis to deal with well-defined crimes and offering maximum guarantees to the defendants, would prevent crises which had adverse effects on entire peoples. A note of caution was however struck in this respect by some representatives, who drew attention to the far-reaching legal and financial implications of the project. A remark was also made that the result of the discussion in the Committee would inform the decision of those States which were not committed to the establishment of an international criminal court on this matter
>
> (Bassiouni 1998, p. 618).

The first sentence of the extract reflects the desire to have a court that could dispense justice equally for all, with as little political manipulation as possible. The next two sentences reflect more ominously on the significant political hurdles to achieving the establishment of an ICC. The reference to "far-reaching financial and legal implications" reflects recognition of the fact that states were contemplating the establishment of the world's first permanent judiciary with the power to hold individual persons criminally responsible for some crimes. The sheer magnitude of that fact had doomed the project to failure on prior occasions, as we saw in Chapter 3. The final sentence cited reflects the exercise of explicit political power, putting pressure on the otherwise communicatively rational debate.

If powerful states did not have their wishes fulfilled in the final draft statute, they would withhold their support from the new institution. The United States chose to pursue that precise strategy between 1998 and 2006. But their effort to influence the actual negotiations or the terms of the final statute by withholding U.S. support for the most part failed. Instead, the vast majority of states preferred to adopt an ICC statute that could be justified through communicatively rational arguments about appropriate ethical norms.

The report goes on to note the central compromise that allowed discussions of an ICC to proceed in the first place, namely, that the new court's jurisdiction should be limited to being complementary to the existing jurisdiction of national courts and "existing procedures for international judicial cooperation in international matters." Finally, it "emphasized that without universal participation the court would not serve the interest of the international community" (Bassiouni 1998, p. 618).

This argument that there were political limitations on what sort of an ICC important states would be willing to accept continued to characterize the discourse of the U.S. delegation throughout the negotiations. In 1995, Jamison Borak said:

> There are many critical issues that need to be explored in greater depth and, we hope, resolved. If we approach the court from an academically pure perspective, without regard for political realities and what States are willing to participate in and fund, we will have wasted our time. The United States has consistently cautioned against unrealistic propositions that would create a court that would be ineffective. Those who wish to accelerate the work of the court need to avoid futile proposals and press for the achievable.[56]

This is a rhetorical move by the United States to attempt to characterize particular proposals for the ICC's design as being impossibly utopian and therefore not worth pursuing. What is remarkable about the ICC negotiations in general is the extent to which this type of appeal to power failed to impact the final outcome of the negotiations.

I have used the criteria of communicative rationality to mark out particular discursive practices by NGOs as rational. But the criteria also allow us to identify discursive moves that cannot be defended on rational grounds. Of course, both NGOs and states may be guilty of this from time to time. But in the case of the ICC negotiations it was frequently NGO claims that met the test for rationality and some state claims that did not.

Italy made a statement in October 1997 focusing on the mechanics of hosting the conference and formally proposing the five-week schedule from June 15 to July 17 that was ultimately adopted for the conference. In their statement they also called for the participation of NGOs in the Rome conference and made note of the extensive contributions that such organizations had already made to the negotiations. Finally, Italy called for the extensive participation of as many states as possible.[57]

The United Kingdom delegate said, "As my delegation made clear at the August Preparatory Committee the new British government is strongly committed to the early establishment of the International Criminal Court."[58] This was a significant policy change, because a few weeks later the British would formally announce that they were prepared to support the Singapore compromise on the relationship between the ICC and the UN Security Council. They were the first permanent Security Council member to take this position. The UK also spoke specifically about the NGO role:

> Lastly a word of thanks to the non-governmental organizations. We have been assisted in our preparations for the different meetings on the Court by studying carefully the papers produced by several of the NGOs. Their presence at the sessions of the Prepcom has led to many interesting informal exchanges, often lively, often useful. We were glad to have been able to host a meeting with NGOs and invited delegates at the August session on the question of the role of the victim. We believe that focused informal meetings such as this are particularly useful in enabling all of us to benefit from the expertise of NGOs.[59]

This passage demonstrates a couple of useful things. One is that the new British Labour government cooperated closely with CICC members from the early stages of their ICC policy development. It also indicates the respect that leading government delegations had for NGO expertise.

Bill Richardson, speaking for the United States in late 1997, recalled Bill Clinton's remarks to the General Assembly in September 1997, when Clinton said that "to punish those responsible for crimes against humanity and to promote justice so that peace endures, we must maintain our strong support for the United Nations' war crime tribunals and truth commissions. And before the century ends, we should establish a permanent international court to prosecute the most serious violations of humanitarian law."[60]

So six months before the Rome conference, there was still no agreement on how cases would be brought to the ICC and what the Security Council's role would be in that process. There was a widespread, but not unanimous, consensus that the ICC should have jurisdiction when states were unwilling to investigate and prosecute, and also an emerging consensus that war crimes, genocide, and crimes against humanity would be within the jurisdiction of the court, although many states wanted to include other crimes as well. The diplomats and activists who gathered in Rome would have their work cut out for them.

6

Building the Rome Statute: 1998

> An International Criminal Court is hereby established. It shall be a permanent institution and shall have the power to exercise its jurisdiction over persons for the most serious crimes of international concern . . .
>
> —Article 1, *The Rome Statute of the International Criminal Court,* adopted July 17, 1998

The Discourse Expands

In 1998, the complexity of the International Criminal Court discourse grew exponentially. Prior to that time, relatively few diplomats, NGO activists, and legal scholars were engaged in the ongoing debates about whether or not to establish an ICC and how to go about doing so. One crucial consequence of the approach of the Rome conference scheduled for June 1998 was that many more people began to discuss and take positions on the ICC issue. For the first time, the developments in the ICC negotiations began to be covered regularly by major newspapers. Consequently, it became much more difficult for any single participant in the ICC discourse to remain fully aware of the positions being taken by all of the other interlocutors in the ICC debate. Also, the supporters of the ICC project quickly realized that delicate compromises worked out in the early stages of the negotiations could become vulnerable to collapse as more individuals, generally with less expertise in the field of international criminal law, began to examine the issues at stake in the proposed ICC statute.

At this point, NGO summaries of the early negotiations and the reasoning behind the development of particular compromises in the early stages of the negotiations were critical in informing newcomers to the negotiations and in keeping the entire negotiating process on track.[1] The NGOs increased access to the dialogue by providing accurate and authoritative descriptions of the conversations that already had taken place. This is a crucial aspect of the way that NGOs' discursive practices contributed to the outcome of the Rome Statute.

In order for a discourse to be communicatively rational, we have noted that it needs to be open to all interested participants. Of course, in world politics, that standard of universal access to the discourse is never met perfectly in practice. The question is the degree to which any actual discursive process approximates this standard. In order for persons, including state delegates, who "arrived late" to the ICC negotiations to understand what had already occurred and what issues would be debated in Rome, they needed to understand the dynamics of the negotiations up to that point in time. The various NGO position papers and summaries of earlier negotiation sessions greatly increased the transparency of these earlier sessions for the new arrivals. This was very important, since only around 60 states had participated regularly in the ICC Preparatory Committee discussions in New York between 1996 and 1998.[2] In contrast, around 150 states were represented in Rome. Of course, NGO analysis is less important for states with a large number of diplomats.[3] It was much more important for increasing the access to the negotiations for less well represented states that otherwise did not have sufficient personnel to follow the complex negotiations. The Bureau of the Preparatory Committee decided as early as its first meeting in 1996 that every effort should be made to increase the participation of states in the negotiations, and this concern led to the adoption of a resolution by the General Assembly that provided for the establishment of a trust fund to facilitate the participation of the least developed states in the conference. Fifty-four delegates from fifty-two states participated in the Rome conference under the auspices of this fund (Lee 1999, p. 9). These states were among the most likely to be influenced by the NGOs' principled arguments about how to design the court's statute because they were less likely to have the legal resources to conduct a full analysis of the relevant legal issues within their own foreign ministries.

At the Rome conference itself, it was a broad-based group of states, known as the "like-minded group," who pushed the consensus positions of the NGO Coalition for an ICC forward. This group included Canada, Germany, Norway, the Netherlands, Ghana, Egypt, South Korea, and Singapore from an early date in the preparatory process. Those delegations in particular played major leadership roles. Members of the like-minded group agreed to support a series of positions on issues in the ICC negotiations that largely matched the CICC's goals for a fair and effective court, including supporting a prosecutor with the authority to initiate prosecutions. The group grew to include nearly 60 states by the third week of the Rome session, and the CICC published a list of like-minded states and wrote that "The Coalition welcomes the recent-growth" of the group.[4] This public listing served both as recognition from the human rights community of the favorable stance that these states were taking and also created pressure on other states to have their names added to the list. Approximately 100 states claimed some association with the like-minded position by the end of the conference. For the founding core group of states, close cooperation with the representatives of nongovernmental organizations was the normal mode of conducting business from early on during the Preparatory Committee meetings (Wippman 2004, p. 160). In fact, the relationship between the CICC and the group of like-minded states was institutionalized in a series of working lunch seminars that were held during the Preparatory Committee, the Rome conference itself, and the sessions following the Rome conference on implementation of the Rome Statute. These sessions were usually hosted by the German government and featured NGO spokespersons addressing particular issues that concerned the NGO community. Delegates from the growing group of "like-minded" states regularly attended. The growth in the number of groups openly associating themselves with the issue positions of the like-minded group reflects the steady success of CICC member NGOs at persuading states to accept their views.

The NGOs made a regular habit of thanking state delegations for helpful comments they made during the state-to-state negotiations. Frequently, these thanks reflected the fact that states had adopted NGO proposals as their own positions. One typical comment, more general than most, came in an HRW 1999 annual report. The year following the Rome conference, HRW said the coalition of like-minded states from Africa, North and South America, Asia, Western and Eastern Europe, and Oceania "drove the ICC negotiating process to its successful conclusion."[5] Other examples include press releases issued by HRW, the most media-savvy of the human rights NGOs, following the introductory speeches by Canada and South Africa on June 15, 1998. HRW praised Canada's Lloyd Axworthy particularly for supporting the concept of an independent prosecutor.[6] Another HRW press release thanked South Africa's Justice Minister, Dullah Omar, who also called for a prosecutor with powers to begin investigations on his or her own initiative.[7] NGOs consistently followed the maxim that it is better in politics to let others take the credit for good ideas, but the written record shows that NGOs regularly put forward crucial proposals first.

Writing in 1998 on the eve of the Rome conference, Bill Pace, the founder of the CICC, described the previous years' negotiations as follows. He said "For the past three years, a partnership of nongovernmental organizations, governments, and international organizations have been leading a quiet but determined effort to create a permanent International Criminal Court" (Pace 1998). At that point he described the pro-ICC NGO coalition as including

> literally hundreds of NGOs from all regions of the world and sectors of society. Relatively small constituents benefit enormously from being associated with leaders of major organizations who join in the common efforts at the negotiations. Nonstate actors such as the International Committee for the Red Cross and NGOs such as Amnesty International, the Lawyers Committee for Human Rights, the International Commission of Jurists, Human Rights Watch, and the International Federation for Human Rights have substantial expertise in international human rights and humanitarian law. They are able to focus deeply on key political, legal, and technical issues.... Among the primary objectives of the Coalition is the circulation and promotion of new research and expert documents prepared by its member organizations. The Coalition Secretariat updates both NGOs and governments on current developments in all fields related to the ICC. Each organization plays a unique role in communicating the Coalition's varied goals. Somewhat surprisingly, the smaller groups are often more effective at networking, information dissemination and coalition-building than the larger international organizations.
>
> (Pace 1998)

Pace went on to describe some of the lobbying techniques employed by the coalition. "Throughout the last two years of negotiation, the Coalition has organized meetings with national and regional delegations to the ICC preparatory committees.[8] In addition to general strategy meetings, which usually include between 50 and 100 NGOs, the caucuses and groups meet individually to develop their positions. These positions are independent of the Coalition as a whole. It is vital to maintain the plurality of ideas and objectives represented by the Coalition's loosely bound constituents."[9]

In the balance of this chapter I analyze the discursive moves of NGOs and elements of the U.S. government, particularly the Department of Defense, in the months before and during the Rome conference. The goal remains to identify discursive moves and characterize them as being communicatively rational or strategic forms of action. Recall that in the constructivist approach to the analysis taken throughout this study, a crucial element of the political process undertaken in Rome is the evolution of new conceptions of state's interests. In other words, an important part of the negotiation involves persuasion about what ends states ought to collectively pursue by creating the ICC. In that sort of a discourse, it is important that states reach agreement about the reasons for establishing an ICC. In these negotiations, communicatively rational forms of argument were particularly efficacious when states were trying to persuade one another of the most important objectives to be sought in the establishment of the ICC.

This chapter also discusses the differences in negotiating styles between states and NGOs in Rome and examines why NGOs often were more able to utilize communicatively rational discursive practices. Finally we will examine the resolution achieved in the final days of the negotiations on the central issues that were discussed in Chapter 5, namely, the definition of the crimes in the Rome Statute, the implementation of complementarity for the court's jurisdiction, the trigger mechanism for initiating prosecutions, and the development of the independent prosecutor not limited by UN Security Council control.

Before I turn to the analysis of particular arguments advanced during the negotiations, I want to describe the process of the Rome conference generally. As was the case during the Preparatory Committee meetings, the working assumption in Rome was to proceed by attempting to reach consensus on every issue. Of course, as we saw in Chapter 5, many of the most crucial issues remained to be decided in Rome, including how cases would be brought to the attention of the court, what the role of the Security Council would be, and precisely which crimes could be prosecuted, along with myriad other issues. Work at the Rome conference was divided into working groups, and the chairs of each working group together constituted the bureau that served collectively as the administrators of the conference.[10] The task of reaching consensus was made more difficult because states' positions on one issue were conditional on the resolution of other features of the statute.

In the first three weeks of the conference, states put forward proposals, many of which were mutually exclusive. A complete consensus on most issues was impossible. Of course, one possible outcome, and perhaps even a strategy pursued by some delegations, was to delay the establishment of a court indefinitely by insisting on positions that were irreconcilable with other states' views. At the same time, it became clear as the conference progressed that the vast majority of states shared "near consensus" positions on many of the crucial issues. In the final week of the conference, the bureau held bilateral meetings with delegations and tried to find each state's bottom line about what features of the court were absolutely necessary for them to accept the total package. Following this, the bureau produced a draft statute, which on the final day of the conference garnered the support of 120 states, and with relatively few adjustments became the Rome Statute. Of course, for delegates participating in the Rome conference, it was impossible to know even fairly late in the five-week period that this dynamic would emerge at the end of the conference. What I show in this chapter is the ways that arguments about particular proposals were deployed and how a near consensus, if never a complete one, gradually emerged. What is surprising is that in substantial measure, that final package compromise addressed nearly all of the principled concerns raised repeatedly by member organizations of the CICC during the negotiating process and set aside the strategic interests of several powerful states.

Preconference Discursive Moves

Justice in the Balance, published by Human Rights Watch in early 1998 in the run-up to the Rome conference, is one of the more extensive statements of the argument in favor of a strong ICC published by a leading member of the NGO coalition. The book's introduction includes seven recommendations that HRW argues must be followed if the ICC is to be an independent, fair, and effective judicial institution (HRW 1998, p. 2). The recommendations follow:

1. The jurisdictional regime should eliminate any need for state consent (on a case-by-case basis);
2. The court must be independent of the Security Council;
3. The court must have an independent prosecutor;
4. While complementarity should be the basis for the court's jurisdiction, the ICC must be able to investigate and prosecute when states fail to do so;
5. No distinction should be made between international or internal armed conflicts;
6. States must clearly be obligated to comply with requests from the court; and
7. The ICC should respect the rights of the accused, suspects, and witnesses.

The best evidence of the NGOs' efficacy is the fact that all of these recommendations were implemented in some form in the Statute.[11] On the most controversial issues, numbers 1 through 4 above, the history of the negotiations summarized in Chapter 4 and below shows that the NGO positions were the crucial starting points for the compromises that were ultimately adopted by the treaty drafters. Still, in the spring of 1998, this agenda put forth by HRW and other NGOs seemed remarkably ambitious.[12]

On March 27, 1998, in the middle of the final Preparatory Committee session, the U.S. Department of Defense began a major diplomatic campaign to persuade other militaries around the world to get involved in the ICC negotiations. This was a potentially very effective strategy for ensuring that the Rome conference would produce a relatively weak ICC because militaries around the world are frequently opposed to internationalist foreign policies (Solingen 1998). The Department of Defense briefs were issued to most foreign military attachés in Washington, and they encouraged military officials to "take an active interest in the negotiations regarding an international criminal court."[13] U.S. officials pointed out their concern that American military forces deployed on UN missions could become the target of frivolous or politically motivated prosecutions. The document warned that military officials in other states could also be the target of future ICC prosecutions, and for this reason encouraged such officials to engage in the ICC negotiating process. HRW's Executive Director responded in a press release to this campaign: "They're calling in the foxes to help build the chicken coop. The Pentagon should not resort to enlisting the Pinochets of the world to lobby against the creation of an independent and effective ICC."[14] HRW also pointed out the safeguards against politically motivated prosecutions, such as the proposed complementarity rules that gave deference to domestic investigations and prosecutions. The Department of Defense proposal could be seen as communicatively rational in a conversation about how to design an ICC court that is sufficiently weak to ensure that it will prosecute military officials rarely if ever. It is difficult to see the argument as communicatively rational in a conversation about how to ensure that perpetrators of war crimes, crimes against humanity, and war crimes would not enjoy impunity. The U.S. Department of Defense quickly found in response to their campaign that the ICC discourse was now focused on the later objective of ensuring an end to impunity, and their appeals ultimately had little effect. But that was not yet obvious in April 1998. Of course, to the extent that Department of Defense lobbying on this issue was accompanied by the suggestion that military-to-military cooperation might be reduced or eliminated if states failed to heed American suggestions, this was a form of strategic action.[15]

The Rome Conference Gets Under Way

On June 15, 1998, Kofi Annan opened the Rome conference as temporary president of the UN Diplomatic Conference of Plenipotentiaries on the Establishment of an International Criminal Court. He gave a speech that sounded very much like an NGO brief on the reasons for favoring a strong ICC.[16] He discussed the history of efforts to criminalize excesses of violence in warfare, and said "the world had come to realize that relying on each State to punish its own transgressors was not enough. All too often, such crimes were part of a systematic State policy and the worst criminals might be found at the pinnacle of State power."[17] This is an example of the ways that nonstate actors and the secretariats of international institutions reinforce each other's power.[18] It seems unlikely that a delegate from any state could make the same statement with such force, or even that a UN secretary general would feel so emboldened as to address his primary constituents, the diplomatic representatives of states, if he was not aware of the larger audience listening to his remarks that included so many representatives of global civil society. Annan said as much himself, noting that "World public opinion had led to the holding of the Conference, stimulated by the hard work of the Red Cross, of many other nongovernmental organizations and of the humanitarian community. The whole world would be watching the Conference, and concrete results would be expected."[19] Annan recognized the difficulty that delegates would face in drafting a statute that would be widely ratified by many states, yet still he argued "The court must be strong enough to carry out its tasks—an instrument of justice, not expediency. It must be able to protect the weak against the strong."[20]

In closing, Annan set the tone for the negotiations by reminding delegates of their unique position in history. He said he hoped the participants would "feel [that] the eyes of the victims of past crimes, and of the potential victims of future ones, were fixed firmly upon them. The Conference offered an opportunity to take a monumental step in the name of human rights and the rule of law, an opportunity to create an institution that could save the lives and serve as a bulwark against evil, bequeathing to the next century a powerful instrument of justice. Future generations would not forgive failure in that endeavor."[21] This sense of historical moment is a factor that I believe crucially contributes to the success of communicatively rational arguments over strategic ones. It is characteristic of efforts at constitution drafting. When people take a long-term view of the consequences of the political actions that they are debating, arguments premised on arriving at norms that can be rationally defended as just and efficacious at promoting social order are strengthened in relation to arguments that instead focus on the particularized interests of actors, even powerful ones. Annan's remarks indicate that he deliberately sought to invoke in the delegates to the Rome conference that sense of historical moment. The results of the conference, and the fact that many delegates were present and attuned to this speech when it was given, suggest that Annan's effort to invoke consciousness of history's judgment was successful.

Persuasive Arguments and Decision Making at the Rome Conference

Below, I trace the ways that arguments presented by the NGO coalition worked their way into the final compromise deal on the terms of the Rome Statute that were presented to the delegations in Rome by the bureau of the negotiations in the final hours of the conference.[22] I argue that the structure of the arguments employed during the ICC negotiations themselves influence the way a great many decision makers reached their decisions, because once the crucial objectives of the Rome negotiations were framed in a particular way by the NGO delegations, certain policy choices in the final statute were much more likely to be adopted than others. Reasons for particular policy choices that could be grounded in achieving widely shared objectives in ways that were rationally consistent with existing understandings of international law were usually much more effective than arguments that focused on protecting particular political interests. The outcome of the ICC negotiations demonstrates that the structure of these arguments, in other words, the logic of communicatively rational arguments, persuaded many of the participants in the ICC negotiations.

This analysis points out the relationship between arguments that were advanced during the ICC negotiations and shows why certain conclusions of the Rome conference were likely to be reached once the logical premises of NGO arguments were accepted. My assertion about the ICC discourse between January 1997 and July 17, 1998 is that it became too complex, with too many speakers and listeners involved, to trace every possible act of persuasion. What I do claim is that NGO arguments in printed form between 1994 and June of 1998 can be logically related to the choices that were made in the final drafting of the Rome Statute on July 17, 1998. My claim hinges on the analysis of the logical relationship between arguments and is buttressed by extensive anecdotal evidence that NGO analyses were repeated in countless conversations leading up to and during the negotiations themselves.[23] Farther on I discuss examples of that process on crucial issues, following the same issues that were covered in the earlier stages of the negotiations in Chapter 5. One hundred and twenty states voted for the statute in Rome, while only seven voted against it. Each of those votes has some formal governmental decision-making process implied in the background. I do not attempt to systematically examine each of those processes, although in an ad hoc way I will mention a few things I have learned about those decisions when space permits. I do show how during the negotiations themselves particular proposals gained widespread support, while other proposals were gradually shown to have very little or no support beyond the states that initially sponsored them.

David Wippman, who worked on developing U.S. ICC policy in 1998 and 1999, has noted that the ICC negotiations included both legal and political forms of argument that were often deployed simultaneously. Wippman defines legal arguments as those that are based on what international law requires or should require as a legal system. Political arguments are those claims that focus on what would or would not advance the interests of particular actors (Wippman 2004). This distinction is similar to the one I make between communicatively rational and strategic arguments.[24] Wippman notes that during the Rome negotiations, many delegates took the perspective that where existing rules of international law were determinative, they were bound to follow those rules in drafting the ICC treaty (Wippman 2004, pp. 153–4). This supports my general claim that the principle that the ICC statute should be grounded in existing international law had become a widely accepted topos for the Rome negotiations by the time they got under way in June 1998. NGOs were able to use that fact to argue for particular proposals by grounding the justification for the proposals in their expert understandings of the existing rules of international law.

The claim that NGO arguments were abundant and generally well received at the Rome conference itself is widely supported by comments made by participants in those negotiations. The following passage, by Cherif Bassiouni, who served as chair of the drafting committee at the Rome conference, is representative. He writes of the NGO role that:

> Non-governmental organizations, and particularly the "NGO Coalition for an ICC" played an important and useful part in the process. Their contributions took the form of aiding the PrepCom through publishing expert NGO papers which contributed to a deeper understanding of the issues and creating opportunities for generating ideas, and for informal meetings with delegates throughout which NGO experts could offer advice to the delegates. Equally, the close attention which NGOs have paid to the proceedings of the PrepCom, the meetings which the NGO Coalition has held during the PrepCom with various states, groups of states, and other influential persons inside the ICC process, and the lobbying which has gone on at the United Nations have all served to sustain and strengthen the momentum of the process. At a broader level, outside of the PrepCom, efforts were undertaken by NGOs to influence political leaders, create world wide awareness of the Court issue, and hence their support for the Court has been crucial, and should be acknowledged as such.
>
> (Bassiouni 1998, pp. 25–6)

During the working group negotiation sessions in Rome, leading states within the like-minded group worked closely with NGO representatives to advance their favored proposals. Fabricio Guariglia, who was a member of Argentina's delegation in Rome, recalled that when a particular proposal he advanced met with a number of questions, he was able to call on colleagues in the NGO movement to prepare a briefing statement educating other delegations about this proposal at only a few hours' notice. Commenting on the role of the NGOs in the negotiations generally, he said that "NGO's were pushing the envelope" in terms of the proposals they put forward.[25]

During the Rome conference, NGOs were demonstrably more able to modify their positions on particular issues. States, particularly those with large foreign policy bureaucracies, are not nearly as able to adjust their positions to ongoing deliberations. David Scheffer, who was appointed to the newly created post of Ambassador-at-Large for War Crimes Issues in August 1997, led the US negotiating team in Rome. He recalled one incident in which he participated in a negotiating session where NGO representatives were present.[26] Immediately following the session, the NGO representatives retired to the Sudan Room at FAO headquarters where the NGOs based their operations during the negotiating sessions. Twenty minutes later, the NGO delegates emerged with a new policy statement on the issue that had just been discussed at the previous meeting. Scheffer recalled that the statement began: "The international community takes the position that . . . " Scheffer personally berated the NGO delegates for claiming that their newly formulated position, developed in less than half an hour, represented the views of the "international community." He explained the long and complex process of vetting that his own statements had to undergo in the U.S. policy making process before he could make a statement that claimed to be the position of the United States of America.

Scheffer is of course quite correct that his own statements, fed through the U.S. government bureaucracy, have a much stronger claim to representative legitimacy than those of his NGO counterparts. However, at the same time Scheffer's story precisely illustrates why NGOs are more capable of engaging in a deliberative negotiating process. A handful of legal experts from a few leading NGOs could quickly analyze new issues raised by state governments and immediately offer counterproposals to particular suggestions put forth. In 20 minutes, these NGO leaders could draft new proposals that both addressed the concerns put forward by states and preserved their own goals, namely, creating a "fair and effective" ICC. Of course, NGO statements cannot be justified on representative grounds. In order to be effective, NGO proposals have to offer persuasive arguments about why they are a normatively better or more practical solution to the concerns other participants in the negotiations have advanced.

NGOs might well have done better to avoid the rhetorical device of claiming that their views were the position of the international community. Their arguments could have been just as effective if they had instead claimed to have a logically defensible solution to problems raised by different states that were easier to justify as fair and legitimate rules.

NGOs also contributed to the realization of communicative action through their efforts to ensure that all states had adequate legal advice and personnel to follow the complex negotiations (Struett 2004). One crucial NGO initiative organized by NPWJ sought to identify experts in international law, including advanced students and faculty from law schools in the United States and Western Europe who would be willing to serve as legal counsel for less developed nations participating in the ICC negotiations. This initiative allowed over 30 less developed states to enjoy expert legal counsel and participate in the Rome conference negotiations on the ICC statute, including Sierra Leone and Bosnia, states that had just recently witnessed the crimes covered by the Rome Statute.[27] This NGO initiative thus deliberately ensured that the perspectives of states that have recently experienced violent conflicts and subsequent efforts to bring the perpetrators to justice would be heard during the Rome conference.

Both of these delegations favored a permanent ICC with a prosecutor with independent authority to bring charges. According to the delegates who represented each of these states, they had only very general instructions from the governments they represented to advance a strong court during the negotiations.[28] They were able to use the latitude that they were given to work toward a progressive definition of the crimes in the statute and otherwise ensure the establishment of an effective court. These delegates were not NGO agents; they saw themselves as legal counsel, representing a client. Still, NGOs' general goals for a strong and effective court overlapped with the goals of these states, so it made good tactical sense for NGOs like NPWJ to work to ensure that such states had an effective voice during the negotiations. These delegates were particularly compelling during the negotiations because they represented states that were already dealing with the legacy of mass violence and with international efforts to bring the perpetrators to justice.

Resolving the Main Issues

The Rome conference began with an ambitious agenda of problems to resolve in the five short weeks scheduled for the conference. The draft statute that formed the working basis for the conference included 1700 sets of bracketed options (Lee 1999, p. 13). Adrian Bos, the chair of the Preparatory Committee negotiations, notes that it was difficult to speak of progress in the negotiations prior to Rome because states deliberately left some of the most contentious issues to be decided at the conference itself.[29]

Covered Crimes and their Definitions

By the time of the Rome Conference, the topoi that the ICC statute should reflect existing international law was well entrenched. This grounding point for the debate left NGO legal experts in a strong position to argue that existing rules of international criminal law already made criminal a number of specific acts. Below I discuss examples. As a preliminary question, I briefly want to discuss how expectations about what crimes the ICC would try had shifted as a result of statements by Amnesty and like-minded groups. The evolution in the formal positions of the American Bar Association demonstrates this trend.

The position of the ABA on which crimes should be included in the jurisdiction of the court evolved over time. The increased specificity of their position on the issue at a latter time reflects the evolution of the general debate on the topic. When the ABA issued its recommendations in favor of the establishment of an ICC tribunal in 1992, they said simply that the ICC's jurisdiction should "cover a range of well-established international crimes."[30] In 1994 the ABA's revised recommendation was only slightly more specific; they spoke of two broad categories of crimes: "crime specified in an international convention" and "crime recognized by the international community as a gross violation of a rule of customary international law widely accepted by states representing all of the world's major legal systems."[31] Their position statement issued in February 1998 closely parroted the positions taken earlier on this issue by Amnesty International and HRW.[32] The U.S. government agreed with the CICC on this issue, arguing that the court should focus on the "most serious" crimes of concern to the international community, a phrase that found its way into the preamble of the Rome Statute.[33]

By the time of the Rome conference, there was a broad consensus among the delegates that the definition of genocide should be copied unchanged from the 1948 convention. Amnesty also worked to update the definition of crimes against humanity by ensuring that emerging variations of crimes, such as "enforced disappearances" were specifically named in the Statute (Amnesty International, 1997, p. 6; Rome Statute Article 7.1, i).

More importantly, a consensus was beginning to form around the idea of giving the court some sort of inherent or automatic jurisdiction over the three core crimes: genocide, war crimes, and crimes against humanity. What was meant by the phrase inherent jurisdiction is that the ICC would have jurisdiction over all the covered crimes when they occurred on the territory of any state party. This was in sharp contrast to the initial ILC proposal for an ICC that would have allowed states to pick whether or not their state would be subject to each class of crimes. Under the emerging consensus, states would not be allowed to choose to give the court jurisdiction over genocide while withholding jurisdiction over war crimes, for instance.

This formula is distinct from universal jurisdiction, which is the jurisdictional theory that certain international crimes, such as piracy, are so widely condemned that they can be punished by any court, regardless of where the crime occurred and the nationality of the accused or the victims. Germany proposed at the final Preparatory Committee meeting in April 1998 that the ICC should exercise this form of jurisdiction over genocide, war crimes, and crimes against humanity, since many legal scholars already hold that individual states have such universal jurisdiction rights over these crimes.[34] This proposal met with strenuous objection by the United States Department of Defense, who faxed the German government with a request that the proposal be withdrawn, and a threat that if it was not, the United States would withdraw its forces from military bases in Germany.[35] This tactic is a prototypical example of strategic action designed to impact another actor's behavior in a negotiation by threatening to take a particular action on another issue rather than by reaching agreement about the desirability of an ICC with the authority to exercise universal jurisdiction. The American objection was apparently motivated by a desire to ensure that if the ICC was designed in a way that the United States did not accept, it should not have the power to try U.S. nationals. Germany did not withdraw its proposal, but in Rome, it was decided that it would be unwise to grant the court universal jurisdiction. Drafters of the statute were sensitive to the concern that the new court should not create new legal obligations for states that chose not to join the court, which would have been a necessary implication of an ICC with universal jurisdiction. This would have violated the topoi that the court should be consistent with existing principles of international law.

Now I turn to an example of some of the ways NGOs used their legal expertise to impact the codification of the crimes at the Rome conference. Amnesty lawyers warned long before the Rome conference against an expansion of the definition of genocide beyond what is contained in the 1948 convention to include the destruction of political or social groups. They pointed out this could create two separate but parallel approaches to the crime of genocide in international law, with different standards under the Genocide Convention of 1948 and the new ICC (Amnesty International 1997b, pp. 4–5). Fairness dictated that such a situation should be avoided. If the definition of genocide was broadened to include political groups, then a much larger number of incidents would potentially be included under the definition of genocide. Deciding which to pursue and which to ignore would tend to politicize the office of the ICC prosecutor, Amnesty argued.

Another Amnesty International paper published in April 1998, titled "The International Criminal Court: Ensuring Justice for Women," called on states to ensure that gender crimes would be specifically enumerated in the ICC statute. The paper begins with an emotional account by a Kurdish woman who was raped by Iraqi soldiers. From there, it turns to making a series of legal arguments about how specific acts against women are already criminal under existing provisions of international humanitarian law, with references to the appropriate legal authorities. The paper argues that rape and forced impregnation can already be acts of genocide if they are undertaken with a genocidal intent. Similar calls were made to specifically list gender-based crimes in the definitions of war crimes and crimes against humanity. These calls were based in part on the emerging practice of the ad hoc tribunals. The result in the Rome Statute is clear; these provisions were included in the definitions of crimes after vocal NGO insistence (Rome Statute, Article 6 d-e, Article 7.1 g, Article 7.2 f, Article 8.2 b xxii, and Article 8.2 e vi).

One of the delegates who worked to include the war crimes provision was the legal advisor from Bosnia and Herzegovina who was recommended to the Bosnian ambassador through the NPWJ program described above. It is important to note that this person was not an NGO activist prior to or during the Rome meeting. She was a legal expert working on a doctoral dissertation at the London School of Economics on the definitions of crimes under international humanitarian law.[36] Her own views on the evolution of international criminal law were probably not shaped by the NGO papers circulated during the ICC negotiations. However, she was a state delegate in Rome, speaking on behalf of Bosnia because of an NGO program, and her arguments carried the day in part because many other delegations had been exposed to these arguments earlier by way of NGO papers circulated by Amnesty and other pro-ICC NGOs.

The permanent members of the Security Council pursued a number of negotiating positions during the Rome conference itself with reference to the definitions of the crimes and the conditions for their exercise that had as their intent to limit the scope of the ICC's authority. For instance, Britain, France, and the United States all continued to object to a widely supported proposal to define a crime against humanity as any of a series of specifically listed acts when committed as part of a widespread *or* systematic attack.[37] Instead these states wanted to require that the definition read *widespread and systematic*, significantly raising the bar of what a prosecutor would have to show in order to prove the commission of a crime against humanity.[38] Crimes against humanity were particularly hard to define during the Rome conference because the precedents in international law for the prosecution of this type of crime are found in a wide variety of sources that are not consistent in their use of terminology (Hebel and Robinson 1999, p. 90). The exact phrasing of the definition of this crime was crucial because if it was defined narrowly, it would be difficult for the court to prosecute those accused of this entire class of international crimes.

As a leading advocate of a fair and effective court, Canada proposed a compromise wording during the third week of the conference in an effort to gain the support of the Security Council countries for the court in general. Canada's proposal suggested the following definition: "For the purpose of the present statute, a crime against humanity means any of the following acts when knowingly committed as a part of a widespread or systematic attack directed against any civilian population." In a footnote, the proposal added that "attack directed against any civilian population" means a "course of conduct involving the commission of multiple acts ... against any civilian population, pursuant to or knowingly in furtherance of a governmental or organizational policy to commit those acts."[39] NGO legal experts were quick to criticize the limitations of the Canadian draft, and an NGO-sponsored newsletter trumpeted the NGOs concerns.[40] NGO experts pointed out that the phrase "knowingly" "means that a perpetrator would have to be aware that he was acting as part of a larger plan in committing a crime. This would be extremely hard to prove and could mean that individual acts—no matter how barbaric or massive—would not be covered."[41] Additionally, NGOs pointed out that acts of omission, such as starving a population or some forms of ethnic cleansing might not qualify as an attack.[42]

With two and a half weeks left in the Rome conference, the French delegation met with a group of French NGOs associated with the CICC. The French delegation announced that they would accept the Canadian proposal on crimes against humanity.[43]

France also continued to advocate a restrictive definition of war crimes and declared that since the definitions France proposed to include in the ICC statute were drafted in different "contexts" from the (more progressive) definitions in protocol I of the Geneva Conventions the two should not be compared.[44] Again, this line of argument violates the by then well-established topoi of the Rome negotiations that the ICC statute should reflect existing international law, and so such arguments ultimately foundered.

In the final Rome Statute, the basic form of the Canadian proposal on defining crimes against humanity is retained, but these concerns raised by the NGO legal experts are mitigated by adjustments to the text. On the face of it, this is a remarkable outcome. Article 7 of the Rome Statute says that a "'crime against humanity' means any of the following acts when committed as part of a widespread *or* systematic attack directed against any civilian population, with knowledge of the attack." The elimination of the adverb knowingly and its repositioning as "knowledge of the attack" addresses the NGOs concern that a prosecutor might have to prove awareness of the whole plan as opposed to awareness of the alleged perpetrators role in the plan. Also, Article 7 makes clear that acts of omission can constitute a crime against humanity by stating that "extermination," one of the expressly prohibited acts, "includes the intentional infliction of conditions of life, inter alia [among other things], the deprivation of access to food and medicine, calculated to bring about the destruction of part of a population."[45] At NGO insistence, the following acts were specifically named as acts that constitute crimes against humanity: "rape, sexual slavery, enforced prostitution, forced pregnancy, enforced sterilization, or any other form of sexual violence of comparable gravity."[46]

Why should the final compromise brokered by Canada and the bureau of the Rome negotiations be closer to the desired position of human rights of the NGOs than the initial positions of the governments of France, the United Kingdom, and the United States? The arguments advanced by the NGOs were focused on ensuring an end to impunity for the perpetrators of mass atrocities, while the arguments advanced by the Security Council powers were clearly intended to limit the range of cases the court could prosecute and to create loopholes that could be used in the future to avoid international prosecutions. In the context of a communicatively rational, legally oriented, type of discourse, the former NGO arguments were widely seen as persuasive, while the powerful states found it impossible to attract adherents to their positions. This was true even though the Security Council powers had considerable leverage to torpedo the entire process by withholding their approval of the resulting court. Such explicitly strategic power was less persuasive than the force of NGO rational arguments.

Many states still sought to have other crimes, including aggression, terrorism, hijacking, the use of nuclear weapons, or drug trafficking included in the statute. But as the meeting wore on, most states came to accept the NGOs' pragmatic warning that to insist on an expansion of the list of crimes would likely result in a failure to create a court at all in Rome.

On the issue of aggression, there was considerable disagreement among NGOs themselves. Some NGOs insisted that an ICC without jurisdiction over aggression would be a betrayal of the Nuremberg precedent. We have seen above that Amnesty International had not taken a position on including the crime of aggression in the statute, partly out of recognition that the difficulties of defining that crime could torpedo the entire negotiations, and the fact that prosecuting aggression would almost certainly involve an enhanced role for the UN Security Council. Norway explicitly advocated this position during the conference itself, openly stating that the crime of aggression should be included in the statute only if it did not antagonize the Security Council, and warned that an effort to force this issue could lead to the collapse of the entire conference.[47] Greece, Russia, and Germany all acknowledged that aggression was one of the most serious crimes of concern to the international community and that it would be a retrograde development of international law to exclude it. Other states, including Pakistan, insisted that only states commit aggression, not individuals, and so it was inappropriate to include that crime.[48] The decision not to resolve this issue in the Rome Statute but instead to postpone it for another day was crucial for establishing a court that could attract widespread support. Article five of the statute explicitly gives the court jurisdiction over the crime of aggression but then forbids the court from exercising that jurisdiction until such time as the crime is defined by a conference of the ICC state parties, to occur no earlier than seven years after the entry into force of the statute.[49]

On the final day of the conference, 120 states set aside their desires for changes and accepted the bureau's compromise proposal that limited the ICC to the core crimes but created a court with strong powers. It is hard not to be struck by the parallels between the approach taken and the approach advocated by Amnesty International in the early years of the debate.

Complementarity and the Jurisdiction of the Court

In the end, the drafters of the statute formulated the complementarity issue so that any case that is "genuinely"[50] being investigated or prosecuted by a national court is not admissible before the ICC (Rome Statute, Article 17). Crucially, it is the court that makes the determination about whether or not a national prosecution is genuine; states have no automatic mechanism to block the ICC from investigating a case. This was the central compromise made in deference to national sovereignty that allowed the ICC to go forward (Holmes, p. 74 in Lee 1999). Many delegates to the Preparatory Committee meetings wanted to avoid establishing an appeals court that could review national decisions. At the same time however, delegates realized that the pretense of a national investigation could be used to block legitimate ICC prosecution of a case unless the court was given explicit authority to find that a state was not genuinely investigating the case (Holmes, pp. 48–49 in Lee 1999). The Rome Statute allows for such a determination to be made by majority vote of the pretrial chamber subject to review by the appeals chamber (Article 18, Rome Statute). The statute also establishes involved procedures that allow states to object before proceedings begin or even during the proceedings that a particular item is inadmissible because it is being handled genuinely by a national judicial procedure, but these state objections cannot automatically stop a case at the ICC. This outcome from the negotiating process, granting such substantive power to the court over determining the limits of its own jurisdiction, can only be understood in light of the fact that the NGO community actively and early on highlighted the fact that complementarity could be used as a mechanism to circumscribe the court's authority before it came into existence.

During the final weeks of the Rome conference, the United States put forward a slightly modified version of a proposal they initially advanced at the last Preparatory Committee meeting in March 1998 that would have institutionalized a much more systematic mechanism to allow states to object to the exercise of jurisdiction by the ICC. The proposal would require the ICC prosecutor to notify any state that might have jurisdiction to prosecute a case one month in advance of his or her own prosecution, whether or not they were parties to the ICC statute.[51] The proposal would include states with the potential to exercise jurisdiction on the principles of territory, nationality, custody, or passive personality principles. Any of these states could block the ICC's investigation and prosecution of a case by opening their own investigation and notifying the ICC prosecutor. Many NGOs expressed concern that such a proposal would create too many safeguards against "frivolous prosecutions" the United States wanted to avoid, and that this would contribute to permitting impunity for serious international crimes. Germany declared that the proposal was simply unnecessary.[52] The Rome Statute actually reflects a system that grants the ICC prosecutor and judges the crucial role of determining for themselves whether or not a national prosecution is really genuine, reflecting the goal of the vast majority of conference participants to design a court that could ensure an end to impunity.

The complementarity regime has had an unintended positive consequence in the eyes of the NGO Coalition for an ICC. As states ratify the Rome Statute, they are taking steps to enhance their national courts' capability to try criminal cases arising out of international law, in accordance with the Rome Statute's complementarity provisions.[53] This is having the effect of dramatically developing the provisions in municipal law for enforcing violations of international criminal law.

For the United States, the complementarity regime ultimately was not perceived as providing adequate protection of sovereign rights. U.S. War Crimes Ambassador David Scheffer has argued that in the case of a frivolous claim against a U.S. peacekeeper deployed in the field, the United States would have to initiate an investigation even if there was no real wrongdoing in order to block ICC jurisdiction. Even then, the ICC could find by a two-to-one vote of the pretrial hearing that the U.S. investigation was not genuine and proceed with its own prosecution (Scheffer 1999, p. 19). This argument is not compelling. If the United States participated in the court, actively cooperating with the other states parties to define the "elements of crimes" and working to ensure that judges and prosecutors of the highest integrity were selected, it could in all likelihood prevent the scenario that Ambassador Scheffer puts forth. It seems that the only real justification for U.S. opposition to the treaty was a fundamental unwillingness to subject U.S. personnel to international review of their compliance with their existing international obligations under international humanitarian law.

This issue nicely illustrates the relationship between communicatively rational and strategic arguments that occurred during the Rome negotiations. The United States made both communicatively rational and strategic arguments to support its contention that the ICC should not exercise its jurisdiction over states except on the basis of the consent of those states or a Security Council referral. The outlines of this issue were presented in Chapter 5. Recall that one of the arguments the United States presented was that there is a long-standing principle of international treaty law that treaties cannot create new obligations for nonstate parties.[54] This is a communicatively rational argument, and interlocutors in the ICC debate largely accepted this claim by the United States. However, supporters of the final text of the Rome Statute argued that it does respect the legal rights of states not to join the ICC, and accordingly, not to be bound by its provisions. Supporters of the ICC argue that this does not mean that the nationals of nonstate parties cannot be held responsible for their actions on the territory of states parties to the ICC if the court prosecutes them.[55]

The United States also advanced a more explicitly strategic argument that the country and its citizens should be exempt from unwanted supervision by the ICC because of the unique role the United States plays in maintaining international peace and security. Supporters of the ICC rejected the premise of this argument and insisted that International Criminal Law should be enforced against all violators, regardless of their nationality. While both the legal and strategic arguments were deployed by the United States to the same end, it is fascinating to observe the difference in the responses received during the debate. The communicatively rational argument was treated seriously by the other parties to the negotiations, whereas the strategic argument was not.

In fact, the decision in Rome not to grant the ICC universal jurisdiction was in part a decision to limit the impact that the ICC statute would have on nonstate parties so as not to violate the principle of international law that the United States had advanced, that treaties should not impact nonsignatories. The issue of universal jurisdiction is closely related to the procedures for initiating a prosecution, or the so-called trigger mechanism. While many states supported the idea of universal jurisdiction in principle, they were ultimately persuaded that if there were enough channels to bring cases before the court, it would not be necessary for the court to exercise universal jurisdiction. I will explain this point in more detail and show how the compromise in the Rome Statute on the mechanisms for triggering the court's jurisdiction reflected the principled argument advanced by the United States that the court could not create obligations for nonstate parties.

Elizabeth Wilmshurst, who was a leading member of the United Kingdom's delegation to the ICC negotiations, notes that after the opening discussions in the committee of the whole in Rome, "it was clear that there was very substantial support in the Conference for conferring automatic jurisdiction on the Court in respect of States Parties to the Statute" (Wilmshurst 1999, p. 133). The more complex issues were when and to what extent nonstate parties would have to consent to a particular prosecution before the ICC could hear a case. In the opening days of the conference, South Korea advanced a proposal on the jurisdictional mechanism that was supported by many NGOs. The South Korean proposal would allow the ICC to prosecute if any one of four states were members of the ICC, or if they were nonstate parties and they agreed to consent to the court's jurisdiction, namely, the territorial state where the crime occurred, the state whose nationality was possessed by the accused, the state with custody of the accused, *or* the state whose nationals were victims of the alleged crimes. This was much more expansive than the ILC's original vision, which essentially would have required all of these states to consent in order for the ICC to proceed.

Although the Korean proposal was not adopted in its initial form, it did have a decisive impact on the final compromise that was reached in Rome.

In particular, the Korean proposal attracted attention from states, including Germany, that would have preferred that the ICC exercise universal jurisdiction (Wilmshurst 1999, p. 133). They quickly recognized that the large net cast by the Korean proposal would come close to giving the ICC a form of universal jurisdiction, since only one of several states that might be related to a particular international crime could confer jurisdiction on the new international court. Of course, elements of the Korean proposal also seemed to create the potential that nonstate parties could have their legal rights impacted by the ICC, thus violating the principle of international law that treaties cannot create obligations for nonstate parties. For example, if a crime occurred on the territory of a nonstate party and then the perpetrator traveled to an ICC state parties territory and was arrested, the Korean proposal would allow the ICC to handle the case, thereby overriding the normal jurisdictional rights of the territorial state to prosecute something that happened on its territory, without the consent of that state.

In meeting with NGOs during the third week of the conference, France continued to insist on some form of state consent before the court could exercise jurisdiction over war crimes, to the chagrin of these French human rights groups. The NGOs did note their pleasure that the French acknowledged the South

Korean proposal on jurisdiction as "one of the most interesting and serious" [the proposal favored by the like-minded states and many NGOs], but French officials also asserted that many governments would resist being bound to the war crimes jurisdiction without granting specific consent.[56] France's final price for accepting the ultimate compromise in Rome was the insistence that states be allowed to opt-out of the ICC's jurisdiction over war crimes for seven years by declaring that intent when they submit their instrument of ratification, a provision that negotiators included as the infamous Article 124 of the Rome Statute.

In the end, the bureau of the ICC negotiations narrowed South Korea's proposal on the conditions for exercising the jurisdiction of the court in order to attract the support of more states to the final outcome. The United Kingdom, France, and possibly Russia are states whose support apparently hinged on this feature. Rather than allowing the ICC jurisdiction if any of the "four states" with existing jurisdiction claims were parties to the ICC or granted the court jurisdiction by an ad hoc act of consent, the bureau narrowed the formula to either the territorial state or the state of nationality of the accused.[57] This was deliberately intended to lessen the possibility that the ICC would impose its jurisdiction on nonparty states (Kirsch 1999, p. 460). This also in principle leaves open the potential for the ICC to exercise essentially universal jurisdiction if all the states in the world choose to ratify the ICC statute.

The Role of the Security Council and the Independent Prosecutor

During the Preparatory Committee negotiations, delegates debated the proposal advocated by many NGOs and a few state delegations that the ICC prosecutor should have the authority to initiate an investigation on their own authority if evidence of crimes came to the attention of the prosecutor's office. The central concern with this proposal was that if prosecutors had such power they would be too autonomous and could therefore pursue politically motivated prosecutions that few if any states desired to see take place. Essentially, the concern was that if the prosecutor were granted this authority, it would be a form of "unchecked" power. Supporters of the independent prosecutor proposal, including NGOs, recognized that this concern regarding the prosecutor's unchecked authority had some merit. At the final Preparatory Committee meeting in April 1998, Argentina proposed a mechanism to permit the prosecutor to initiate investigations, while introducing a mechanism that would help ensure this power would not be abused. The proposal called for the prosecutor to request the approval of the pretrial chamber of judges before initiating an investigation using this independent authority (Wilmshurst 1999, pp. 132–3). This was intended to provide the assurance that nonmeritorious investigations could be blocked at an early stage. Argentina's proposal was included in the package advanced to the Rome conference for final decision. France also advocated this proposal during the Rome Conference, and conditioned its acceptance of some form of *proprio motu* (on his own authority) powers for the ICC prosecutor on the inclusion of this pretrial chamber's check on the prosecutor.[58]

The United Kingdom was the first permanent member of the Security Council to abandon the idea of strong Council supervision over the ICC.[59] In part this policy change came about because of new Prime Minister Tony Blair's desire to have a strong human rights based foreign policy. There was also pressure on both the United Kingdom, and France to bring their positions into line with the common European foreign policy.[60] Lars Van Troost, who attended the Rome Conference with Amnesty International's delegation, recalled that in 1997 with ten European Union members having joined the like-minded group, it was clear to all that the United Kingdom and France were holding back the European Union consensus.[61] The statements of the European Union's common position were noticeably weaker than the like-minded position, even though most European states clearly adhered to the stronger like-minded platform. In December 1997, the United Kingdom became the first permanent Security Council member to join the like-minded group.[62]

The Singapore Compromise

We saw in Chapter 5 that the compromise ultimately adopted in the Rome Statute on the role of the Security Council was first proposed by Singapore in August 1997. That proposal did not require Security Council action in order for the ICC to act. Instead, it permitted the Security Council to block any particular prosecution before the ICC for up to 12 months at a time by taking an affirmative vote of the Council ordering such a hiatus. This was a modification of a rule first proposed in the ILC draft that would have automatically barred the ICC from commencing a prosecution if it arose from a situation that was being dealt with by the UN Security Council "as a threat to or breach of the peace or an act of aggression" under Chapter VII of the UN Charter. Under the ILC proposal, the Council could wave this condition if it so chose.[63] The CICC directly advocated the Singapore compromise.[64]

The United States claimed that because it often put its own forces in harm's way in order to defend world order, it should not be subject to international prosecution before the ICC (Orentlicher 1999, p. 495). This approach was unacceptable for the vast majority of states and NGOs involved in the process. Because they wanted a court that could argue it was applying a legitimate rule system backed by reasons, it was logically unacceptable to grant de facto exemption to a single powerful state.[65] For other states to accept the sort of exemption that the United States sought, they would have needed to accept as a matter of principle that war crimes and crimes against humanity should not be punished if they are carried out by powerful states seeking to maintain the existing international order. Such a position is logically inconsistent with the norm that these crimes should always be punished.

NGOs partnered with like-minded governments in order to articulate their concerns about the Security Council's exercising undue control over the ICC. *Terraviva*, a newspaper published by NGOs at the Rome negotiations, ran a cover page article during the third week of the conference that highlighted the concerns of Burundi's government with the Security Council's exercising control over ICC prosecutions.[66] Burundi was the subject of a 1995 UN Security Council commission of inquiry that found genocide had occurred in that country in 1993, but the Council refused to create a tribunal to judge the perpetrators, breaking with the precedents of the ICTY and the ICTR. Burundi's Justice Minister, Therence Sinunguruza, argued that this showed that the Council was driven by fundamentally political concerns and so could not be depended on to enforce international criminal law in a neutral way.[67] By highlighting this argument in their newspaper, NGOs assured that delegates to the Rome conference would have to consider its implications. Many states ultimately accepted the principled argument that the Security Council should not have complete control over the process of initiating prosecutions at the ICC.

Three weeks into the Rome conference, the meeting seemed to have reached an impasse over the Security Council role, with near consensus for the Singapore compromise but adamant continued opposition by a few permanent members of the Security Council (Kirsch and Holmes 1999, p. 5), including the United States, China, and sometimes France. Only the final vote of the conference would demonstrate how isolated China and the United States had become on this issue[68] (Benedetti and Washburn 1999). Both Russia and France ultimately accepted the Singapore compromise. In the final days of the conference, the bureau of the Rome conference that was responsible for drafting the final text met with many delegations individually. It was at this point that France insisted that it could only accept the independent prosecutor and the limited role of the Security Council if a clause was added to the statute that allowed for states to exempt themselves from war crimes for seven years. This was clearly strategic action by France. As a Security Council power, France's support for the statute was important. No principled argument can be made for why citizens from some states should be exempted from prosecution for seven years. However, in the long run, this compromise on principle is self-limiting, because the time will run out, and then all ICC state parties will be subject to the court's jurisdiction over war crimes. This compromise was granted in order to broaden support for the final statute. A great effort was made to secure a similar compromise that would have ensured United States support for the final statute, but no such formula could be found (Lee 1999).

Conclusion

In hindsight, it is perhaps easy to underestimate the magnitude of what was achieved by the delegates in Rome. Five weeks earlier, it was not clear what law the court could enforce, what judicial procedures it could use, and under what circumstances it would have jurisdiction. The technical challenge of merging so many different legal cultures remained immense. Many observers assumed states would not be willing to cede such significant sovereign rights and the negotiations would have to be postponed, as had happened before in the 1950s. The fact that 120 states found common ground and that the compromise very nearly fulfilled the wish list of the members of the NGO Coalition for an ICC must be taken as ample demonstration of the efficacy of these nonstate actors in writing new international law.

The principled issues raised by the NGOs in the years and months prior to and during the Rome conference achieved widespread support in the final compromise. It should be clear that the NGOs' countless written and verbal interventions, in formal and informal settings, decisively shaped the final result on virtually every provision of the statute. That outcome can only be explained through the logical force of the communicatively rational arguments put forth by NGOs.

7

Principled Discourse and the Drive for Ratification: 1998–2002

They are the most lethal pair of foes for human rights everywhere in the world—ignorance and indifference.

—Senator William Proxmire, *"Pledge to Plead Daily for Ratification of Genocide Treaty"*[1]

Discourse and Ratification

In the immediate aftermath of the Rome conference in 1998, it was not at all clear how many states would be willing to ratify the ICC statute, and when, if ever, the sixtieth ratification would occur, triggering the entry into force of the Rome Statute.[2] NGOs, once they decided that the ultimate compromises in the Rome Statute were ones that they could accept, decided to mobilize a worldwide campaign to secure signatures and ratifications of the Rome Statute.

On July 17th, 1998, not all human rights NGOs were immediately pleased with the outcome of the Rome Statute, particularly because it did not have a provision for exercising universal jurisdiction and it was not clear when, if ever, it would exercise authority over aggression. Also the final compromise included the curious Article 124 "Transitional Provision," which allows states to reject the court's jurisdiction with respect to war crimes for seven years after joining the court. This last point in particular violates the topoi of ending impunity and ensuring equal justice under the law and thus cannot be reconciled with NGOs' principled beliefs. By August 1998, NGO leaders had the chance to review all the provisions in the Rome Statute as a whole and realized that on balance, the provisions of the final statute very nearly met the NGOs principled concerns, and the CICC made the decision to campaign aggressively for ICC ratification.[3]

This chapter has two purposes. The first is to document the way that NGOs used their discursive practices to increase global support for the ICC. The essential strategy was to make as much information about the ICC statute as possible available to political leaders in various states so that they could understand the principled basis for the delicate compromises in the Rome Statute. NGOs correctly anticipated that informed persons would be more willing to accept the modifications to state sovereign privileges that were inherent in joining the ICC. This chapter also has a second purpose, which is to examine the cooperation in this case between NGOs that are based in developing states and NGOs that are based in the Organisation for Economic Co-operation and Development (OECD) countries. I argue that such cooperation is important because it shifts the discursive structure of world politics. Routinized communication between NGOs from the advanced industrial economies of the North and the developing economies of the global South allowed for dramatically broader participation in the discourse about the establishment of the ICC when compared to the level of discursive participation in more typical diplomatic discourses.

Constructivist research has gone a long ways toward demonstrating that NGOs influence the interests and identities of states and other actors. This has led to increased concern about their legitimacy. Who do they represent, which voices are amplified, and do some remain unheard? The most widely recognized international NGOs tend to have memberships and headquarters that are concentrated in Northern developed states, such as the United States and the European Union, but does this mean that voices from developing states are systematically excluded? This chapter analyzes the organization and structure of NGO coalition-building during the campaign for ratification of the ICC treaty and finds that in this case, NGOs from the North and South built alliances that strengthened the influence of groups from both parts of the world.[4] Northern-based international NGOs enjoyed legal and media resources that are impossible for Southern-based NGOs to match. However, the local knowledge of NGOs based in single states in the developing world was crucial for the international NGOs to stay informed of the political situation in the various governments where debates were under way about whether or not to ratify the ICC statute. This chapter continues to draw methodologically on interviews, participant observation, and analysis of the discursive practices of NGOs involved in the ICC statute ratification campaign. As of August 2007, 105 states have ratified the ICC statute across Latin America, Western and Eastern Europe, and much of Africa, as well as a handful of Asian states including Japan and South Korea.

The literature on epistemic communities (Haas 1990), transnational advocacy networks (Keck and Sikkink 1998), and sociological institutionalism (Finnemore 1996) all suggest nonstate actors can sometimes convert knowledge into power. However, it is less clear how and under what circumstances nonstate actors are influential and why some are more influential than others. One recurring theme is that NGOs are influential through their technical expertise or rational analysis of existing problems and pragmatic solutions (Boli and Thomas 1999). Another claim is that NGOs' statements grounded in appeals to widely accepted moral principles carry persuasive normative force (Wapner 2000).

Here I argue that in the case of the NGO campaign for the ratification of the ICC, NGOs were effective because their discursive practices altered the structure of the international political discourse on this issue in a way that facilitated increased participation in that discourse. Because of this increased participation in the international discourse, principled normative arguments about why an ICC was needed and how it could be made effective were widely diffused. This discursive activity probably contributed to decisions by policy makers in a large number of states to sign and ratify the ICC statute.

Of course, factors that contribute to a decision in a particular state to ratify or not to ratify a particular treaty are many, and the interrelationships between them are complex. One crucial factor that impacts decisions about treaty ratification is the content of the treaty itself. We have already seen that NGO discourse had a decisive impact on shaping the content of the ICC statute. Because this activity sent the ICC negotiations on a particular path that they would not have taken otherwise, we could have said that the NGO community impacted the ICC ratification debate, even if they had closed their offices and stopped working on ICC issues in July of 1998. This is the idea that political outcomes are inherently path-dependent. Of course, pro-ICC NGOs did not stop their activities in July 1998. This chapter describes some of the further efforts that the NGO community took to ensure that as many states as possible would ratify the ICC statute as quickly as possible.

How Long Would Ratification Take?

When the Rome conference concluded with a climactic and euphoric sense of achievement on July 17, 1998, it quickly became clear that states had negotiated the statute in a way that would give the new court rather substantial powers.[5] This led to fears on the side of court supporters that ratification of the statute might take a very long time. After all, many human rights treaties have faced long delays before their entry into force. For example, both the International Covenant on Civic and Political Rights (ICCPR) and the International Covenant on Economic, Social and Cultural Rights (ICESCR) were adopted in 1966 but did not enter into force until 1976, and they each required only 35 ratifications.[6] The Rome Statute, in contrast, required 60 ratifications. The Genocide Convention entered into force in 1951, only three years after its adoption, but the United States failed to ratify it until 1988 (Ratner and Abrams 2001, p. 28). However, many states attached reservations to their ratification of the Genocide Convention, complicating the picture for determining who legally is obliged to meet its requirements (Ratner and Abrams 2001, pp. 39–41).

The Rome Statute allowed states to sign without ratifying for just over two years, until December 31, 2000. After that time, states would have to accede to the treaty. Bassiouni said optimistically that "by then, [December 31, 2000] it is hoped that 60 required ratifications will have occurred and the treaty will enter into force" (Bassiouni 1998, p. 33) when explaining the deadline for signing the Rome Statute without simultaneous ratification. This was by most accounts an extremely optimistic (and presumably politically motivated) estimate. For most observers, the entry into force in April 2002 was earlier than had been anticipated. Writing at the time, Jennifer Elsea commented it was "years earlier than had been predicted" (Elsea 2003, p. 1).

The Signature and Ratification Campaign

After the adoption of the Rome Treaty in July 1998, NGOs moved to a new political game. Now, the campaign began to focus on securing the signatures of states and ultimately ratifications. Again, the coalition of NGOs that supported the establishment of the ICC focused on ensuring the widest possible dissemination of arguments for and against the court.

Different states employ a wide variety of different mechanisms for deciding whether or not to ratify treaties. A variety of local, regional, and structural factors shaped the outcomes of the decision to ratify or not to ratify the ICC statute in different states.[7] A full analysis of all the different factors that impacted the decision to ratify or not in nearly 200 states is beyond the scope of this chapter. Still, NGOs' discursive campaigns were clearly a factor in the ratification process for a number of states. Their international campaign undoubtedly strengthened individual pro-ICC campaigns at the national level in a variety of states. More importantly, NGO strategies created an international dimension to the campaign for ICC ratification that allowed the policy discourse in many states to transcend the confines of a more limited discourse about whether or not treaty ratification was in the national interest of a particular state, instead allowing a focus on whether or not the ICC was desirable for world order more generally.

One essential element of NGOs' success was their effort to contribute to the communicative rationality of debates about the ICC. NGOs again played an educative role, explaining how the ICC interacted with existing provisions of international criminal law and how its procedures were intended to work in practice. This is not the only strategy that NGOs used in the international ICC ratification campaign. In some situations, they relied on other well-understood NGO tactics, such as shaming or threatening voter mobilization (Keck and Sikkink 1998). This chapter focuses primarily on the communicatively rational strategies and continues with a general description of the discursive strategies that NGOs employed worldwide, with a particular focus on the interaction between Northern and Southern NGOs. In the final section of the chapter, I briefly consider the particular dynamics of the ratification process in three states that are exemplars of types of states that ratified the ICC statute, states that were early advocates of a strong ICC, states that are permanent members of the Security Council, and those authoritarian regimes that were among the states most likely to see ICC investigations on their own territory in the near future. I discuss Argentina as representative of the first group, the United Kingdom in the second group, and Uganda in the third category.

NGOs initially focused on securing signatures to the Rome Statute rather than full ratifications. Signatures imply that a state intends to ultimately ratify an international treaty and obliges that state not to act in ways contrary to the purpose of the treaty, but they do not make the terms of the treaty fully binding on the signing states. As in American practice, typically a head of state, head of government, foreign minister, or their delegate can sign a treaty, but an act of the legislature or other more formal process is required to ensure ratification (Aust 2000, pp. 57–65). Because of this fact, signature is a much simpler political process that can normally

Figure 7.1 State signatories to the ICC by July 17, 1999. These states were the first to indicate their support for the ICC statute by signing it in the first year after the text was negotiated. Most of the early support came from Western European states, Canada, Australia, and parts of Latin America and sub-Saharan Africa, with Jordan the lone signatory in the Middle East.

be taken on the authority of a single political leader. Understanding this, NGOs chose to focus on getting signatures initially rather than ratifications. Signatures have little immediate legal consequence, so it is politically a "cost-free" way for state leaders to gain the approval of human rights NGOs and other groups that supported the ICC. At the same time, signing the statute indicates support for its general principles and goals, so this signing process had the effect of putting important world leaders on the record as favoring the ICC and also provided a way for NGOs to show growing worldwide support for the Rome Statute as more and more states signed. Figure 7.1 shows the states that had signed the Rome Statute after one year, in July 1999. Figure 7.2 shows how the number of signatory states had grown by December 31, 2000.

For the CICC the signature process had another important benefit. For most states, the signature on a treaty is a first step toward beginning the ratification process under domestic law. Once a state signed the Rome Statute, this would typically give activists working on the ICC ratification process within the state leverage to persuade legislators or newspapers to make statements regarding the Rome Statute. Signature itself could provide the sense of occasion that was necessary for NGOs to organize conferences in particular countries on the ICC.

Figure 7.1 shows the earliest group of states to sign the ICC statute, those that signed within the first year after the Rome Statute was adopted. These were typically the governments that had most consistently favored the ICC during the negotiation phase. By the end of the Rome conference, most of these states had chosen to affiliate themselves with the like-minded position that paralleled the positions of the major NGOs. Notice that the West European states, Australia, and Canada, that formed the core of the like-minded group of states were among the first to sign. Argentina also was a dedicated member of the like-minded group and signed in early 1999.

Australia and some of the Western European states took much longer to finalize their ratifications, usually reflecting differences between the executive and legislative branches on the ICC issue. Also, governments in these democracies were involved in the negotiations and understood the provisions of the ICC statute, whereas legislators frequently needed more time to be informed about decisions that were made in designing the Rome Statute. NGOs particularly excelled at performing this educational work with legislators in the established democracies. Chile is an interesting example of this divided government phenomenon. The center-left government of Ricardo Lagos, who gained political notoriety in Chile during the struggle against Pinochet's dictatorship, openly supported the ICC and Chile's early signature reflects this fact. Chile's legislature, however, which is electorally biased toward conservative forces associated with Pinochet's government, has, as of late 2007, blocked Chile from ratifying the Rome Statute.

Figure 7.2 shows the near global support for the ICC that was indicated by signatures on the Rome Statute by the end of the year 2000. That date was significant because it was the deadline for states to sign the statute without ratifying at the same time. This had some practical importance because states that signed the Rome Statute but were not yet ratifying parties could participate in the preparatory commission meetings that were continuing to work out the practical rules for the court's operation. The United States, Israel, and Iran signed the ICC

Figure 7.2 State signatories to the ICC by December 31, 2000. These states signed the Rome Statute before the December 31, 2000, deadline, signaling their intent to join the ICC through ratification. The broad pattern of signatures covering most of the globe indicated the breadth of international support for the ICC. However, the lack of signatures in Asia showed an important limitation to the ICC's support in that region of the world.

statute in close succession in the final hours before the time for doing so without simultaneously ratifying expired.[8] Notice the nearly complete pattern of signatures across Eastern and Western Europe, Africa, and both North and South America. Only in Central and Southern Asia and parts of the Pacific were there substantial areas where governments were not willing to sign the Rome Statute.

NGOs made use of this nearly universal signature pattern to convince states that in fact the ICC was likely to be established, and that once it came into being it would enjoy widespread support across regions of the globe. Notice that perhaps somewhat surprisingly, four of the five permanent members of the UN Security Council signed the Rome Statute.[9]

Widespread support and ratification of the ICC treaty is necessary in order for the Rome Statute to make good on the promise that it would deliver equal justice under the law. Recall that arguments in favor of particular provisions on the design of the court during the negotiation phrase were often based on the topos that the ICC should provide equal protection under the law. So the fact of widespread signatures on the ICC statute allowed NGOs to persuade doubters that the ICC would not be a court that was imposed on a few states that were foolish enough to ratify but that instead ratification might indeed ultimately be universal or at least nearly so. If advocates of the ICC had not been able to show widespread support for the ICC from an early stage in the process, this crucial argument in favor of the court would have been dramatically undermined. Because the ICC's jurisdiction is substantially restricted by the geography of the ratifying states, it is important to the normative justification for the court that nearly all states ultimately be willing to join.

Figure 7.3 shows the states that had actually ratified by the signature deadline of December 31, 2000. While it is a much smaller group of 27 states, advocates of the court could then point out that they were nearly halfway to the threshold of 60 states joining the court that was necessary to trigger the entry into force of the Rome Statute.

Just over two years later, the CICC helped accomplish that goal. A formal ceremony was held on April 11, 2002 at UN headquarters in New York and 11 states agreed to simultaneously deposit their ratifications, bringing the total to 66 and triggering the establishment of the court. Figure 7.4 shows those states. In the months prior to that date, NGOs pressured states that were close to ratifying to accelerate their process so they could be among the states that were founding members of the court. After April 11, 2002, NGOs moved the goals and pressured states to ratify by July 1, 2002, the date the court would legally begin to exist, so that they could be among those states voting at the first Assembly of States Parties. Figure 7.5 shows the 105 states that ratified the Rome Statute as of September 2007.

NGOs affiliated with the CICC organized and sent delegations to an astonishing number of conferences and seminars between 1999 and 2002[10] in order to generate upport for the ICC and disseminate information about its provisions and goals. For example, No Peace Without Justice, a group based primarily in Italy, organized or sent delegations to meetings in various cities in Italy, The Hague, and Amsterdam, (the Netherlands), Freetown (Sierra Leone),

Figure 7.3 States ratifying the ICC by December 31, 2000. The early decision by these 27 states to ratify the Rome Statute before the end of 2000 raised the possibility that the goal of 60 ratifications could be achieved within a few years' time and thus, that the ICC might actually become a political reality.

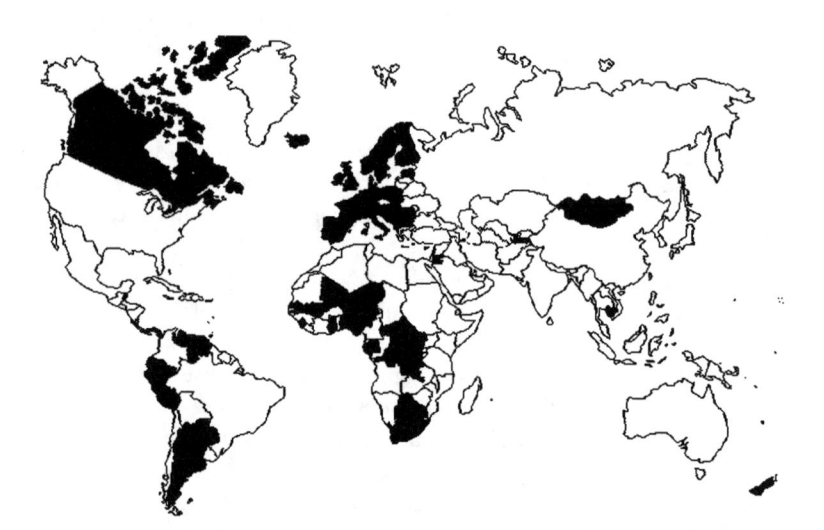

Figure 7.4 States ratifying the ICC by April 11, 2002. These are the 66 states that agreed to join the ICC by April 11, 2002, and in so doing, triggered the establishment of the court by breaking the required threshold of 60 states.

Bamako (Mali), Manila (the Philippines), Seville (Spain), Mexico City (Mexico), and Phnom Penh (Cambodia), among others.[11] NPWJ, according to their website, "is an international committee of parliamentarians, mayors and citizens, whose objective is the establishment of an effective system of international justice."[12] Their active membership includes the noted European Union parliamentarian

Figure 7.5 States ratifying the ICC by July 17, 2007. These states are the current 105 member states of the ICC as of late 2007. Japan is the most recent state to ratify, and its participation in the court's work is critical because it will become a leading contributor to the financial needs of the ICC.

Emma Bonino. The group receives funding from the European Union but their website includes a disclaimer that "The views expressed herein are solely those of NPWJ, and can therefore in no way be taken to reflect the views of the European Union."[13]

NPWJ was of course not the only major NGO based in a developed state to organize such international conferences in order to generate support for the ICC statute. HRW, Amnesty International, International Committee of the Red Cross, and other major groups also organized and participated in similar meetings around the globe. These international NGOs magnified the effectiveness of their voice by partnering with local NGOs based in single countries. These groups often had more direct access to local political leaders in the executive and legislative branches of a particular government. Consequently, local NGOs sometimes had good intelligence about the political status of ratification in particular states. The international NGOs brought other assets to the partnership. They had the legal staff needed to analyze the arguments surrounding the ICC and a greater familiarity with the issues being raised about ICC implementation and how early ratifying states had confronted those issues. By disseminating that international information to their local partners, the international NGOs empowered the local groups to be much more effective in lobbying for signatures and ratifications on the ICC treaty.

These conferences organized by NGOs often were regionally based, and brought together ICC experts from neighboring countries. This led to a form of peer pressure where states became more willing to take action on signing and ratifying the ICC statute because their neighbors were doing so. Also, legal traditions tend to transcend national boundaries and cover entire regions of the globe. Often states that share a colonial linguistic heritage also share common legal customs. NGOs organized conferences in French-, Portuguese-, English-, and Spanish-speaking regions of Africa, America, and Asia. Frequently, local legal scholars in such areas would have similar concerns about integrating the Rome Statute into their own legal systems or securing whatever constitutional amendments might be necessary for the state to ratify the statute. Accordingly, conferences held on a regional level allowed for useful sharing of ideas about how to address such concerns.

For example, on March 13 to 15, 2002, HRW and *La Coalición Guatemalteca por la Corte Penal Internacional* (The Guatemalan Coalition for the International Criminal Court) cosponsored the first Central-American Meeting For the International Criminal Court in Guatemala City that was attended by representatives from Nicaragua, El Salvador, Honduras, and Guatemala. I list the names of the groups that participated to convey a sense of the types of organizations that cooperated with the larger international NGOs in the ICC ratification campaign. They were:

From Nicaragua,

CENTRO NICARAGUENSE DE DERECHOS HUMANOS (CENIDH)
CENTRO DE LA MUJER DE LA UNIVERSIDAD DE LAS REGIONES AUTÓNOMAS DE LA COSTA CARIBE NICARAGUENSE (URACCAN).[14]

From El Salvador,

COMISION DE DERECHOS HUMANOS DE EL SALVADOR (CDHES)
INSTITUTO DE DERECHOS HUMANOS DE LA UNIVERSIDAD CENTRO AMERICANA
SIGLO XXIII
PAZ SUSTENTABLE
CENTRO PARA LA PROMOCION DE DERECHOS HUMANOS
Madeleine Lagadec, TUTELA LEGAL DEL ARZOBISPADO DE SAN SALVADOR
UNIVERSIDAD DE EL SALVADOR (UES)
PROCURADURIA PARA LA DEFENSA DE LOS DERECHOS HUMANOS (PDDH).[15]

From Honduras,

COMITÉ PARA LA DEFENSA DE LOS DERECHOS HUMANOS EN HONDURAS (CODEH).[16]

And from Guatemala,

GRUPO DE APOYO MUTUO
FUNDACION MYRNA MACK
FUNDACION RIGOBERTA MENCHU TUM
ALIANZA CONTRA LA IMPUNIDAD

CENTRO DE ACCION LEGAL EN DERECHOS HUMANOS
INSTITUTO DE DERECHOS HUMANOS DE LA USAC
INSTITUTO DE ESTUDIOS COMPARADOS DE CIENCIAS PENALES DE GUATEMALA (ICCPG)
MAESTRIA DE DERECHOS HUMANOS DE LA URL
ASOCIACION LA CUERDA
OFICINA DE DERECHOS HUMANOS DEL ARZOBISPADO
OFICINA DE LA PASTORAL SOCIAL DEL ARZOBISPADO
COORDINADORA NACIONAL DE DERECHOS HUMANOS DE GUATEMALA
COALICIÓN INTERUNIVERSITARIA POR LA C.P.I.[17]

The final statement from this conference read in part that "We, the delegates, . . . having in mind the lack of political will of the States that have not promoted the analysis, process of discussion, socialization, and ratification of the Statute of Rome, consider it important and urgent that organized civil society contribute and work to ensure that Central America does not remain outside of the international jurisdictional context."[18] Thus the NGOs from this region were self-consciously aware that the governments in Central America were reluctant to move toward joining the ICC. They understood that pressure from nonstate actors would be essential to ensure movement on these issues. The statement also sought to create a sense of regional solidarity by emphasizing that Costa Rica and Belize had already ratified the ICC statute and that Panama was in the process of doing so. Panama ratified the Rome Statute on March 21, 2002. Four months later, in July 2002, Honduras ratified the ICC statute just in time to be one of its founding members. The other states have still not joined the ICC, but the NGO campaign to encourage those states to ratify continues.[19]

Such conferences took place around the world at various times during the ICC campaign. For example, an Expert's Conference on the International Criminal Court was held in Manila on Oct. 16 to 18, 2001 with senior government officials from various Southeast Asian and Pacific Island states. Delegates attended from Brunei, Cambodia, Indonesia, Laos, Malaysia, the Phillipines, Singapore, Thailand, Vietnam, the Fiji Islands, Palau, the Marshall Islands, Samoa, Tonga, and Tuvalu.[20] Several of those states are now ICC members, including Cambodia, Fiji, the Marshall Islands, and Samoa. This meeting was initiated by the Centre for Restorative Justice in Asia in cooperation with the International Committee of the Red Cross. This event included panel discussions on Sharing of Experiences in the Ratification and Implementation of the ICC. NGOs were well aware that arguments that had been advanced by ICC opponents in some of the first countries to ratify the ICC statute would likely be repeated in future ratification debates. By educating ICC supporters about those arguments in advance and the various legal strategies that had been adopted in order to overcome the objections of ICC opponents, the pro-ICC NGOs were able to give their local supporters a crucial advantage during the ratification debates.

Latin American constitutions typically require action by the legislative branch of government in order for the state to ratify a treaty (Comisiâon Andina de Juristas 2004, pp. 32–3). NGOs found that the resulting congressional deliberations created a useful entry point for diffusion of arguments in favor of the ICC. In Colombia, it was necessary to amend the constitution in order for the ICC statute to be ratified (Comisiâon Andina de Juristas 2004, p. 37). In Chile, the Constitutional Court ruled on April 8, 2002, that a reform of the Chilean Constitution would be necessary prior to ratification of the ICC statute. This was seen as necessary because ratifying the ICC statute implied submitting to the authority of an autonomous court and the incorporation of the rights and duties listed in the treaty; so the court felt this required review of the constitutional provisions regarding pardons, amnesties, parliamentary immunity, and the competence of judges (Comisiâon Andina de Juristas 2004, p. 37).

European Union Support for the ICC and Cooperation with NGOs

On March 1, 2002 the European Parliament passed a resolution encouraging the widespread ratification of the Rome Statute and "inviting" the U.S. president and U.S. congress to reconsider their opposition to the ICC.[21] This was only five weeks before the ceremony held in New York on April 11, 2002, marking the sixtieth ratification of the ICC statute and triggering the entry into force of the statute. This resolution was in line with the already established policy of the European Union favoring the widespread ratification of the ICC. The Council of the European Union adopted a common position on June 11, 2001 that called on all European Union states to use their diplomatic leverage to encourage non–European Union states to ratify the ICC statute and to pass implementing legislation toward fulfilling the objective of widespread ratification of the ICC statute. The resolution specifically noted the need for states from Asia and Africa to ratify to ensure that the court would have a universal character.

The CICC worked closely with various European Union entities to promote ICC ratification. The CICC's leading program officer in Europe, Brussels-based Irune Aguirrezabal, lobbied for that European Union parliament resolution and was present for the debate on the ICC in March 2002. She said:

> It is critical that the European institutions boost the momentum, as in a few months the ICC Statute will enter into force and major issues need to be addressed. The EU support will be critically important. We are satisfied that this resolution echoes our concerns on the need to ensure universality of the Court. Unfortunately, although the debate showed deep concern for the US position, political considerations won against a much stronger appeal to the United States not to legislate against the ICC in the final resolution.[22]

Of course, the European Union also directly supported the work of several NGOs that favored the establishment of the ICC. It provided direct funding for that purpose to the CICC, NPWJ, and Parliamentarians for Global Action.

In fact, as Aguirrezabal noted, the European Union was very diplomatic in its language reproaching the United States for its opposition to the ICC and the passage of legislation forbidding U.S. cooperation with the court. The resolution said only that the European Union parliament "Is convinced of the importance to the ICC of full support from the USA; invites the US executive and legislative powers to reconsider their position on the ICC."[23]

Examination of patterns of ICC ratification over time illustrate the regional trends in ratification. Figure 7.4 shows that Spanish-speaking South America, Western Europe, and the Cold War border states just east of the Iron Curtain, West Africa, and the Caribbean were the primary regions that drove early ratification of the Rome Statute. Of course, many of these places are areas that have experienced war crimes, crimes against humanity, or genocide within living memory.

Another crucial aspect of the NGO campaign during the ratification process was an effort to have states develop progressive implementing legislation in their domestic legal systems to enhance their ability to try ICC crimes under their own national legal jurisdictions. This served the CICC goal of ensuring an end to impunity by providing one more mechanism for criminals to be brought to justice. The complementarity design of the ICC created an incentive for states to do this, to ensure that the ICC would not find their national legal systems was "unable" to prosecute such crimes. Canada and Argentina developed implementing legislation in close cooperation with NGO experts, and subsequently these states and NGOs promoted those two pieces of national legislation as a model. Canada, in particular, provided significant financial and diplomatic backing to these efforts.

ICC Ratification Campaigns in Three States

As was mentioned in the introduction to this chapter, a wide variety of local political and institutional factors, as well as history and regional culture, influenced the ICC ratification campaigns in each state. In a separate research project that cannot be reported on fully here, we have identified a number of significant structural predictors of whether or not a particular state is likely to ratify the ICC statute (Struett and Weldon 2006).[24] The important determinants that make states more likely to ratify the Rome Statute include high levels of democracy, low shares of global defense spending,[25] high levels of participation in other international organizations, states with relatively few veto players in the legislative process, and states that have recently emerged from conflict. States with ongoing conflict situations are less likely to ratify the Rome Statute. While the extent of NGO organization and activity probably varies from one state to the next, I have been unable to identify a systematic way of effectively measuring the amount of such activity.[26] Consequently, I am unable to make definitive claims about the extent to which NGO activity increases the likelihood of ratification by particular states while holding other factors constant.

Accordingly, the claims for the NGO role in promoting ratification of the ICC statute must be more modest. The following cases are briefly discussed to illustrate the ways that NGO activity may have contributed to the ratification process in three different types of settings. Also, it is probable that NGO activity has had a cumulative effect over time. NGO success in persuading early states to ratify may well have contributed to decisions by other states to ratify later on in the process. Another way of thinking about this relationship is to point out that we simply do not know how many states would have ratified the ICC statute if there had been no lobbying by pro-ICC NGOs after 1998. It is possible that all states would have been equally less likely to ratify in the absence of such lobbying activity. Efforts to quantitatively measure the impact of various factors on the likelihood of ICC ratification may miss the impact of constant effects, if for instance the existence of the NGO campaign in essence impacted all states relatively equally. There is a sense in which the NGO campaign's overall effect may indeed have impacted every state, at least to some minimal degree, because pro-ICC position papers by Amnesty International and other groups were routinely circulated to all UN member states.[27]

Argentina

Argentina was an early supporter of the ICC statute. There was some controversy about the ICC issue within the Argentine government at the time of the Rome Conference in 1998; however, government officials from the Ministry of Justice and the Ministry of Foreign Affairs who favored a strong and independent ICC were largely able to control Argentina's official position in favor of a fair and effective court.[28] As discussed in Chapters 4 and 5, Argentina was a key player in the coalition of like-minded states.

Under Argentine law, a simple majority vote is needed in both the Senate and the Congress for ratification of a treaty. After the votes of approval, the treaty is sent back to the president, and then to the Foreign Affairs Ministry, which deposits it at the UN. The ratification act must be published in the official gazette of the government in order to make an international treaty part of the domestic law.[29] That step was taken in late January 2001, and the instrument of ratification was deposited on February 8, 2001.

Argentina has an active human rights movement as a result of its experience with brutal military dictatorships in the 1970s and 1980s. The CICC found natural allies with these groups and capitalized on these relationships during the ratification campaign. Local Argentine human rights groups have strong contacts in the Argentine legislature, and they used those contacts to serve as conduits of information from international NGOs based in New York and London to and from Argentine officials.

Following the ratification of the Rome Statute, Argentina played a leading role in persuading other states to ratify. Cooperation between the NGO community and Argentine government officials toward this end continued after Argentina's ratification. From June 20 to 22, 2001 a major Latin American regional conference was held in Buenos Aires. Leading experts on the ICC from the Argentine government and the leadership of the CICC spoke to an audience that included government officials from Honduras, El Salvador, Colombia, Mexico, Ecuador, Panama, Uruguay, Bolivia, Chile, Venezuela, New Zealand, Portugal, Spain, and France. Legislators from several states also attended. The conference reviewed all of the major issues with the ICC and problems and challenges when dealing with ratifying the statute and drafting implementing legislation (Human Rights Watch 2001).

NGOs have also been extensively involved in the debate within Argentina about drafting implementing legislation to ensure that Argentina can prosecute crimes of international concern within its own judicial system. Draft ICC implementing legislation was circulated by an interministerial commission in 2000, and since that time there have been several rounds of public comment in which human rights NGOs participated fully. These exchanges have involved government ministers and both houses of the Argentine congress.[30] Versions of the proposal that are particularly favored by the CICC community have been circulated internationally as "model" legislation for other states considering legislation to implement the complementarity provisions of the Rome Statute. HRW and other NGOs have long favored the adoption of such legislation if it is well drafted because it increases the likelihood that perpetrators will be prosecuted in some court.[31]

United Kingdom

Under British custom, treaty ratification requires that a bill be presented to Parliament containing all the necessary changes to domestic law that would be required prior to ratification. This involves coordination among the different ministries, particularly the Foreign Office, the Home Office, and the Ministry of Defense in the case of the ICC. These agencies examine existing legislation and draft the changes required. The legislative procedure includes debates in the House of Commons and the House of Lords and finally royal assent after approval by both houses.

The ICC Act of 2001 allowing ratification incorporated into British law the offenses in the Rome Statute and made provisions for them to be dealt with domestically in the Crown Court.[32] Furthermore, the Act contains provisions for the arrest and surrender of persons in the United Kingdom charged by the ICC as well as for having them serve their custodial sentences in the United Kingdom if convicted by the ICC.[33] This legislative process in the United Kingdom was closely monitored by pro-ICC NGOs. Some parliamentarians argued forcefully that the ICC statute involved an unacceptable erosion of British sovereignty. However, since the Rome Statute had the support of Prime Minister Tony Blair, who made its ratification a central element of his human rights—based foreign policy, the ultimate passage of the Ratification Bill was virtually assured. NGOs offered critical political support to Blair and his government during this debate.

Uganda

Uganda ratified the ICC Statute on June 14, 2002, becoming the sixty-eighth state party only two weeks before the Rome Statute entered into force. This was a result of considerable pressure from other governments and human rights NGOs and other humanitarian relief organizations to improve the government's record on human rights.

According to the CICC, legislation to give effect to the ICC statute under Ugandan law was presented to parliament on June 25, 2004. "Civil society is expected to be involved in the debate on the bill and will also present a memorandum to the relevant parliamentary committee."[34] In April 2002, the initial memorandum on ICC ratification prepared by the minister of justice and constitutional affairs and submitted to the Cabinet in 1999 had lapsed. A new memorandum was prepared and was submitted by the attorney general. No implementing legislation was prepared at this stage. The ratification bill was then submitted to and approved by the cabinet and parliament. At the time, NGOs in favor of the ICC did not anticipate that the legislature would be a significant obstacle to ratification, and indeed, that proved to be the case.[35]

Uganda has witnessed massive political violence in recent years and at varying levels over the last two decades. As I mentioned in Chapter 1, the government has been involved in a civil war with a group called the Lord's Resistance Army (LRA) in the north, and that group has at times received support from the Sudan. According to HRW, there was a great deal of violence associated with parliamentary elections in Uganda in 2001, and while the level of violence diminished somewhat in 2002, it nevertheless continued. Civil and political rights are regularly violated by the government in Uganda, and political organization is heavily restricted by law and actively suppressed by the police.[36] It is in that political context that Uganda's government chose to ratify the ICC statute in 2002, under pressure from human rights groups to do so. It is difficult to ascertain the precise motives of the decision maker in Uganda for ratifying, but three lines of plausible speculation stand out.

One possibility is that Ugandan officials perceived that the ICC could be of direct value in suppressing the rebellion led by the LRA in northern Uganda. Perhaps these officials understood that Uganda would be a likely first location for ICC trials but also thought that such trials would play to their political advantage. Another likely factor is that Ugandan government officials perceived joining the ICC as something that they could do to improve their international reputation with human rights groups. NGOs certainly made use of shaming strategies in attempting to persuade Uganda to join the court. Finally, Uganda's government may have perceived the ICC as a form of international financial assistance. To the extent that the international community absorbs the costs of investigating and prosecuting serious cases of political violence in Uganda, the society stands to benefit from this assistance. Uganda's officials may simply have believed that the ICC could be useful in reducing or ending political violence in that country. The ratification cannot be taken, however, as a sign that the government is prepared to eschew the use of political violence to maintain itself in power.

The ICC opened an investigation into war crimes and crimes against humanity in Uganda in January 2003 at the request of the Ugandan government. That investigation is ongoing and raises complex political issues for the ICC prosecutor's office because of periodic progress and digression in peace talks between the government and LRA. The ICC issued indictments against five top officials of the LRA, including its leader, Joseph Kony, in July 2005. Kony subsequently has insisted that the LRA will only lay down its arms if the ICC process is stopped. Thus far, the Ugandan government, the United Nations, and the officers of the

ICC itself have been steadfast in their refusal to grant amnesty to Joseph Kony and other LRA leaders accused of ICC crimes in exchange for peace. It seems to this observer that the threat of ICC trials and ultimately jail time is one reason that the LRA has been willing to negotiate in the first place.

NGO Campaign for Universal Ratification Continues

The CICC did not suspend their work after the Rome Statute entered into force in July 2002 following the 60th ratification. Instead, the regional meetings and campaigns targeted on ensuring ratification in particular countries continued. As of August 2007, there are 105 states that have ratified the ICC statute. NGOs have continued their campaign to disseminate principled arguments justifying the court's design. This work continues on to this day, as the following example illustrates.

The following announcement from the CICC European coordinating officer is an example of the information transmitting techniques that NGOs have now perfected. Turkey is a likely candidate to ratify at some point in the future because it is under considerable pressure to do so in order to strengthen its bid to join the European Union. Of course, that is a compelling form of strategic pressure that Brussels can apply in Ankara. Still, NGOs are involved in the process by presenting information about the ICC's structure in order to anticipate sovereignty concerns that some Turkish leaders may have. The CICC's project officer in Brussels for Southeastern Europe recently announced a roundtable on the "Ratification and Implementation of the International Criminal Court Statute in Turkey" organized by the *Fédération Internationale des Ligues de Droits de l'Homme* (FIDH), the Human Rights Foundation in Turkey, and the Turkish Human Rights Association in cooperation with the CICC on June 16 to 17, 2005, in Ankara.

The agenda for the meeting is attached as Appendix 7.1. Even though this example is later in time than the ratification debates in many states, from June 2005, it is an excellent example of the type of informational session that NGOs held in hundreds of forums since early 1999 to promote ratification of the ICC. I have included it to make several points. First of all, the topics of discussion center around the same principled issues NGOs sought in the courts design during the drafting of the statute. The first session on the first day focuses on the ICC's complementarity provisions, the crucial feature of the court that strikes the balance between maintaining state sovereign prerogatives and ensuring that perpetrators of serious international crimes are brought to justice. In these presentations, local experts are programmed to explain how the ICC is designed to defer to local proceedings when they are available. They would also explain the complex rules for the ICC to take up a case if the prosecutor can prove that national courts are unable or unwilling to pursue a particular case. These informational sessions allocate time to present the principled arguments that this feature of the court's design was necessary to ensure an end to impunity. All of this educational work serves to ensure that Turkish politicians in this case, or in any of the other states where the CICC held similar meetings, would not object to aspects of the ICC's design without understanding how all of the court's jurisdictional and procedural rules were designed to fit together and the goals they were designed to achieve, primarily ensuring an end to impunity.

Conclusion

During the campaign for ratification of the International Criminal Court treaty, NGOs from the North and South built alliances that strengthened the influence of groups from both parts of the world. Northern-based international NGOs enjoyed legal and media resources that are impossible for Southern-based NGOs to match. However, the local knowledge of NGOs based in single states in the developing world was crucial for the international NGOs to stay informed of the political situation in the various governments where debates were under way about whether or not to ratify the ICC statute. In this case, the participation of nonstate actors seems to have expanded the number of perspectives included in discussion of the establishment of the ICC, ensuring that voices that are not always well represented in formal intergovernmental policy discussions were still heardin this discourse. The partnership found in this case suggests that one way to evaluate global policy debates is to analyze the structure of communication, drawing on communicative action theory to assess the extent to which voices from different parts of the world are represented in various policy-making discussions.[37]

Appendix 7.1

AGENDA

Thursday 16 June, 2005
9.30–10.00—OPENING CEREMONY

- Remarks by Sjoerd I. H. Gosses, ambassador of the Netherlands in Turkey on behalf of the European Union
- Remarks by Marc Van Rysselderghe, ambassador of the Kingdom of Belgium in Turkey (TBC)
- Remarks by Yusuf Atalas, president of IHD[38]
- Remarks by Yavuz Onen, president of TIHV[39]
- Remarks by Souhayr Belhassen and Akin Birdal, vice presidents of FIDH[40]

SESSION 1 (10.15–13.00)
THE ICC IN THE NATIONAL AND INTERNATIONAL JUSTICE SYSTEM

Chairman: Att. Sukran Buldu, general assistant of IHD president
Rapporteur: Att. Aygul Demýrtas, IHD branch Diyarbakir

10.15–11.30   Introduction to the ICC and its Jurisdiction—Complementarity Principle
Exercise of Jurisdiction. Cooperation. ICC/UN Relations
Prof. Dr. Gökçen Alpkaya Tunalý, Ankara University—Political Science Faculty

Definition of Crimes and General Principles of Criminal Law
Mr. Murat Önok, 9 Eylül University—law faculty (Ýzmir), research official

11.45–12.15   Victims' Rights before the ICC
Participation, Representation, Reparation, Protection
Jeanne Sulzer, international Justice program director, FIDH

12.15–13.00   Questions and Answers

SESSION 2 (14.30–7.30)
TOWARD TURKISH RATIFICATION OF THE ICC STATUTE

Chairman: Att. Dr. Kerem Altýparmak, Ankara University, Political Science Faculty
Rapporteur: Att. Meryem Erdal

14.30–15.30   Worldwide Efforts in Favor of the ICC

Worldwide NGO Support for the ICC
Work of the Coalition for the ICC
Maria Cavarretta, Program Officer for Southern and Eastern Europe,
Coalition for the International Criminal Court

The European Union Support to the ICC
[Representative from the European Union]
The United States and the ICC
ASPA, Bilateral Immunity Agreements, Security Council
Jeanne Sulzer, international justice program director, FIDH

Questions and Answers

15.45–17.00   Toward the Turkish Ratification of the ICC
Political, Constitutional Efforts and Civil Society Campaign
Günal Kursun, Turkish Coalition for the ICC
Hakan Ataman, Human Rights Agenda Association

Questions and Answers

Friday 17 June 2005

SESSION 3 (10.00–13.00)
IMPLEMENTING THE ICC STATUTE INTO TURKISH DOMESTIC LAW

Chairman: Dr. Mithat Sancar, Ankara University, Law Faculty
Rapporteur: Att. Faruk Duran

10.00–10.30   Turkish Legislative Reforms and the ICC
Reform of the Interministerial Working Group, etc.
Günal Kursun, AI/Turkish Coalition for the ICC

10.45–13.00   STRATEGY SESSION: Turkish Coalition for the ICC
Moderator: Souhayr Belhassen, vice president of FIDH
Rapporteur: Maria Cavarretta, CICC European Office

- Amnesty International Turkey—Gunäl Kursun
- IHD- Yusuf Alatas
- Human Rights Agenda Association—Hakan Ataman
- Helsinki Citizen's Assembly—Aycin San
- Maazlum Der—Ayhan Bilgen
- Turkish Human Rights Foundation—Sedat Aslantas

DEBATE

SESSION 4 (14.30–17.30)
ADOPTION OF AN ACTION PLAN

14.30–16.00   Discussion and Adoption of an Action Plan
Representative of the Turkish Coalition for the ICC
Jeanne Sulzer, International Justice Program, FIDH

16.30   Press conference at Dedeman Hotel, Ankara
Buklum Sokak Number 1 Akay

8

The Legitimacy of the International Criminal Court

Introduction

War crimes, crimes against humanity, and genocide are inherently political offenses, so both legal and political factors come into play when the ICC prosecutor makes choices about whether or not to prosecute these crimes. A crucial question, then, is how much institutional legitimacy the new International Criminal Court can expect to enjoy.

As we have seen in the preceding chapters, opponents of the ICC complain that its prosecutor is insufficiently accountable and has too much latitude in deciding which cases to prosecute.[1] Supporters argue that this prosecutorial independence is the crucial strength of the court's design because it weakens the ability of states to block particular prosecutions for political reasons (Gurmendi 1999). In fact, the rules of the ICC statute give the prosecutor substantial discretion to consider whether or not pursuing justice is wise in a particular political context.[2] Still, this discretion exists under real constraints. The ICC's rules, and the court's need to work with state governments, provide checks on the prosecutor's authority, thereby lessening the likelihood of capricious exercise of the prosecutor's discretion.

In previous chapters we saw that this balance resulted from the contributions of nongovernmental organizations to the negotiations that led to the court's establishment. Those organizations were sensitive to the need to balance an empowered independent judiciary with the complex political issues that arise in trials dealing with mass violence (Elster 2004). Human rights groups, religious communities, and lawyer's associations around the world unfortunately have a great deal of experience with the challenges of bringing political leaders to trial for mass crimes. Their voices contributed to an ICC statute with enough judicial independence to ensure an end to impunity but under the guidance of procedural rules that limit the likelihood of prosecutions that are politically motivated or that unnecessarily intervene in the judicial and political processes of sovereign states.[3]

There are two specific principles in the ICC's design that create this balance in the prosecutor's discretion and therefore contribute to the potential legitimacy of the court. The first is the court's permanence. One aspect of that permanence is institutional. Another aspect of permanence is the authoritative definition of crimes in the statute to ensure that like criminal acts will be punished alike in the future. The second principle is the court's complementarity features, which establish that the ICC is a court of last resort. In other words, the ICC is only to be used when other mechanisms for ensuring accountability for ICC crimes are not available. Both of these principles were developed by states negotiating the statute of the ICC in broad dialogue with NGOs. The breadth and openness of this discourse are responsible for the careful balance of prosecutorial discretion that resulted in the Rome Statute for the ICC.

The foregoing chapters demonstrated that the ICC negotiations were remarkably open and were generally characterized by communicatively rational discussions. This fact contributes to the legitimacy of the ICC. Many of the NGOs involved in the ICC negotiations were human rights groups that have worked internationally or in societies that have recently experienced violent repression; they brought their familiarity with transitional justice issues to bear on the ICC negotiations.[4]

NGOs have little formal legal role in drafting treaty law, and some observers note that NGOs have a "legitimacy deficit" because it is not always clear who they represent and how they are funded, and their internal decision-making procedures usually lack transparency (Castelos 2003, pp. 1050–51). Nevertheless, NGOs have one important attribute that allowed them to make a unique contribution to the overall legitimacy of the legal system embodied in the ICC statute. NGOs are fundamentally oriented toward securing the public interest. As advocates of the public interest, they rely on rational arguments that can be justified through principled reasons. Of course, the leaders and members of NGOs may have private interests, such as increasing group membership and funding, individual career motivations, or personal friendships, for pursuing particular courses of action. Still, NGOs do not decide public policies of their own accord in national or international fora. This simple fact means that in order for NGOs to be effective, they must persuade other decision makers, and consequently, they are uniquely disposed toward giving reasons that logically support their preferred outcomes.

In the negotiations on establishing an ICC, this mode of communicative action was particularly efficacious. Arguing about norms that could be defended as just was at least as important during the ICC treaty negotiations as bargaining about which norms various states would be willing to accept. States, unlike NGOs, often are constrained and forced to pursue the more narrow interests of the constituencies that they represent. Reasons based on interests that are salient for particular states may not be a concern to other parties in the negotiations. Rather than persuading based on reason then, states are likely to use traditional carrots and sticks and the threat of withdrawing from negotiations altogether to alter the cost/benefit calculations of other actors engaged in the negotiations.

The NGOs often cannot effectively pursue those bargaining strategies because they typically do not have sufficient power resources to modify state behavior. Consequently, they are peculiarly inclined to use persuasion based on reasons that appeal to their interlocutors. Arguing based on reasons that are accepted by everyone present is a form of communication that is uniquely disposed toward establishing the legitimacy of rule systems.[5] This is particularly true when the threat of violence does not explicitly or implicitly influence the behavior of negotiators in a constitution drafting exercise (Elster 1998). The negotiations for the Rome Statute of the ICC were almost entirely free of such coercion, and when such appeals to power were implicitly or explicitly made, most of the participants in the negotiations chose to ignore them.

Legitimacy Defined

Before we define legitimacy, it is useful to remember what it is not. Legitimacy is not the same thing as institutionalization (Jepperson 1991). Institutionalization refers to the process whereby social patterns are chronically reproduced through relatively self-activating social processes (Jepperson 1991). It is important to recognize that institutions can be perceived by many as illegitimate and yet continue to be maintained as institutions.

Legitimacy is the belief "in the legality of patterns of normative rules and the right of those elevated to authority under such rules to issue commands" (Weber 1957, p. 328). This definition is drawn from Max Weber's conceptualization of rational-legal authority. For the ICC, legitimacy is the extent to which people in the world perceive it as legal and are prepared to accept its commands as binding. Of course, what is most important is the extent to which officials of states who are parties to the ICC statute comply with formal directives from the judges and prosecutor of the ICC. However, in assessing the ICC's overall legitimacy, we are also interested in the extent to which other persons expect and consider it right for such officials to comply with those commands. To that extent, the legitimacy of the ICC also rests in part on the beliefs of state officials that are not a party to the ICC statute and of other persons generally. Of course, a crucial grounding for rational-legal authority as Weber defined it was peoples' voluntary acceptance of the expediency and/or rational values of an established order.

The prospects for the widespread perception of legitimacy of the ICC are strong because of the careful elaboration of the principles of permanency and complementarity in the Rome Statute. NGOs played a crucial role in that dialogue, particularly by ensuring that it tended toward communicative rationality. The legitimacy of the ICC is developing in the world notwithstanding the sustained diplomatic campaign by the United States to exempt its own nationals from the ICC's jurisdiction.[6] Since the ICC is a permanent court, it can avoid many of the criticisms of ad hoc war crimes tribunals.[7] Because of its permanence, it can build on its successes over time. This permanence strengthens the ICC's pretensions to be enforcing universal norms, and as such it is logically in a position to command greater legitimacy. The second crucial feature is the ICC statute's careful deference to national legal systems. If the ICC attempted to provide a universal solution to all future mass crimes committed, it would be more vulnerable to criticisms that it is overreaching and is unaccountable to local populations. Instead, the ICC is designed to encourage national governments or even regional associations to bring the perpetrators to justice in line with local political conditions and will exercise its own authority only when local conditions allow impunity. The balance between these two principles of the court's permanence and complementarity provisions may not be perfect, and a number of observers have criticized the design of the institution. I examine those critiques in more detail, but I conclude that the balance struck between prosecutorial independence and accountability in the design of the ICC statute is one that is likely to build the legitimacy of the court over time.

The ICC enjoys widespread legitimacy because of the inclusive nature of the negotiations that led to the drafting of the court's statute, including the prominent participation of NGOs. As of August 2007, 105 states have ratified the Rome Statute, and this fact is considerable evidence of widespread acceptance of the court's rules.[8] Because of NGO participation, a much broader range of voices had the opportunity to participate in the negotiations than typically occurs in international treaty negotiations (Struett 2004). The openness of discussions about drafting rule systems to all interested parties is a crucial criterion for communicative action. By communicative action, we mean simply actor's speech acts that are oriented toward reaching shared understandings with others about the validity of facts or normative rules. This is opposed to strategic action where speech acts may deliver warnings, threats, or promises intended to coerce others into the speaker's desired course of action regardless of whether or not the other party agrees with the speaker's reasons. As a result of the openness of these negotiations and their reliance on communicative action, the law and legal institutions embodied in the ICC statute will tend to enjoy *rationally motivated agreement* (Habermas 1996, pp. 153–68).

The compliance pull of modern legal systems rests simultaneously on two forces. One is the probability of enforcement through sanctions that motivate individuals to comply with the law. The other is the assertion of the rational validity of the law, as embodying norms that diverse individuals can agree ought to be obeyed for the general good of all concerned.[9] For international law, including international humanitarian law and international human rights law, the legitimacy of the legal order has historically suffered from weakness of enforcement efforts and a lack of clarity and consensus about how international legal norms apply to particular circumstances. Thomas Franck has noted that the heavy reliance of the international legal system on voluntary compliance offers an opportunity to build a world legal order primarily on the basis of consent rather than coercion (Franck 1988, p. 710). Thus, political and legal theorists from various perspectives have argued that a key factor in establishing the legitimacy of rule systems is ensuring that every person impacted by the rule has a voice in the process that leads to adoption of a rule. Having a voice is not merely the opportunity to speak but an assurance that claims will be taken seriously and responded to as part of a rational communicative process.[10]

Many of the NGOs that participated in the ICC negotiations were international or national NGOs that have had direct experience with seeking accountability for mass atrocities. Human rights groups that were established in domestic contexts to document the abuses of totalitarian regimes and then survived through democratic transitions were natural allies for the international NGOs such as Amnesty and HRW that sought to advocate a strong and independent ICC. We saw in Chapter 4 how HRW issued an action alert in 1997 directly targeted at persuading such NGOs to join the CICC (Human Rights Watch 1997). Consequently, human rights activists with transitional justice experience had extensive input into the ICC negotiations.

In what follows we turn to some criticisms of the ICC's main features,[11] followed by an elaboration of the NGOs' role in the negotiating process, particularly with respect to the specification of the principles of permanency and complementarity in the ICC statute. Then I develop my argument that these principles as written in the statute create a well-designed balance between constraining the prosecutor from unwise prosecutions that are insufficiently sensitive to local political conditions, even while they grant the prosecutor enough independence to ensure that prosecutions take place when relevant politicians are reluctant. Finally, I conclude that if an ICC prosecutor, with the tacit support of the ICC judges, used his authority in a capricious way, the likely result would be the ineffectiveness of the court itself but not the unwarranted detention of persons unjustly accused or the disruptive interference of the ICC in local peace-building efforts. This balance is a result of the contributions of NGOs to the negotiations on developing the ICC.

Major Criticisms of the Court's Design

Criticisms of the ICC's design have focused on a three main issues. One is that the court will be insufficiently sensitive to local political concerns and the need to reestablish political order, particularly in the wake of regime transitions characterized by mass violence. A second objection focuses on the concern that the Rome Statute creates new legal obligations for nonstate parties to the treaty in violation of international law. A third category of criticisms claims that the ICC prosecutor and judges are insufficiently accountable to others, and therefore the exercise of the ICC's powers is potentially antidemocratic.

The objection that the ICC will intervene in ongoing political conflicts with insufficient regard for the impact of criminal prosecution on other public policy values is perhaps the most serious objection to the structure of the ICC. The prosecutor's *proprio motu* power to initiate investigations and trials is at the center of this objection to the court's design. Critics argue that this feature amounts to placing the ICC's legal system outside of any controlling political context (Czartnetzky and Rychlak 2003). The ICC prosecutor, with the consent of the ICC judges, is in a position to legally pursue cases, free of the control of the political authorities in the state where crimes occurred. Proponents counter that the ICC statute only allows for the court to take jurisdiction if there is no genuine local investigation or legal proceeding; local authorities can always block ICC action by genuinely prosecuting a case in local courts. However, as a result of the negotiations discussed in Chapter 6, the ICC prosecutor and judges retain the authority to determine in a formal hearing that a domestic legal proceeding occurred merely for the purpose of shielding the accused (Article 19).

The prosecutor and judges of the new permanent ICC will face many decisions that are roughly analogous to those confronting transitional regimes when they decide whether or not to pursue criminal justice. Those decisions are often controversial, particularly when conflicts are perceived between the goals of pursuing justice and promoting the stability of new regimes (Becker et al. 1995).

Of course, the ICC will never be the only mechanism for achieving justice in the wake of politically motivated atrocities. The ICC statute's complementarity provisions mean that the ICC is only to be used as a court of last resort. Truth commissions, trials in national courts, and even future ad hoc international courts may all be used from time to time as mechanisms for holding people responsible for the most egregious violations of human rights. The ICC's complementarity provisions ensure that national tribunals or courts in third states may continue to play an important role. Still, the existence of the ICC as a possible option for achieving justice during times of transition will change the dynamics of future discussions about how to deal with transitional justice issues. The simple existence of the court means that policies that ignore ICC crimes at the local level are unlikely to be the last word. The implications of this aspect of the court's design are discussed below.

Another central objection to the ICC's design, raised primarily by the U.S. government, is the fact that the court could conceivably try to punish citizens of states that have not ratified the court's statute (Scheffer 1999a). As such, it has been argued that the statute unfairly creates legal obligations for states that have not accepted the treaty. If citizens of nonstate parties commit crimes on the territory of state parties, or if the Security Council refers a case to the attention of the court, as has now happened with respect to Sudan, it is true that the court can try the citizens of states that have not accepted the treaty.[12] Legal scholars continue to debate the whether or not this amounts to a violation of the international law rule that treaties create obligations for nonstate parties.[13] I review that discussion below.

The final concern that the ICC prosecutor is insufficiently accountable is closely related to the issue that the prosecutor will not be sensitive enough to local political considerations when deciding whether or not to prosecute particular cases. The ICC prosecutor or individual judges can be removed from office for misconduct by the Assembly of State Parties, which is formally the highest authority within the court.[14] Each member state has one vote in this body. But this extreme penalty will likely be used only rarely, and in any case gives only very limited voice to the societies that are most directly involved in an ICC investigation. A closer examination of this concern is the focus of the later section on the principle of complementarity in the Rome Statute.

The next section examines the role of NGOs in negotiating the crucial principles of permanence and complementarity in the ICC statute and explains the ways that their contributions added to the legitimacy of the resulting principles. Then, we turn to a reexamination of those principles in light of the above objections frequently raised to the ICC statute and discuss the prospects for the continued widespread acceptance of the ICC's legitimacy.

NGOs' Role in Legitimizing the ICC

I have argued that one of NGOs' main sources of power is their ability to advance persuasive reasons for the adoption of particular legal norms.[15] Thus, the cumulative effect of their extensive participation in the ICC negotiations was to move the debate toward communicative action rather than strategic action. The result is that the ICC statute embodies a set of legal norms that are deserving of *rationally motivated* consent and not simply strategic compliance driven by the threat of sanctions. As long as the new officers of the ICC act consistently with the principles of the Rome Statute, there are theoretical reasons to expect that the ICC will enjoy widespread legitimacy in the world community.

As we saw in the previous chapters, arguing based on reasons tended to be more effective in the negotiations that led to the Rome Statute than bargaining based on coercion or exchange. We saw that efforts were made to keep the discussions open to all interested participants, including NGOs, and that most actors tended to orient their communications toward achieving intersubjective agreement about what law and procedures would ideally be best for the court. For example, a topos emerged in the negotiations that it would not be wise to create new international law in the ICC statute. The major NGOs in the pro-CICC used their legal expertise to make assertions about the existing state of international criminal law, ensuring that the codification of crimes occurred in a progressive way.[16]

Rules have legitimacy when diverse members of a society can agree in the abstract that such rules are fair to all concerned, before particular interests come into play. Diplomats representing states find it difficult to take this abstract position, behind Rawl's famous "veil of ignorance" (Rawls 2001). The problem of creating a new ICC is a difficult one for governments representing states. Governments must always be concerned with the immediate and future interests of the states they represent. The United States has to consider the potential political fallout if an international court labels its former leaders as war criminals or attempts to punish its generals for future decisions made in the context of interventions around the world. The other major powers face the same sets of problems. NGOs, by contrast, can take principled positions about the desirability of certain formulations of rules without having to concern themselves with the consequences for any particular constituency to whom they are pledged to be loyal.

The authority of a state delegate involved in international negotiations turns on her claim to be the official representative of a particular set of interests, a government, and its people. The NGOs enjoy no such assumption of representative legitimacy. Their arguments only carry the day if they can be justified as rational to all relevant listeners. It turned out that in the context of trying to develop a charter for a new institution that would punish individuals for egregious violations of international criminal law, the type of rational persuasive legitimacy claimed by NGOs was as important and influential as the representative legitimacy enjoyed by delegates representing states. As we saw earlier, NGOs also contributed to the realization of communicative action through their efforts to ensure that all states had adequate legal advice and personnel to follow the complex negotiations.

The establishment of the ICC is a case where we can see clear and fairly rapid change in the norms for dealing with the perpetrators of mass atrocities in the world political system. It is also a case in which NGOs, through their discursive practices, have played a crucial role in shaping the content of emerging norms. NGO influence was surprising because it came at the expense of the desires of powerful states, such as the U.S. government (Scheffer 1998). The court's statute adopts early proposals from the NGO community on a number of issues that were contentious during the ICC debate.

We have seen that NGOs lobbied for and won approval for the ICC to have a strong, independent prosecutor. States remain primarily responsible for enforcing international criminal law under the complementarity provisions of the ICC statute. But in order to ensure that serious atrocities would not continue to go unpunished because the relevant states were unwilling or unable to act, most states accepted the idea that the new international institution should have substantial powers.[17] As we noted above, under the ICC statute, the prosecutor with the permission of judges of the pretrial chamber is authorized to bring charges on her own authority.[18] This procedural independence means that decisions to prosecute are at least partially isolated from the short-term political pressures of interstate politics.[19] States' behavior in constructing an ICC with these powers can only be understood in the context of NGO discourse on this issue (Amnesty International 1994).

On the principle of complementarity, NGOs understood that an effective ICC would be one that heard few cases because most ICC crimes would be dealt with adequately by national legal systems.[20] But for such a happy situation to emerge, NGOs argued that the ICC prosecutor and judges had to have sufficient authority to begin prosecutions on their own if relevant political leaders were reluctant to do so.

Now I examine in more detail the principles of permanency and complementarity as they are embodied in the ICC statute. I have shown that a broadly accessible discourse contributed to the elaboration of these principles in the ICC statute. Now we can examine those rules and consider whether or not the amount of discretionary authority granted to the ICC prosecutor under the ICC rules can be considered legitimate.

The Principle of Permanence in the ICC Statute

The ICC will likely achieve a greater degree of institutionalization than other ad hoc mechanisms created to punish or account for atrocities. That is because the ICC will be constituted as a permanent supranational entity, with sitting judges and prosecutors. Consequently, the ICC will have the opportunity to build operating procedures and create shared expectations in the larger world community over time.

One of the many crucial challenges to projects that attempt to ensure justice during times of transition has been the need to establish courts or truth commissions in a short amount of time under intense political pressure. The permanence of the ICC may make it an attractive option in the future because it will not face these start-up costs or the political challenges associated with developing a new institution. The institutional permanence of the ICC will tend to strengthen the norm that the acts criminalized in the statute should always be punished. The International Military Tribunals at Nuremberg and Tokyo never fully escaped the charge that they only imposed "victor's justice" and not the impartial rule of law.[21] Recent reports from the former Yugoslavia suggest that many citizens there still question the ICTY's legitimacy.[22] If a criminal norm is universally recognized, it is valid even if not always punished. But ad hoc tribunals are too inconsistent to persuade doubters that the norms are really universal principles and not just propaganda of the powerful punishing the defeated. This same problem often is faced by truth commissions or special courts established in times of transition. The claim that the enforcement of international criminal law is the implementation of universal principles is often suspect when courts are imposed by powerful outsiders on conflict-torn societies or by newly established regimes within a society in transition. In the future, however, the ICC need not face this charge because it represents an institutional commitment to ensure that certain crimes are punished regardless of the prevailing political situation.

The ICC's permanence is central to the court's ability to claim legitimacy. The permanence of the court raises the likelihood that occurrences of war crimes, crimes against humanity, and acts of genocide will be punished. Of course, no legal system created by human societies can expect to punish every violation that occurs. Indeed, the ICC is much less ambitious. It is designed as a court of last resort that will punish these crimes only when national legal systems fail to do so. The upshot is that permanence by itself will not ensure the perception of legitimacy of the ICC. It must also embody a set of procedures and norms for deciding which cases to prosecute and when to convict that diverse observers recognize as fair and just.

Accordingly, the provisions of the Rome Statute that provide for its procedural jurisdiction are critical for understanding how the ICC will interact with domestic processes for attaining justice during times of transition. In previous chapters we saw the ways that NGOs helped bring those procedures into existence. We will turn to an examination of the implications of those procedures for the court's ability to aid with efforts to impose justice in times of transition.

Nullum crimen sine lege (no crime without law) is the widely recognized principle of criminal law that a person cannot be held criminally responsible for an act that was not legally recognized as criminal at the time it was committed. Nuremberg and Tokyo struggled with this issue, but more or less convincingly the judges were able to persuade themselves that the conduct in question before them was recognized as criminal at the time it was committed (Ehard 1949; Hosoya et al., 1986). Crucially, the ICC is a permanent court, and its very permanence promises that violations will be judged by the same standards in the future. ICC negotiators were careful in defining the crimes in the ICC statute to limit themselves to those that were already recognized as part of either customary or treaty-based international law. NGOs were insistent on this point during the negotiations. NGOs understood that focusing only on existing crimes would strengthen the legitimacy of the permanent court, and they reminded state delegations that it would be wise to avoid attempting to create new international law crimes (Amnesty International 1997b).

When charges under international criminal law are adjudicated and decisions are rendered, it is always both a retrospective and prospective act. The judge finds guilt or innocence of a particular individual for a past act. But by enforcing a rule and offering the reasoning for that decision, the judge also holds out a promise that in future cases with similar facts, the legal rule will be applied in the same way (Stone Sweet and Brunell 1998, pp. 63–5). Consistent application of the rules to future cases is a logical necessity for our sense of justice and the rationality of our normative rules (Alexey 1989, pp. 65–79, 100).

Third-party dispute resolution, when it is exercised effectively, tends to increase the legitimacy and authority of the judicial decision-making body. As judges successfully resolve problems, other actors with similar problems are also likely to seek decisions of the court as well (Stone Sweet 1999). Consistent third-party dispute resolution is crucial for individual actors to achieve stable expectations about how others will behave in the future. Over time the successful settlement of disputes increases the legitimacy and authority of the judge or law–giver (Stone Sweet and Brunell 1998, p. 63).

Transitional justice issues arise after violent civil wars or when governments commit atrocities on their own territories. However, states have historically been reluctant to extend the protections of international humanitarian law to internal armed conflicts. The 1949 Geneva Conventions made important distinctions between international and civil conflicts, limiting crucial provisions of the convention to "international armed conflicts."[23] Consequently, we are on relatively new ground in considering how crimes against humanity and war crimes as defined in international law may be relevant to efforts to achieve justice in times of transition. The ICC's charter *does* define each of these crimes in a way that makes clear they can be committed and prosecuted, even when there is no nexus to an international conflict.[24] As noted above, this outcome in the ICC negotiations was something that NGOs campaigned for aggressively. By the 1990s it was clear that much of the death, destruction, and hardship caused by warfare during the twentieth century had occurred during civil wars or other conflicts not of an international character. Given their commitment to ending impunity for the individuals responsible for such acts, human rights NGOs insisted that the ICC should have jurisdiction over the core crimes even when there is no link to an international conflict.[25] Even near the end of the negotiations in Rome, many important states, including Russia, China, India, and Mexico, argued against giving the ICC jurisdiction over crimes committed during conflicts that were entirely within the confines of one state.[26] NGOs prevailed on this point despite the continued reluctance of many states to permit international oversight of their internal use of force. They argued that logical consistency demands that internationally recognized crimes must be punished equally regardless of whether or not they occur during international warfare or the much more common civil warfare of recent decades. Ensuring consistent punishment of war crimes and crimes against humanity is part of the effort to ensure the universality of the criminal normative standards enshrined in the ICC statute.

For international criminal law as it was practiced in the twentieth century, the promise that future crimes would be treated similarly was usually extremely tenuous. Gary Bass has noted that a complex set of political circumstances had to coincide before tribunals would be allowed to go forward. According to Bass, only liberal states support bona fide war crimes tribunals. However, liberal states will only do this when their own soldiers are not at risk, and they are much more likely to do so when their own citizens have suffered greatly in the recent conflict. Public outrage increases the likelihood that liberal states will pursue trials. Bass notes also that the mobilization of nonstate pressure groups makes trials more likely. The conjunction of all these criteria obviously has been a rare historical occurrence. Consequently, tribunals rarely have been established, and the perpetrators of many atrocities escaped criminal accountability (Bass 2000). But it is a mistake to assume that the political challenges to the ICC will be of the same kind as those that constrained the establishment of ad hoc war crimes tribunals.

The tremendous difference is the permanence of the ICC. This means that time will tend to serve the interests of justice rather than the interests of impunity. Ad hoc courts, particularly after World War II, depended on the imposition of superior force from the outside to document the crimes that had occurred (Griffin 2001). In the case of the former Yugoslavia, local cooperation was ensured in large part through outside coercion by the Western powers. Ad hoc tribunals require significant military backing because they need to be established quickly before political momentum is lost.

In contrast to the relatively authoritarian Security Council procedure used to establish the UN tribunals, the ICC statute was drafted on the basis of consensus, with the extensive input of NGOs. The permanent ICC can afford to be patient; with its rules and judges and officers in place, it can gradually build a case prior to indicting and detaining a suspect. This means that even without total military control over the territory where evidence exists, witness testimony and documentation can nevertheless be accumulated gradually when opportunities arise. The ICC can indict suspects and wait for a politically appropriate time for a state to arrest the suspect and/or turn over evidence. As the Yugoslavia tribunal has shown, even intermittent and half-hearted cooperation with international prosecutions over time will lead to the detention of many suspects and the production of sufficient evidence for prosecution (Scharf 1997, p. 149).

Since the ICC's rules and procedures have been adopted through a process of open, consensus-driven debate, they already enjoy a great deal of support from the governments that adopted them. Because the permanent court will enjoy the diffuse support of many in the global community, it has less need for a particular great power or coalition of great powers to support its edicts. For this reason, United States opposition to the ICC will not necessarily doom the court to irrelevance in its early years.[27]

The court will be constrained by political realities. Indeed, the establishment and enforcement of law is always and everywhere a political activity. There is no such thing as a judicial system that operates completely free of political constraints. But the constraints and limitations that will set the agenda for the ICC will be different in kind from the political circumstances of the Nuremberg or Tokyo tribunals. The ICC will not face the perception that it is being established simply for the purpose of punishing the leadership of a national group that has lost political favor internationally.

It is crucial that the ICC prosecutor and judges work to punish violations of the Rome Statute wherever they occur, and not only on one continent or with respect to some parties to a conflict and not others. The Rome Statute's authors went to great lengths to anticipate this problem in crafting the jurisdictional rules of the ICC. Partially because of NGO insistence, the Rome Statute only allows states to refer *situations* to the ICC prosecutor's office and not individual criminal acts. This ensures that if a government is engaged in conflict with an armed group within the borders of the state and ICC jurisdiction is invoked, crimes committed by the government as well as crimes committed by groups in open rebellion can be considered by the prosecutor's office.

The permanence of the ICC strengthens its claim to legitimacy relative to ad hoc methods of achieving accountability for mass crimes. Conduct norms are logically more valid if there is an institutional commitment to punishing their violation(s) consistently. Of course, every political situation is different, and accordingly in the future it will continue to be necessary to adapt to local conditions in order to achieve justice for particular acts of mass violence. While the ICC's permanence promises some minimal level of consistent punishment, it would be presumptive of the ICC founders to assert that the ICC was the best institution to deal with every situation. This recognition was embodied in the complementarity provisions of the ICC statute. NGOs with on the ground experience in conflict situations recognized this reality and so worked with states to develop the ICC's principle of complementarity in a balanced way that would lessen the likelihood of continued impunity for these crimes but still be deferential to local political needs.

Principle of Complementarity in the ICC Statute

As we saw above, a crucial concern with some critics of the ICC has been that the institution will be insufficiently attentive to local political situations in deciding which cases to pursue. Since the court will not be directly accountable to the existing authorities in societies in which it is investigating and prosecuting war crimes, genocide, or crimes against humanity, there is concern that it will not sufficiently consider other values, such as establishing peace and order, as it pursues justice. The complementarity principle in the ICC statute provides some relief against these concerns, because to the extent that local societies have legitimate legal procedures for achieving accountability, the ICC will not take jurisdiction. NGOs drew on their experience with transitional justice issues in the positions that they took during the ICC negotiations about how the complementarity system should work.

Each time a new court or truth commission is established, a host of concerns emerge about who should be prosecuted, for what acts, and whether or not amnesties should be granted in exchange for truth. The justice of ad hoc tribunals is always a function of the political forces that are willing to impose trials at a given point in time. Consequently the justice that is meted out often is perceived as political and potentially unjust. To the extent justice is imposed by outsiders, it may not be perceived as justice at all. And because many arguably similar cases are not tried, charges of political selectivity are a recurring problem. The net result is that for groups who feel trials have unfairly been imposed on their leaders, international tribunals have scant legitimacy. Still, because of its permanence, there is reason to think the ICC can avoid the perception of selectivity if the procedures for selecting cases are defensible and implemented fairly. This is the crucial issue, whether or not the prosecutor exercises his discretion in a way that is widely acceptable.

Because the prosecutor and the ICC more generally will need state cooperation to carry out arrests and detain suspects, there are built-in incentives for the prosecutor to act in ways that can be justified to a broad set of outside observers. Examination of the ICC complementarity procedures suggests that they are fair.

Observers have noted that pursuing justice for the victims of authoritarian regimes sometimes conflicts with the goal of strengthening democratic institutions (Kritz 1995). Some scholars conclude that where democracy itself is at risk from an authoritarian backlash and the reformers are too weak to undertake prosecutions, it is best to forgo justice and allow democracy to gain strength without directly threatening the deposed forces (Kritz 1995).

International prosecutions of human rights crimes have been described as challenges to the sovereign authority of states because international legal efforts to prosecute human rights crimes may threaten the delicate political bargains that are often struck between outgoing authoritarian regimes and reformers. This point was made with respect to the Chilean case while General Pinochet was still under house arrest in London (Roht-Arriaza 2005). In early 2001, newspapers filled with a similar debate over the wisdom of the ICTY's indictment of Slobodan Milošević. In March 2001 he was arrested in Yugoslavia on domestic corruption charges. The rump Yugoslavia ultimately surrendered Milosevic to the ICTY, but that move resulted in a domestic political crisis that nearly toppled the sitting government. Milosovic's case, like Pinochet's, raised the question of whether and when it is wise for the international community to press for international prosecutions of human rights crimes given their potential to exacerbate domestic political instability.

Even when national circumstances force pragmatic concessions on the issue of dealing with violations that occurred during the outgoing regime, it is not logically necessary for the international community to recognize, defer to, or respect any national compromises that the transition government may be forced to make (Kritz 1995, pp. 47–8). The crucial challenge facing the ICC prosecutor in exercising discretion about the pursuit of particular cases is precisely this decision about when the "interests of justice" will best be served by pursuing prosecution.[28] The justice versus democracy debate has tended to assume that prosecutions for human rights violations will be undertaken by the state in which crimes occurred. Prior to Pinochet's arrest in London, there was insufficient consideration of the differences between international and national prosecutions. The case of Pinochet suggests that the tradeoffs involved for new democracies may not be nearly as painful if prosecutions are undertaken internationally.[29] If international courts pursue cases of past atrocities, it makes little sense for aggrieved domestic groups to retaliate against other domestic actors. A wise ICC prosecutor will allow groups that do cooperate with international investigations to do so quietly and when necessary out of the public eye. Indeed, this desire for internationalization of criminal prosecutorial responsibility was a reason why many conflict-ridden states supported the creation of the ICC. For dictatorial leaders who maintain power in part to ensure their own immunity from prosecution, international accountability poses a fundamentally different set of challenges than potential prosecution or retaliation by their political opponents in their domestic society.

Whether or not the dictator gives up power in the domestic society, he cannot travel abroad without fearing the police power of other states.

Benomar has written on the tension between the goals of retribution and reconciliation. For those who favor retribution, anything less than punishment of the violators risks signaling that human rights violations are acceptable in some circumstances, thereby increasing the risk that such violations will occur again in the future of the society. For those who favor reconciliation, amnesty and or clemency can play a role in beginning a national healing process, and they also emphasize that it might be impractical to prosecute if that risks the collapse of the new government (Kritz 1995, pp. 32–41).

There is a difficulty in framing the conflict as a tradeoff between retribution and reconciliation. In many cases, failure to have a legally compelling and just accounting and punishment for past violations may increase the likelihood that aggrieved social groups will take it upon themselves to avenge the past in violent ways. Moreover, there is grave danger in signaling that some human rights abuses can be forgiven, which has ominous implications for the ability to deter future crimes.

A group of mental health professionals working with the victims of political repression in Chile noted that Pinochet's police state not only created "extreme trauma" for the direct victims of repression "but also produced trauma at a macrosocial level" (Becker et al. 1995, p. 584). While families were impacted by unemployment and loss of housing, the structural breakdown of social groups, political parties, and communities "made collective responses [to the trauma] chaotic and ineffective" (Becker et al. 1995, p. 586). Becker and his colleagues report that when the victims of political violence take legal action against the police responsible for political killings, it can have a therapeutic effect (Becker et al. 1995, p. 588). All of which suggests that pursuing criminal justice may be important not only for achieving retribution but also for laying the groundwork for social reconstruction.

The existence of a permanent international judicial institution now modifies considerably the relationship between international law and domestic decisions to provide amnesty or prosecute. The case of Pinochet's London arrest suggests that international dismissal of such national bargains may be resisted by national transition governments but also ultimately strengthen their hand in the national context vis-à-vis forces that want to protect those who are guilty of past abuses.

The ICC statute is silent on the question of recognizing amnesties issued by national courts, partly because NGOs pressured states to ensure that all human rights leaders would be prosecuted (Dugard 2002, p. 700). If they are issued only in an effort to shield the accused, as in Pinochet's case, they could be considered by the ICC as legal proceedings designed to shield the accused from prosecution, thereby providing legal grounds for the ICC to take up the case. In a case like that of the South African Truth and Reconciliation Commission, where amnesties were traded for truth, the ICC is probably not legally barred from prosecuting a case but would have discretion to defer to the national legal process. Because the ICC is a court of last resort, within the context of its complementarity provisions the ICC statute provides its prosecutor and judges with a great deal of discretion about whether and when to pursue prosecutions.[30] The ICC will have substantial resource constraints, and early indications suggest that there will be no shortage of cases that the ICC might investigate.[31] Resource constraints mean that the prosecutor will need to defer to any local judicial process that comes anywhere close to meeting international standards for providing accountability.

In the future, the ICC will provide a mechanism that may allow for international prosecutions even when domestic stability in a transitioning regime is still in question. It will be up to the ICC's officers to make the determination about whether or not the interests of justice are served by prosecuting immediately. Within the rule framework laid out by the Rome Statute, the ICC prosecutor will be forced to make these choices about who to prosecute for what particular acts and when to defer to domestic trials or truth commissions. It is worth noting that this prosecutorial discretion could in principle allow the ICC officials to take into consideration "redeeming acts" as discussed by Elster (2006). The "interests of justice" clause in Article 53 of the Statute provides significant latitude in this respect.

NGO advocates sought to ensure that no states, such as the permanent members of the UN Security Council, could interfere in these decisions in a politically motivated way. To do that, they helped establish a system in which the ICC prosecutor's authority to bring charges is balanced against the authority of the ICC judges to determine whether or not the charges have merit and meet the limited conditions under which the ICC has jurisdiction. The ICC remains deferential to national sovereignty in its complementarity provisions; it does not have jurisdiction where national legal systems genuinely investigate or prosecute an alleged instance of an ICC crime. However, the court does have the strength to initiate prosecutions when states are unwilling to do so.[32] This careful balance did not emerge by accident. Many states sought a court with more limited jurisdictional rules. However, NGOs who have experienced the reluctance of political leaders to provide accountability for crimes of mass violence sought to ensure that the independent prosecutor would have enough independent authority to pressure states to act, even when it might be politically easier to allow crimes to go unpunished.

For the ICC to be legitimate, it must create the impression that war crimes, crimes against humanity, and genocide can be prosecuted regardless of who commits them, be they citizens of impoverished failed states or great powers. For this reason, the authors of the ICC statute understood it was better to have an ICC without the United States rather than an ICC that effectively exempted U.S. citizens from prosecution. The purpose of the ICC is not primarily to try American citizens or the leaders, citizens, or soldiers of any other state with well-functioning judicial institutions. Nevertheless, the framers of the statute of the new permanent ICC realized that the new court would only be perceived as legitimate if *all* the founding states accepted the court's authority. Even powerful states must open themselves up to judgment in theory. A court that procedurally exempted the permanent members of the Security Council would continue to face the legitimacy crisis of Nuremberg and the other ad hoc tribunals, namely, the perception that international humanitarian law crimes will only ever be punished when committed by leaders from relatively weak states and only when the powerful see it as in their interest to back an international tribunal with force.

Of course, the imposition of justice by the ICC will require the exercise of political power, and at times that power will need to be backed by force. The ICC cannot detain suspects, secure evidence, or compel witness testimony without cooperation from states, and particularly at least some cooperation from the state where the alleged crimes have occurred. Such "cooperation" from the territorial state may only be secured through diplomatic, economic, and even military pressure from other states. We considered above that this pressure may come from a variety of states, and lack of cooperation from the world's "one remaining superpower" (Wedgewood 1998) is not by itself a bar to other states creating enough leverage to convince recalcitrant states to comply with the ICC.

Consequently, there are substantial external political checks on the ICC's prosecutor and judges. They will only be successful in bringing criminals to justice if they husband their moral authority and focus on charging law breakers who have clearly violated international standards. If they are too aggressive, they risk losing international support, and the likely result is that they will be unable to carry out even basic investigative functions.

In future (and ongoing) cases of regime transition, it is likely that the ICC may have a useful role to play. Where relatively liberal governments have recently attained power but may remain threatened by the remnants of authoritarian regimes, government leaders may have every incentive to cooperate with the international tribunal in arresting suspects and preserving evidence while allowing the ICC itself to undertake the prosecutions. When new regimes are fragile, it is logical that they could easily be found to be "unable" to carry out prosecutions, thereby triggering the ICC's complementary jurisdiction. In cases of transitional justice, there are often elements of the political elite in the state where crimes occurred who favor the prosecution of the alleged criminals. In some cases, the accused leaders themselves may find that detention and trial in The Hague, even facing possible lifetime imprisonment, is a preferable outcome compared to what they might expect at the hands of their former victims. Additionally, in a case where a new weak regime has taken power following a violent transition, the existence of the ICC will give the new leaders an added incentive to comply with international human rights standards when they find themselves in control of the state's force apparatus. By taking the moral high ground and complying with international human rights standards, new regimes can distinguish themselves from their authoritarian predecessors while allowing the ultimate judicial determinations of guilt and innocence to be made by neutral international judges.

In cases where the present government is uncertain about or even opposed to cooperating with the ICC, other states may be able to bring sufficient pressure to ensure cooperation. Even without superpower support, coalitions of middle-sized states can bring resources to bear to compel cooperation with the ICC. Because the norms that the ICC embodies have been accepted by the world community in advance, the court begins its life with diffuse legitimacy and an expectation that many actors will be willing to cooperate with its requests. As the number of states who ratify the ICC statute rises, the places that will serve as harbors to fugitive subjects will decline accordingly. Of course, given the limited resources that the ICC prosecutor will have at his disposal for the foreseeable future, it will be wise to focus on prosecutions in which a relatively high level of cooperation can be expected from the government on whose territory the alleged crimes occurred.

Still, it is important to recognize that the ICC and its member states have the option of pressuring recalcitrant governments to cooperate.

The ICC remains entirely dependent on cooperating states to pursue investigations and to arrest the accused and surrender them to the court. Therefore, political leaders of states retain significant authority to weigh for themselves whether or not a particular case ought to be prosecuted given political concerns. Of course, state parties to the court will have a *legal* obligation to cooperate with an indictment duly issued by the court. Nevertheless, the court remains constrained by the extent of the cooperation it can muster. The most effective way to secure prosecution is to focus on cases where the responsibility of particular individuals for gross violations of international criminal law is clear and abhorrent and the prospects for achieving justice are real. If the overall political and justice concerns that prevail in a particular case weigh heavily against proceeding with prosecution before the ICC, it seems highly unlikely that a crusading rogue prosecutor would pursue such a case.

Even though ICC prosecutors enjoy independence, assuming good conduct in office, they remain constrained by the views of the world community. Formally, the prosecutor can be removed by majority vote of the Assembly of States parties in the case of misconduct.[33] Far short of that extreme penalty, prosecutors will have an ongoing need to promote the reputation and respect for their office in the global community. Without cooperation from states, the ICC prosecutor will be powerless to investigate cases and detain suspects.

The prosecutor will also probably want to take advantage of the resources of NGOs in developing cases and deciding which to pursue. In part this will be a simple resource issue. NGOs often are able to interview witnesses and systematize evidence of atrocities more efficiently than formal prosecutors.[34] When there are many victims and potentially many perpetrators, NGO assistance can help prosecutors decide which cases warrant the attention of their office. The first ICC prosecutor, Luis Moreno Ocampo, has a history of working successfully with NGOs.[35]

Finally, of course, we should consider cases where a transitional government succeeds in establishing a genuine truth commission or judicial process for holding individuals accountable who probably are guilty of international law crimes. In such a case, particularly given resource constraints, the ICC will have every incentive to defer to the outcome of the domestic legal process. This may even apply to a situation such as a future version of the South African Truth Commission, where punishment was specifically suspended in exchange for truthful information. A future situation like the Chilean military's "self-amnesty," however, should be subject to much closer review by the ICC.[36]

State Sovereignty and the ICC Statute

It has become popular in recent years to suggest that state sovereignty, as a phenomenon in the international legal system, is in decline.[37] One such challenge to state sovereignty is the empowerment of international organizations or institutions to make binding decisions in areas that historically have been the prerogative of sovereign states. A prime example of this would be the ICC. We have seen that the states party to the ICC statute grant the court considerable authority over the prosecution of war crimes, crimes against humanity, and genocide when those crimes are committed by the member state's citizens or on its territory. It has been alleged by the United States that, in addition to the voluntary sacrifice of sovereign authority by states party to the ICC, the new ICC also infringes on the sovereign rights of nonstate parties.[38]

State sovereignty, however, remains a foundational norm of the international legal system. In what follows I examine the challenges to state sovereignty that are brought about under the Rome Statute of the ICC but will argue that these are developments of the concept of state sovereignty and not a radical departure from it.

Viewed from this perspective, arguments by the United States government that the Rome Statute violates the sovereign rights of nonstate parties[39] have little merit, as the principles of the ICC statute are well in line with the traditional state sovereignty norms that are the foundation of international law. The essential impact on nonstate parties' sovereignty is that nationals of such states who commit crimes on the territory of states party to the ICC statute could potentially be punished for their crimes before the new international court. However, under the traditional rules of international law, nationals of a foreign state are normally subject to the laws of the state where they are traveling (Oliver 1991).

Consequently, to the extent that the establishment of the ICC creates obligations for nonstate parties, it does so in a way that is consistent with the foundational international law norm of state sovereignty. States that consent to become parties to the Rome Statute of the ICC do engage in a significant redefinition of their sovereign rights and responsibilities, but they do so in a way that is consistent with the gradual evolution of the concept of state sovereignty over the centuries. Therefore, the establishment of the ICC does not radically undermine the concept of state sovereignty; instead, it modifies sovereignty norms in a direction that promises to permit the continued utility of the concept for international law in the twenty-first century.

The Concept of State Sovereignty

Sovereignty as a Social Construct

State sovereignty is a foundational legal concept of international law that holds that states should have autonomy to act and be free from unwanted intrusions by other states. However, the precise rule content of the sovereignty concept has changed a great deal over time. For instance, it was once accepted that one of the privileges of sovereign states was the right to use force in world politics. Today, in contrast, the concept of state sovereignty includes the right to be free from armed attack on a state's sovereign territory (Werner 2004, p. 127). I accept the notion articulated by Werner and others that sovereignty is a conceptual category of international law whose specific content changes over time through the discursive practices of states (Werner 2004, pp. 131–33). As Werner states clearly:

> State sovereignty is not a descriptive concept which stands for ("mirrors") a pre-given state of affairs and which can be measured and counted in an objective way. The very

fact that collapsed states still count as sovereign states in international law suggests otherwise. Rather than being a representation of a state of affairs, state sovereignty is a *claim to authority;* a claim which has been institutionalized, defined and redefined within the framework of international law.[40]

This perspective is at odds with the view that sovereignty is an actual political characteristic of independent political entities that have de facto political autonomy. In such a view, international law simply takes note of that empirical situation.[41] I assume, instead, that the discourse of international law has substantiated the conceptual category of sovereignty. The existence of a body of law based on the principle of the independence of sovereign states has legitimized and institutionalized the existence of political forms that claim the status of sovereign states. Moreover, the particular bundle of rights and duties that sovereign states claim to possess as a result of qualifying for legal sovereign status has changed considerably over time.

Biersteker and Weber elaborate on the view that sovereignty is a socially constructed legal concept whose exact content changes considerably over time. They assert that

> Sovereignty provides the basis in international law for claims for state actions, and its violation is routinely invoked as a justification for the use of force in international relations. Sovereignty, therefore, is an inherently social concept. States' claims to sovereignty construct a social environment in which they can interact as an international society of states, while at the same time the mutual recognition of claims to sovereignty is an important element in the construction of states themselves.
> (Biersteker and Weber 1996, pp. 1–2)

Thus, sovereignty is a social fact. States exist as meaningful entities because they are constituted by international law rules of recognition. At the same time, states constitute those institutional rules of international law by interacting in ways that develop and modify the meaning of sovereignty over time. The relationship between states, as agents, and international law, as an institution, is mutually constitutive.[42] I accept the notion that, while the specific rules of conduct for sovereign states shift over time, the sovereignty idea always refers to some capacity of the state to act independently from other sources of authority (Biersteker and Weber 1996, p. 14).

One consequence of the view that sovereignty is a socially constructed phenomenon is that it is no longer necessary to view the international norm of state sovereignty and the norm of individual human rights as existing in opposition to one another.[43] Instead, constructivist scholars of international relations have argued that, since 1945, with the era of decolonization and self-determination, the obligation of sovereign states to protect the individual human rights of their citizens has become essential to legitimizing the existence of the international state system itself (Reus-Smit 2001, pp. 519–20, 531–36). The reason for the legitimacy of the state system in earlier centuries was the divine right of kings, but, since the middle of the twentieth century, the foundational reason for the existence of modern states is to protect the most basic human rights of their populations. As Reus-Smit puts it: "Far from being a categorical right with no strings attached, therefore, the post-1945 right to self-determination was deliberately and explicitly tied to the satisfaction of basic human rights" (Reus-Smit 2001, p. 536).

Liberal legal scholars have articulated the principle that international law rights, including state sovereignty, have as their fundamental aim to promote and protect the rights of individuals. As such, mass violence perpetrated in the name of the state itself cannot be a protected act under international law because it clearly and abhorrently tramples the rights of all human beings to be secure in their person. This view has been advanced most articulately by Fernando Tesón (1998).[44]

Sovereignty and the Juridical Equality of States

Of course, a crucial aspect of the legal concept of state sovereignty is the juridical equality of the states in the international system. However, Michael Byers notes the fiction of legal equality masks significant differences in a state's actual power, and those power differences suggest that states have differing abilities to influence the content of international law (Byers 1999, pp. 35–40). Byers argues that powerful states tend to be more engaged in the international system, and therefore their acts have a disproportionate impact on the evolution of customary international law. Additionally, they tend to maintain larger diplomatic corps that give them added influence in bilateral and multilateral treaty drafting. As I argued in Chapter 1, one of the consequences of the establishment of the ICC is that it gives the judges of that court substantial authority to direct the evolution of the practical application of the laws of war.[45] I elaborate on this power of the ICC below. This power to define the law comes partly at the expense of powerful states that have historically determined the application of the rules of international humanitarian law through their own practices of discourse and prosecution.

Critical legal theorists have noted that international law, like virtually all legal orders, is not inherently fair in its application precisely because power plays a role in the development and application of the law (Kairys 1998). One important change in the legal rights of sovereign states that ratify the Rome Statute of the ICC is that they grant significant authority to the court's prosecutor and judges to determine whether or not particular actions carried out by individuals constitute violations of international humanitarian law. As a consequence, the establishment of the court shifts real legal control from the great powers toward this newly constituted international judiciary. Since military powers historically defined the application of international criminal law standards to their own soldiers, personnel, and citizens, they exercised enormous discretion over the practical definition of the crimes mentioned under the Geneva Protocols of 1949 or the Genocide Convention.[46] If the judges of the ICC are fair and professional in their application of the standards, this development could weaken the argument that international law ultimately is a legal system that serves the interest of only the most powerful states that participate in the international legal system.

Sovereignty and Individuals as Subjects of International Law

Historically, individuals were not recognized as subjects of international law, and it was assumed that only states, and not individuals, had rights and obligations under international criminal law (Bentham 1786–89). Chinese writers on international law have recently reiterated this view, claiming that international law gives no status to individuals on Chinese territory to claim rights against the state (Chiu 1988). However, this argument has been widely criticized as being the obvious manipulation of international law by totalitarian states to preserve their own absolute power (Chen 1989). Moreover, in the twentieth century, the view that individuals have both rights and obligations under international law has gained widespread acceptance (Falk, Kratochwil, and Mendlovitz 1985, p. 205). Indeed, since international law, like any legal system, is ultimately a standard for human behavior, it would seem to be a logical necessity that it would regulate individual human conduct, even if its formal constitution is premised on specific acts undertaken by states as corporate entities (Falk, Kratochwil, and Mendlovitz 1985, p. 205).

International criminal law as a field rests upon the reality that states have deliberately created rights and duties for individuals under international treaties and customs.[47] The ICC is a direct challenge to traditional conceptions of state sovereignty because it creates a supranational judicial authority with the power to rule whether or not particular uses of force by state officials are criminal violations of international law, subject to punishment.[48] This means that the court, and not states alone, will have the authority to help determine what constitutes a legal use of force. Of course, the notion that states have a monopoly on the legitimate use of force within their territory is central to the legal concept of sovereignty. That circumstance is not undermined by the establishment of the ICC because the court does not constitute any new authority with police power. However, states that ratify the statute give the court a role in determining which particular uses of force are legitimate. Consequently, the legal privileges of sovereignty are altered by the court's establishment. In effect, states that are parties to the ICC statute limit their own autonomy in determining whether or not the conduct of their public officials comports with obligations that states have adopted to limit their use of force.

Popular Sovereignty and the Legal Concept of State Sovereignty

State sovereignty is increasingly conceptualized as a phenomenon that creates both rights and responsibilities for governments.[49] In effect, there is an emerging norm in international law that states owe certain obligations to their own citizens and to the international community. The political liberty that comes with state sovereignty has to be tempered by a responsibility to exercise that liberty in a way that is not severely detrimental to people living inside or outside of the sovereign state's jurisdiction. For example, the emerging preference in the international legal system for democratic forms of government suggests that sovereign states have a legal obligation to consider the needs of the citizens of their state. In all the states where the United Nations has recently been involved in "state-building" exercises after a period of war or other upheaval, democracy has repeatedly been the form of government preferred by international organizations and their members (Murphy 2000, 123). This pattern of state practice suggests an emerging standard that participatory forms of political organization are to be preferred over forms of government where a political elite is not accountable to the general populace (Fox 2000, pp. 71–86).

This suggests that the legal concept of sovereignty in international law now focuses increasingly on the popular sovereignty of the citizenry rather than on the political sovereignty of the government. The now extensive pattern of international treaties that recognize participatory political rights means there has been a shift in the locus of sovereignty. As Greg Fox writes, this "shift in the locus of sovereignty undermines arguments against participatory rights based on an infringement of sovereignty. For a nondemocratic regime to claim that participatory rights violate its national sovereignty begs the question of whether that regime has legitimate authority to make such a statement" (Fox 2000, p. 89).

Another example of the increasing significance of the norm of state responsibility overtaking the rights aspect of state sovereignty can be seen in the emergence of "The Guiding Principles on Internal Displacement" adopted by the UN Commission on Human Rights.[50] In this case, we are not dealing with legally binding law. Still the development of workable norms in this area, their adoption by a major UN body, and their use in the field by NGOs and other actors all serve to reinforce the notion that sovereign states have responsibilities and not just rights. The question of internally displaced persons is a classic example of a lacuna created in international law by the doctrine of absolute state sovereignty (Cohen 2004). Of course, persons displaced across international boundaries now benefit from a number of international law rights and privileges. Conversely, persons displaced from their homes by armed conflict who remain within the boundaries of a sovereign state have more limited international legal rights because such persons are traditionally at the complete mercy of their sovereign state governments (Cohen 2004). "The Development of the Guiding Principles for Internally Displaced Persons" is a study in the growing recognition that states have obligations to their own citizens. Roberta Cohen writes: "[w]hile acknowledging that primary responsibility rests with national authorities, the Guiding Principles recast sovereignty as a form of national responsibility toward one's vulnerable populations with a role provided for the international community when governments did not have the capacity or willingness to protect their uprooted populations" (Cohen 2004, p. 459). We are witnessing the gradual strengthening of the notion of popular sovereignty in the international political normative order at the expense of strict privileges of state sovereignty. State sovereignty is increasingly only viewed as legitimate to the extent that it gives expression to the popular sovereignty rights of the people.

The ICC creates new norms that are of precisely this type. The primary effect of the ICC on member states' sovereign rights is to create an important institutional incentive for member states to prosecute genocide, war crimes, or crimes against humanity when they occur on the states' territory. Since the ICC only has jurisdiction if states fail to prosecute themselves,[51] the existence of the court puts pressure on states to exercise their own criminal jurisdiction over these crimes. In the absence of the ICC, other things being equal, states would have more latitude to decide for themselves whether or not it was politically desirable to prosecute these types of cases. Of course, states had already accepted the legal obligation to punish or extradite for genocide if they ratified the 1948 Genocide Convention, and grave breaches of the war crimes law if they ratified the Geneva Conventions of 1949.[52] What is new about the ICC is that it threatens to proceed with international enforcement of these crimes if states fail to punish violators. In effect, the ICC promises to uphold a certain minimal standard of compliance with the requirement on states to punish violations of international criminal law. This can be viewed as recognizing the rights of the citizens of states to be free from victimization as a result of crimes recognized under international criminal law. As such, it is a modification of the meaning of state sovereignty.

Of course, in some cases, states will be glad to shift the burden of prosecution to the ICC rather than undertake such prosecutions themselves. This possibility is discussed later on. But for the majority of states, the incentive will clearly be to handle such matters within their own legal systems.

Sovereignty Implications of the ICC for State Parties

The ICC is dependent on sovereign states in order for it to function effectively. However, it also creates incentives that are likely to modify state behavior in significant ways. Over time, that modified behavior will likely change peoples' expectations around the world about the enforcement of criminal sanctions for gross human rights abuses. These changes will be brought about through the exercise of individual states' sovereign rights and privileges, not by undermining them.

The ICC creates incentives in two different directions. First, as its founders intended, it creates an incentive for states to be more consistent in punishing violations of international criminal law that occur on their territory. However, the first few investigations that the ICC has undertaken in Uganda and the Congo and the recent request for court action in Burundi suggest another dynamic that is likely to develop between states and the ICC.[53] Second, for weak states that have difficulty maintaining law and order on their own territory, the ICC creates a tremendous incentive and a standing mechanism to request international assistance in carrying out investigations and trials of gross human rights abusers. This is a type of burden shifting that transfers responsibility from the individual state to the ICC.

Of course, given its own resource constraints, the ICC will be tremendously limited in the number of such cases that it can take on this basis. To combat this problem, the ICC is permitted to take funding donations from private sources.[54] One hopes that a sufficient number of governments, foundations, and/or private individuals will be willing to donate funds to ensure that the most egregious cases of violations of international criminal law will be adequately investigated and prosecuted. However, it is far from certain that the potential donor pool is equal to the task of providing enough funds to deal with what may be an unfortunately large number of war crimes or crimes against humanity for the foreseeable future.

For state parties, the most intrusive changes in sovereignty norms will appear when the ICC prosecutes a case with respect to events that took place on that state's territory or involving its citizens. The power of the ICC prosecutor to conduct on site investigations under Part 9 of the ICC statute was an extremely contentious issue during the ICC negotiations (Guariglia 1999, p. 231). The Rome Statute envisions two different scenarios for the capacity of the ICC prosecutor to conduct on-site investigations (Guariglia 1999). In the ideal situation, the state party on whose territory the investigation is being conducted will be willing to cooperate with the investigation. In that case, the Rome Statute provides for an elaborate set of notification requirements designed to facilitate close cooperation between the prosecutor's office and the relevant state party (Guariglia 1999). However, it was also felt that it would be important for the prosecutor to have some power to conduct interviews even when the state was either completely ineffective, and therefore unable to facilitate the ICC prosecutor's investigation, or in situations where the state was unwilling to cooperate. In those cases, the ICC statute gives the prosecutor's office some authority, in carefully limited circumstances, to conduct interviews of witnesses on the state's territory without the presence of states' officials, but only under the close supervision of the judges of the ICC's pretrial chamber (Guariglia 1999, pp. 232–3). This power of the ICC prosecutor can only be exercised on the territory of state parties.

This later scenario is a substantial change from the normal sovereign prerogatives of states. Still, it is an arrangement that states only enter into by voluntarily ratifying the ICC statute. A state's willingness to do this can be understood when looked at in conjunction with the emerging standard of popular sovereignty discussed above. By ratifying the ICC statute, sovereign governments are attempting to ensure that if the rule of law should break down in their societies, resulting in massive violations of international criminal law, they, via the international community, have the capacity to bring the individual perpetrators to justice. This international intervention could be interpreted as a step toward restoring the legitimate sovereignty of the people, since in a time of lawless conflict, the true sovereign authority of the people would be incapable of expression. Because of this, the sovereign states feel a need to ratify the ICC statute, granting investigative powers to the ICC prosecutor and judges in advance.

Sovereignty Implications of the ICC for Nonstate Parties

The central legal implication for states that have not ratified the Rome Statute is that their nationals could be tried by the ICC if they commit crimes encompassed by the ICC within the territory of a state that has ratified the Rome Statute.[55] Additionally, nonstate parties could be tried through the Security Council mechanism, even with respect to events that happen on the territory of a nonstate party.[56] These developments, while significant, do not substantially change the *legal* situation that United Nations member states faced prior to the establishment of the ICC. As a matter of power politics, the ICC may command more authority to bring suspects to justice than would be the case with municipal legal systems of many less powerful states. As a result, the ICC may make deliberate political action by states to shield persons from accountability more difficult. However the view that the ICC statute creates new legal obligations for nonstate parties cannot be sustained. To the extent that the court may have an impact on the exercise of nonstate parties' sovereign rights, it does so in a way that is perfectly consistent with existing international law.

In the closing days of the Clinton administration, David Scheffer lobbied for states supporting the ICC to agree to limit the ability of the court to detain the official personnel of nonstate parties. He said: "we believe there should be a means to preclude the automatic surrender to the Court of official personnel of a nonparty state that acts responsibly in the international community and is willing to exercise and capable of exercising complementarity with respect to its own personnel" (Scheffer 2000). Scheffer referred to this as a "fundamental issue [that] needs to be resolved ... [whose] outcome would open the door for the United States to become the good neighbor to the Court" (Scheffer 2000). Of course, this issue was never resolved in a way that was satisfactory to the United States' government, even under the Clinton administration.

International law is based on the foundational rule that a state cannot be obligated to obey a treaty unless it agrees to so obligate itself.[57] Diane Amann has argued forcefully that the ICC creates "non-consensual" legal jurisdiction in a way that violates the principle that treaties are not binding on nonsignatory states.[58] As Amann rightly points out, it is essential to the quasidemocratic legitimacy of international law that states cannot be made to accept international legal obligations except through their own consent. However, I simply disagree with her assessment that the ICC statute violates this principle.

The only legal difference for citizens of nonstate parties who commit war crimes or crimes against humanity after the entry into force of the ICC statute and those of ratifying states is the increased choice of forums in which such persons might be tried. As a legal matter, it seems there is little difference between individuals being held responsible for violations of municipal law in states they visit versus being held responsible for violations of international law in states they visit. The traditional rules of international law have long maintained that states have the jurisdiction to prosecute foreigners for conduct on their territory.[59] As many advocates of the ICC have pointed out, there is no logical reason why such states should be barred from cooperating by a multilateral treaty to punish conduct that each of them had a clear right to punish individually.

Amann offers a series of arguments to prove that this transfer of jurisdiction from national legal systems to a supranational court is illegitimate. The central line of reasoning is that ICC jurisdiction is substantially different from one state transferring its territorial judicial authority to another. Here the argument relies on the fact that many states have been reluctant to grant such authority in the context of European judicial cooperation (Amann 2004, p. 194). However, arguing that states have been reluctant for political reasons to engage in this practice is not the same thing as arguing that there is a well-recognized rule of international law that disallows the practice. If this were the case, the entire concept of extraterritorial jurisdiction would necessarily be moot.

Amann goes on to argue that the ICC is different from states exercising jurisdiction over crimes on their territory individually because ICC decisions are much more likely to have precedent-setting effects (Amann 2004, p. 194). She cites as evidence of this the decision by the U.S. federal ninth circuit court in *Doe 1 v. Unocal*,[60] where the judges relied in part on a legal standard developed by the UN ad hoc criminal tribunals.[61] However, it is simply incorrect to consider this as an imposition on American sovereignty. The judges in the American court were not compelled to follow the international precedent in this case. Instead, they *chose* to do so. In so doing, they were exercising U.S. sovereign rights by voluntarily complying with emerging international standards. This is a consensual acceptance of the legitimacy of international norms, not an imposition by a supranational court that is compelled against the will of a state sovereign.

If the ICC develops into a globally respected judicial institution, there is every reason to believe it will issue decisions interpreting the laws of war in ways that diverse legal scholars will find persuasive. The ICC may indeed have a definitive impact on shaping the legal enforcement norms concerning these international crimes. Politically, this undoubtedly weakens the ability of the United States and other great powers to shape the development of these international norms to their own liking. This fact is at the core of some of the opposition to the court within the U.S. government. Of course, the United States can resist normative developments that occur at the ICC and limit their tendency to be enshrined in customary international law by consistently objecting to the ICC's practice. This is undoubtedly part of the unstated logic behind the campaign of the Bush administration to belittle the ICC at every available turn. But the precedent-setting effects of the ICC could always be resisted by U.S. judges. The Rome Statute clearly states that its contents cannot "be interpreted as limiting or prejudicing in any way existing or developing rules of international law for purposes other than this statute."[62] This gives sufficient latitude to municipal judges to reach their own interpretations of provisions of international humanitarian law, even if they are at odds with rulings by ICC judges.

All of this means that the complaints that the ICC creates unfair legal effects on nonstate parties, through precedent or some other mechanism, are really not substantial.

The ICC and the Relationship Between Law and War

Since 2001, the policy of the U. S. government has been to defend the idea that the United States is entitled to use force preemptively as an extension of the traditional right to self-defense enshrined in Article 51 of the UN Charter.[63] A number of American legal scholars have perplexingly defended the legality of this proposition.[64] The American position does not recognize a similar right on the part of other states to use force against the United States if they feel similarly threatened. This lack of reciprocity will ultimately undermine the credibility of international law itself if the United States continues to pursue this route. Curtis Doebbler and Maha Eid argue persuasively that, at best, the legal reasoning behind these arguments involves a selective interpretation of existing law, and, at worst, an attempt by respected scholars to ensure their own access to the corridors of power by saying what powerful government officials want to hear (Doebbler and Eid 2004). The issue is relevant here because it is essential to understand the legal debate about the impact of the ICC statute on nonstate parties in the context of this larger political question regarding the relationship between U.S. national security strategy and international law. Much of the world is now quite convinced that the United States aims to exempt itself entirely from compliance with the rules of international humanitarian law. The United States need not accede to the ICC statute if it does not believe it is in American interests to do so. Still, it is unnecessary for the United States to complain that the establishment of the ICC unfairly impinges on U.S. sovereignty. The U.S. may not like the existence of the court, but it has no legal right to prevent other states from establishing it and attempting to develop the ICC into an effective institution.

Others have argued that the debate between the United States and supporters of the ICC about the effect of the Court's statute is, in effect, a conflict between two differently valued positions: preserving traditional sovereignty rules of international law versus ensuring an end to impunity for the perpetrators of severe international crimes.[65]

However, I would argue that the Rome Statute was actually careful to balance these values. As we have seen it is true that the existence of the court potentially impacts the citizens of nonstate parties. However, it does so in a way that does not substantially change their legal rights. As a practical matter, however, it increases the likelihood of prosecution because it establishes an independent court. This is the real source of the hostility toward the ICC's impact on nonstate parties, and it really is not a legal complaint but rather a political one. The establishment of the ICC may very well lessen the capacity of powerful states to use extralegal political pressure to block the prosecution of persons accused of ICC crimes when they see such prosecutions as contrary to their national interests. This is an objection to the ICC's political impact on (some) sovereign states' de facto autonomy. It is not a reasonable legal objection to the ICC's impact on transforming the legal concept of state sovereignty.

Conclusions

Ad hoc efforts to enforce international criminal law in the wake of mass killings have succeeded in establishing the concept of *individual* responsibility for these crimes. However, such trials have by definition occurred only irregularly and consequently have struggled to establish the legitimacy of the normative order they seek to enforce.

The negotiations that led to the development of the ICC statute and the normative rules it contains were characterized by an open discussion in which many NGOs took part. The rules, procedures, and crimes embodied in the ICC statute are the result of a broadly consensual, rational, communicative discourse. Consequently, the ICC stands in a considerably stronger position to gain worldwide respect and legitimacy. This is because the ICC's rule system embodies the principles developed through open discussion to ensure logical coherence and practical functionality.

The complementarity principle in the Rome Statute gives broad powers to the ICC prosecutor and judges to determine whether or not their international jurisdiction should be exercised. This means that political authorities in the relevant state cannot block prosecution simply by failing to bring charges. Importantly, the permanence of the Rome Statute affirms the international law norm that no perpetrators of war crimes, crimes against humanity, or genocide should escape justice. At the same time, however, because the ICC is a court of last resort, it also leaves international judges and prosecutors with a great deal of discretion about whether or not to proceed with a particular prosecution when some judicial or truth and reconciliation process is undertaken at the national level. This also allows the prosecutor to take into account more practical if less legal concerns.

If the prosecutor determines that investigating a particular leader who is involved in ongoing hostilities is likely to reduce the chance of a negotiated peace settlement in the short run, he can decline to open an investigation. Experience shows, however, that it will not always be wise to do so. Leaders who rely on mass violence to maintain power rarely modify their behavior of their own accord. The ICC also has the option of quietly collecting evidence and biding its time. It will be possible for the ICC to choose its moments for taking action. If the prosecutor misuses his authority, the result will likely be isolation and weakness of the court. If the prosecutor's discretion is used wisely, the permanence and complementarity rules of the ICC mean that time is now on the side of justice, not impunity.

Postscript: Construction Continues

Habermas's theory of democracy creates an interesting tension between the boundary of the political community and the preservation of democratic decision making itself (Hayward 2007). This creates a particular challenge when applying his thoughts on the legitimacy of law to the international arena because it is difficult to conceptualize the boundaries of world citizenship. He writes, "Unlike moral rules, legal rules do not norm possible interactions between communicatively competent subjects *in general* but the interaction contexts of a concrete society (Habermas 1996, p. 124).

This raises a significant issue of how we can conceive of the legitimacy of international law in general, or the international criminal court in particular, on the basis of Habermas's thought on the generation of valid legal norms through the exercise of communicative rationality. Clearly, the international political system is not perfect at reaching the standards that Habermas's normative theory argues are ideally necessary. I have argued instead that we can assess the degree to which particular discussions of international legal norms approximate the standard that Habermas proposes. In the case of the ICC, the actual negotiations of the text came closer than scholars of international politics would expect is possible.

Habermas says:

> Legal norms stem from the decisions of a historical legislature; they refer to a geographically delimited legal territory and to a socially delimitable collectivity of legal consociates, and consequently to particular jurisdictional boundaries. These limitations in historical time and social space result simply from the fact that legal subjects cede their authorizations to use coercion to a legal authority that monopolizes the means of legitimate coercion and if necessary employs these means on their behalf. Every earthly monopoly on violence, even that of a world government, has finite dimensions, which remain provincial in comparison with the future and the universe. Hence the establishment of a legal code calls for rights that regulate membership in a determinate association of citizens, thus allowing one to differentiate between members and nonmembers, citizens and aliens.

In the case of the ICC negotiations, it is particularly difficult to conceptualize the boundaries of such a citizenry. To the extent that drafters of the ICC statute sought to create an institution that would apply to all human beings, it would seem that the de facto citizenship they had in mind was indeed all living human persons.

We could also treat the relevant political community in a more limited way, as including only the citizens of those states that have ratified the ICC statute.

Potential

The jurisdiction of the International Criminal Court will likely be limited for some time by the failure of some states to ratify it. But this should not be viewed as a failure of the ICC to establish universal norms. It is difficult to imagine that anyone would really claim that the acts proscribed by the ICC treaty should be accepted. Instead, the mere existence of the ICC should come to serve as a warning to all that the age of impunity is coming to an end. Even in states that have not ratified the ICC, there will be pressure to enforce these minimal standards of international justice. It may take decades for the ICC to live up to its potential. Problems with financing the court's operations, obtaining evidence, and arresting suspects will be frequent.[1] Still, the potential of an international court, administering widely respected justice, to transform the relationship between law and war is great. Consequently, we must nurture the court's early successes and be patient with its failures.

Scholars like myself who argue that norms are an important element in explaining outcomes in world politics ultimately must demonstrate that the existence of norms alters the behavior of significant actors. Much research has done exactly that (Klotz 1995). However, for the most part, this book has set aside the question of determining whether or not the norms institutionalized by the process of establishing the ICC have already begun to change the way state leaders make choices regarding the use of force. Primarily, that was necessary because I undertook a separate task here of analyzing the political process through which these norms were institutionalized, and because with the court's formal establishment in July 2002 coming well after this project was first conceived, it seemed impractical to address this question fully here.

However, in the first years of the court's operation some significant preliminary evidence has begun to emerge that individuals responsible for carrying out the war in Iraq in 2003 worried a great deal about the existence of the new court. Various British peace movement groups, including the Stop the War Coalition, Peacerights, and Military Families Against the War, have filed briefs with the ICC accusing British forces of war crimes. In its submission to the ICC on May 5, 2005, Peacerights said it had a "particular concern that attacks, and methods used, were pursuant to the impermissible military objective of regime change rather than dealing with the threat to international peace and security of Iraq's alleged weapons of mass destruction". It added: "There may have been attacks and weapons systems used (particularly cluster munitions) in locations where civilians were particularly at risk (for example, urban areas) where the military objective pursued was intrinsically connected to regime change."[2] Because of the ICC's complementarity rules, it is unlikely that the court will take up these charges formally. However, as a result of the charges, some United Kingdom government sources have revealed information about their thinking regarding the ICC in March 2003.

While the failure of the United States or Iraq to ratify the ICC statute meant that their soldier's acts would not be subject to ICC scrutiny, British forces enjoyed no such guarantee. Lord Michael Boyce, who was chief of the defence staff in Britain in 2003, was quoted in newspapers as having been concerned about ICC prosecution when preparing for the Iraq war in 2003.[3] Apparently Boyce requested a legal opinion from Attorney General Lord Peter Goldsmith establishing that the attack on Iraq was legal. He did this precisely because he thought it would offer some defense against prosecution at the ICC, apparently not understanding that the ICC did not as of yet have jurisdiction over the international law crime of aggression.

Attorney General Lord Goldsmith issued advice to the prime minister in 2003 that was recently leaked to the press in which he noted the court "would only be able to exercise jurisdiction over UK personnel if it considered that the UK prosecuting authorities were unable or unwilling to investigate and, if appropriate, prosecute the suspects themselves."[4] The Goldsmith advice to Prime Minister Tony Blair on March 7, 2003 also included the comment that "given the controversy surrounding the legal basis for action, it is likely that the [international criminal] court will scrutinise any allegations of war crimes by UK forces very closely."[5] In another recent newspaper interview Lord Boyce, the concerned military official, said "I wanted to make sure that we had this anchor which has been signed by the Government law officer . . . It may not stop us from being charged but, by God, it would make sure other people were brought into the frame as well," by which Boyce meant that he felt this ensured the civilian political leadership would be made as vulnerable to prosecution as military officials.[6]

Of course, the fact that British military and political officials took steps to assess and minimize their vulnerability to ICC prosecution is not the same thing as demonstrating that the existence of the ICC significantly impacted decisions about how to wage the war or whether or not to wage the war at all. Still, this evidence does demonstrate that the existence of the ICC has become a significant factor in the decision-making of some state leaders when developing policies that call for the use of military force.

There is also some preliminary evidence from the work of the ICTY and ICTR that international trials can have a positive impact on postconflict peace-building. While a number of factors clearly contributed to declining support for Slobodan Milošević and his forced removal from power, the existence of the ICTY and its condemnation of atrocities carried out by nationalist extremists was apparently one of those factors. Payam Akhavan has noted that the arrest of Momčilo Krajišnik, a founding leader of the nationalist Serb Democratic Party, did not lead to any significant outrage among other Serb leaders. He argues that this is considerable evidence of the success of the ICTY in discrediting virulent nationalism as a political strategy (Akhavan 2001).

Of course, war crimes trials are not a panacea. The worst incident of violence in Bosnia, the Srebrenica massacre in 1995, took place after key Serb nationalist leaders involved in the attack had already been indicted by the ICTY (Meron 1997). This evidence suggests that war crimes tribunals may not be enough of a deterrent to change the behavior of leaders who are already committed to a strategy of violence, but they may be a significant force in discrediting leaders who pursue those strategies over time. David Wippman voiced a similar sentiment when he wrote that international criminal justice likely will "strengthen whatever internal bulwarks help individuals obey the rules of war, but the general deterrent effect of such prosecutions seems likely to be modest and incremental, rather than dramatic and transformative" (Wippman 1999, p. 488).

Notes

Chapter 1

1. Robertson 2000, p. 179.
2. WARRANT OF ARREST FOR JOSEPH KONY ISSUED ON 8 JULY 2005 AS AMENDED ON 27 SEPTEMBER 2005 No. ICC-02/04-01/05; 27 September 2005. pp. 1–23. PRE-TRIAL CHAMBER II Before Judge Tuiloma Neroni Slade, Judge Mauro Politi, Judge Fatoumata Dembele Diarra. Registrar: Mr Bruno Cathala. SITUATION IN UGANDA. (Public redacted version.) Available at http://www.icc-cpi.int/library/cases/ICC-02-04-01-05-53_English.pdf.
3. Ibid.
4. Hobbes, Flathman, and Johnston 1997.
5. As of 2007, there are 105 states that are party to the Rome Statute. See Figure 7.5 on p. 139. For updates, see http://www.un.org/law/icc/.
6. See Article 15, The Rome Statute of the ICC, UN Doc. A/Conf. 183/9, available at http://www.icc-cpi.int/library/about/officialjournal/Rome_Statute_English.pdf.
7. Making arrests and gathering evidence for the ICC is not so isolated from political pressure, because the court relies on states for these functions. Since normally judges are not eligible for reelection, they have little obvious need to please the states' parties. Ibid., Article 36, Paragraph 9.
8. Perry's example is from the Balkan wars of the early 1990s, but the twentieth-century list of atrocities is long and many incidents could be used to make the same point.
9. For a much earlier analysis of the role of argument in world politics, see Lasswell 1935/1965.
10. The Rome Statute of the ICC, UN Doc. A/Conf. 183/9, is available at http://www.icc-cpi.int/library/about/officialjournal/Rome_Statute_English.pdf and is reprinted in Schabas 2001 and Lee 1999. Schabas also includes the draft Elements of Crimes and the draft Rules of Procedure and Evidence, which were adopted without amendment by the Assembly of State Parties in New York, September 3–10, 2002.
11. Some early advocates of a permanent ICC suggested that the court should be established through an amendment to the UN Charter (Broms 1995). In Chapter 4 we see why that did not come to pass.

Chapter 2

1. Albert Camus, "Neither Victims nor Executioners," in Combat, cited in Zinn 1997.
2. Process tracing, as it is used in this study, is explained below on pp. 34–35. For a discussion of the method generally, see George and Bennett 2005, Ch. 10.

3. Thick description is explicated in Geertz 1973.
4. For an authoritative review of the provisions of the Rome Statute and the text itself, including a discussion of the central complementarity provisions, see Cassese, Gaeta, and Jones 2002; and Lee 1999.
5. See Article 15, The Rome Statute.
6. Though making arrests and transferring suspects to the ICC may not be so isolated from political pressure, because the court will rely on states for these functions. Judges are not normally eligible for reelection. Ibid. Article 36, Paragraph 9.
7. I discuss the unique role of NGO discourse in more theoretical detail in the section on agency and throughout the discussion of the empirical case material in the later chapters.
8. It should be clear from the foregoing discussion that it is not my assertion that NGO discourse, or some other NGO action, caused the establishment of the ICC in the sense of being a necessary or sufficient condition for producing an ICC.
9. For discussion of another recent case where international NGOs may have played some role in the construction of a new multilateral institution, the European Monetary Union, see Van Esch 2001.
10. For instance, Waltz classically assumes that states pursue power first to maintain or improve their security in a self-help world (Waltz 1986, p. 117). Progressing from a neoliberal position, Goertz has made an impressive effort to develop a theory of international institution formation that recognizes that purposes or policy problems are socially constructed. See Goertz 2003.
11. In Searle's words, "Institutional facts are, in this sense, ontologically subjective, even though they are epistemically objective" (1995, p. 63). In light of Searle's observation, the claim by King, Keohane, and Verba that questions about obligation, legitimacy, citizenship, and sovereignty are philosophical and not empirical, and therefore not subject to processes of scientific inference, is inexplicable (1994, p. 6). More precisely, many questions about intersubjective phenomena like these are empirical in nature, though there also are some philosophical questions related to these phenomena. This view of social facts takes as foundational the view of language first elaborated by Wittgenstein (1968).
12. As of 2006, the ICTY spent $1.25 billion total, and indicted 161 suspects, for an average cost of about $7.8 million per indictment (Combs 2007, pp. 27–28).
13. On the conceptual difference, see Bull 1977, Ch. 2. At the time of writing Bull did not see much evidence for a Kantian transnational society of individuals, but much in the world has changed since 1977. On the implications of the ICC for the concept of the society of states in the English School, see also Buzan 2004.
14. Importantly, these "laws of nature" are not derived from utility, formal logic, or metaphysical fiat; for Pufendorf, Kratochwil, and myself, they rest on the fact that they are widely socially accepted as moral principles: "The moral quality of an action [. . .] results from the attitude people take toward the action, rather than in the act or its physical properties" (Kratochwil 1989, p. 139).
15. This is consistent with approaches taken in a great deal of more recent normative work, including Brysk 1994; Finnemore 1993; Keck and Sikkink 1998; Klotz 1995; Lynch 1999; Risse-Kappen, Ropp, and Sikkink 1999; Sandholtz and Stone Sweet 1998; and Wapner 1996.
16. For an excellent genealogy of police power and its application to world politics, see Dubber and Valverde 2006.
17. See also Boli and Thomas 1999.
18. Keck and Sikkink 1998, p. 204. Footnote references removed from original.
19. For an elaboration of the distinction between communicative action and strategic action, see Habermas 1984, esp. pp. 286–338.

20. On this point see also Hopf 1998, p. 184; and Klotz and Lynch 2007.
21. Frost makes an interesting observation that the "'unmasking' role of critical theory is itself supposed to be objective and explanatory," because it seeks "to explain (objectively)" how existing theories (i.e., Realism) uphold status quo power arrangements (Frost 1996, pp. 32–33).
22. For a recent empirical approach to discourse analysis that emphasizes the structural side of discourse, see Sjöstedt 2007.
23. The concept of a critical juncture was developed in Collier and Collier 1991. On path dependence see Arthur 1994; and Liebowitz, Margolis, and Lewin 2002.
24. By "social context" here I mean what Habermas refers to as the "lifeworld."
25. For a different approach to the formal analysis of discourse in the history of international politics see Alker Jr. 1988. Alker's piece makes a number of points, one particularly important one in this context being that the content of arguments matters in political outcomes, and normative justifications for actions are bound up with actors' behaviors as "reasons for actions" in the political world.
26. More specifically, some of the ineffective arguments advanced by members of the U.S. delegation were not well grounded in normative ethical principles. U.S. delegates did make principled arguments about due process concerns, and many of those recommendations for due process protections for the accused were accepted in the final compromise on the Rome Statute. See Scheffer 1998.
27. Since the second Bush administration officially rescinded the United States' signature to the Rome Statute in April 2002, the argument for U.S. exemption has been made more explicitly by officials at every level of the U.S. government. See for instance U.S. Ambassador for War Crimes Issues Pierre-Richard Prosper, Foreign Press Center Briefing (May 6, 2002), available at http://ftc.state.gov/9965.htm.
28. Below I describe these source materials in more detail.
29. For an excellent discussion of these issues, see the introduction to Douglas 1986.
30. See Kratochwil 1989, for elaboration of this argument.
31. For instance, the U.S. Department of Defense sent faxes to Germany, South Korea, and Argentina during the negotiations, threatening U.S. military withdrawal from the first two countries and opposition to developmental bank loans to the third if those countries did not withdraw ICC proposals that the U.S. Department of Defense found objectionable. All three states ignored the U.S. threat. (Two anonymous sources.)
32. Indeed, language itself depends on such commonly shared understandings; see Wittgenstein 1968.
33. Aristotle 1928.
34. The author thanks Alison Brysk for helping to develop this description of the topoi concept.
35. I have excluded Alexy's description of possible forms of normative argument and his transitional rules, which, while interesting for the development of his theory, are not particularly important for my proposed actual analysis of the discourse surrounding the founding of the ICC. Alexy's intervening discussion of these rules has also been omitted.
36. Audio recordings of the interviews were made to facilitate analysis.
37. A theme of central importance was the position taken by the U.S. government on various aspects of the negotiations and the dynamics of various elements of the large U.S. delegation.
38. On the importance of looking for disconfirming evidence, see King, Keohane, and Verba 1994, p. 19.
39. She focuses on Keck and Sikkink 1998; O'Brien et al. 2000; and Wapner 1996.

40. On the relationship between knowledge of world politics and its practice, see Haas 1997.
41. Here, admittedly, my own choices are constrained and limited by the fact that English is my first language and I have been educated with respect to particular academic discourses.

Chapter 3

1. Harry S. Truman, Address in San Francisco at the Closing Session of the United Nations Conference, June 26, 1945, San Francisco, CA.
2. On the role of nonstate actors in shaping discourses about world order generally in the interwar period and the foundation of the United Nations in particular, see also Lynch 1999, Ch. 7.
3. For a good, brief review of constructivist research efforts that tackle this problem, see Ruggie 1998, p. 19; see also Finnemore 1993; Klotz 1995; and Nau 2002.
4. On the agency of social actors in the creation of global institutions, see Lynch 1999, p. 177.
5. Cites the United Nations Secretariat, Historical Survey of the Question of International Criminal Jurisdiction, 8-12, UN Doc. A/CN.4/7/Rev. 1 (1949).
6. Specifically, the chief U.S. prosecutor, the U.S. Supreme Court Justice Robert Jackson, concluded his opening statement with the following appeal to the universal validity of the norms he sought to enforce: "And let me make clear that while the law is first applied against German aggressors, the law includes, and if it is to serve a useful purpose, it must condemn, aggression by any other nation, including those which sit here now in judgment"; cited in Persico 1994, p. 137.
7. Indeed, the Soviet Union attempted to make use of the Nuremberg trials to cover up its own responsibility for the Katyn massacre of Polish prisoners of war during World War II, by blaming the Nazis (Persico, 1994, pp. 250, 359; see also Abarinov 1993).
8. Morton undertakes an empirical study of the extent to which ILC members' positions are reflective of their national origins. While his ultimate conclusions are more nuanced than my summary suggests, this general statement is justified by his findings.
9. It is possible that Truman's decision to refer the issue of a permanent ICC to the United Nations was an effort to kill the proposal by prolonging the discussion of it. On the other hand, in the first week of his presidency, he argued forcefully for using a judicial process to deal with Nazi leaders rather than summary execution as the British preferred (Smith 1982, pp. 138–9).
10. See the Spiropoulos report from April 26, 1950, reprinted in Ferencz 1980, vol. 2, p. 185.
11. A. M. Rosenthal, "UN Seeking a World Code," *New York Times*, October 4, 1953.
12. Ibid.
13. Ibid.
14. United Nations 1954, para. 17.
15. United Nations 1954, Annex, Article 2.
16. United Nations 1954, Annex, Article 27.
17. United Nations 1954, Annex, Articles 28 and 9.
18. United Nations 1954, para. 18.
19. I wish to avoid the teleological suggestion that the emergence of an ICC was inevitable at any point or that it is the necessary logical outcome of any truly communicatively rational discourse. Neither Habermas nor myself think that communicatively rational political discourse leads inexorably to particular outcomes. Instead, my focus remains to show, in Weber's formulation, why things were so, and not otherwise, at a particular point in time. I do think that the extent to which political discourse approximates or fails

to approximate Habermas's model of communicative rationality is a factor that influences particular political outcomes.

Chapter 4

1. Woetzel et al. 1973.
2. For a review of the linguistic turn in IR scholarship, see Debrix 2003.
3. Bush 1991.
4. The Dispute Settlement Mechanism of the World Trade Organization (WTO) is an interesting exception where, for the most part, U.S. policy favored the judicialization of international trade disputes. The Uruguay Round treaties that established the WTO entered into force on January 1, 1995.
5. Cited in Meyer 2002.
6. Statement by William Jefferson Clinton authorizing the US signing of the Rome Statute of the International Criminal Court. December 31, 2000. Camp David, Maryland. (Emphasis added).
7. Another contextual factor for the ICC debate that was unique to the American political context in the 1990s was the dual meaning of the term "independent prosecutor." While NGOs and others argued in favor of creating an ICC with a strong "independent prosecutor," Kenneth Starr, the independent prosecutor appointed by Attorney General Janet Reno to investigate links between President Clinton and allegedly illegal Whitewater real estate transactions, had begun by 1998 to use his independent authority to pursue other matters, including the famous accusations of perjury committed by President Clinton. Even though the design and structure of the prosecutor's office as created under the ICC has nothing to do and very little in common with the structure of the office of an independent prosecutor under U.S. law, criticisms and fears of Starr's office became linked to the ICC project for at least some officials in Washington.
8. Hereinafter, the Genocide Convention.
9. From the Liberty Lobby newsletter *Spotlight* cited in Power 2002.
10. This is Senator Proxmire's observation, reported in Power 2002.
11. The legal effect of the U.S. reservations on the Genocide Convention is probably moot, since genocide is now a crime under customary international law and is therefore binding whether or not particular states have ratified the convention (Robertson 2000), and because the U.S. reservations are contrary to the purpose of the convention itself (Paust 2000). By 1999, 133 states had ratified the 1948 Genocide Convention, including the United States (Robertson 2000).
12. Convention on the Prevention and Punishment of the Crime of Genocide, 1948, Article VI.
13. Decisions in the UN's Sixth Committee about establishing an ad hoc committee and ultimately the preparatory committee to begin multilateral negotiations on drafting an ICC statute were taken by consensus, and U.S. support for proceeding was seen as essential. (Personal communication, Adrian Bos.)
14. Ruggie,1993b and 1996.
15. During the prior 35 years "a few lonely voices, such as [Prof.] Ferencz and Professor Bassiouni and one or two others held the torch aloft," urging the creation of an ICC as a standing body (Rosenstock 1994). However, for the most part, there was little serious diplomatic discussion of establishing a permanent ICC between 1955 and 1990.
16. Morton 2000. According to Morton, terrorism was a major motivating factor behind the few ICC discussions in the 1980s.

17. UN General Assembly, Provisional Verbatim Record of the eighth meeting, UN Doc. A/46/PV.8, at 29–30, cited in Ferencz 1992, p. 386.
18. See remarks of U.S. Representative Robert Rosenstock, UN GAOR 6th Comm., 46th Sess., 31st mtg., at 3, UN Doc. A/C.6/46/SR.31, 1991, cited in Ferencz 1992, pp. 386–7.
19. Ibid., cited in Ferencz 1992, p. 387.
20. The ILC's draft statute is reproduced in Morton 2000.
21. First published in 9 *Nouvelles Études Pénales* 1993, reprinted in Bassiouni, 1998.
22. In addition to the International Law Association effort mentioned above, Cherif Bassiouni's International Institute of Higher Studies in Criminal Sciences adopted a draft statute in 1991, and the ABA's International Law Section recommended the establishment of an ICC with jurisdiction over treaty crimes (Morton 2000).
23. Marc Grossman, "Remarks to the Center for Strategic and International Studies," Washington, D.C., May 6, 2002.
24. Perhaps this move was driven by concerns about the U.S. invasion of Panama. Further examination of this linkage would be informative.
25. Interestingly, drug trafficking is not included as crime within the jurisdiction of the court in the Rome Statute.
26. After the U.S. invaded Panama in 1989, Noriega was tried and imprisoned in the United States for violating drug trafficking laws. See Albert 1993.
27. During the first Persian Gulf War, the Allied leadership emphasized that the conflict was with the "war criminal" Saddam Hussein and not with the Iraqi people. Indeed, the U.S. administration rhetoric was sometimes criticized for overpersonalizing the conflict between G. H. W. Bush and Hussein.
28. In 2006, Saddam Hussein was convicted of "crimes against humanity" and sentenced to death in an Iraqi national court established following the U.S. occupation of that country. The definition of crimes against humanity employed by that court was adopted nearly verbatim from the definition used in the Rome Statute of the ICC. For details on the trial and its claim to legitimacy, see Moghalu 2006. Hussein could not be tried at the ICC because most of his crimes occurred prior to the court's establishment in July 2002.
29. In addition to the discussion of these events in Bass, see also Hagan 2003 and Scharf 1997a.
30. Klaus Kinkel, Germany's foreign minister, proposed a tribunal for Yugoslavia to avoid the need for armed intervention by Germany and to prevent a split that would result between his party and Kohl's Christian Democrats (Bass 2000). Bass cites Cassese, *Path to the Hague*, p. 67.
31. Scharf worked in the U.S. Department of the State Office of the Legal Advisor from 1989 to 1993. While he argues he was a wordsmith for policy mandates from higher level State and Justice Department officials, others have described him as the "architect" of U.S. policy; see Ferencz 1992.
32. Of course, this is only one anomaly in "an ocean of anomalies" confronted by rationalist IR theory, as Keohane and Martin acknowledge, referencing Lakatos's bountiful phrase (Keohane and Martin 2003).
33. That decision was taken by consensus. While China was still reluctant to proceed with an ICC treaty conference, they did not want to be the only state blocking the formation of a consensus interview with Bos, May 14, 2002 in The Hague. None of the other Security Council powers or Sixth Committee members, including Russia and the United States, opposed proceeding at this point in the process.
34. According to Bill Pace, the convener of the NGO coalition, his assistant Bettina Pruckmayr was the only person in the world working full time on the ICC issue in 1993. Personal communication, November 11, 2000.

35. Pace 1988, pp. 26–30.
36. Charles Trueheart, "Clout without a Country: The Power of International Lobbies," *The Washington Post*, June 18, 1998, p. A32.
37. Rik Panganiban, "A Permanent International Criminal Court: The NGO Coalition for an ICC," *UN Chronicle* 34, no. 4 (1997): 36.
38. Foundation Statement of the Faith-Based Caucus for an International Criminal Court, 1997, available at http://www.amicc.org/docs/Faith_causus_stmt.pdf.
39. Ibid.
40. This degree of NGO participation was facilitated by the deliberate efforts of the secretariat of the negotiations to facilitate open participation whenever possible. Interview with Bos, May 14, 2002, in The Hague.

Chapter 5

1. Kratochwil 1989. References, Greek spelling, and emphasis in the original have been removed.
2. This list may not be complete, but it is my judgment that it is nearly so, and that all of these premises had widespread acceptance during the negotiations in Rome and subsequently.
3. By "illegal" I mean acts of violence explicitly prohibited under international criminal law.
4. Of course, sometimes, interlocutors prefer not to commit particular statements they make to writing and may not even want particular arguments attributed to them at all. I became aware of a few such instances in the ICC debates during my interviews with the participants. In general, these comments suggest that there were relatively few claims that negotiators were prepared to make in private but not in public, and with a few notable exceptions discussed below, the things that they were reluctant to have released were not ultimately particularly important to the direction of the negotiations.
5. See discussion of January 1997 Amnesty International paper for a sophisticated use of this strategy.
6. Interview with H. Hebel, May 17, 2002, in The Hague; Interview with F. Guariglia, May 21, 2002, in The Hague.
7. UN General Assembly Resolution 50/46.
8. United Nations 1996.
9. UN General Assembly Resolution 51/207.
10. UN General Assembly Resolution 52/160.
11. ILC. 1994 draft ICC Statute, Articles 21 and 22, reproduced in Morton 2000.
12. Specifically, this Amnesty paper referenced Common Article 3 of the Geneva Conventions or Protocol II to the Geneva Conventions of 12 August 1949.
13. Other NGO papers subsequently picked up, reiterated, and developed this argument. See, for instance, Lawyers Committee for Human Rights (U.S.), 1997.
14. See pp. 72–73 in Chapter 4.
15. United States 1995.
16. Interestingly the Russian Federation was among the states that expressed some support for including the crime of terrorism under the jurisdiction of the court. See Russian Federation 1995.
17. Malaysia 1995.
18. In the language of the ICC negotiations, "treaty crimes" means simply acts that are made criminal under a particular treaty, often with less than universal ratification. This is in contrast to acts that are recognized as being criminal under customary international law and therefore apply to all states.

19. The NGOs that were part of the coalition disagreed among themselves about whether or not it was wise to insist that aggression should be a crime within the court's jurisdiction. One group that opposed including the crime of aggression was Lawyers Committee for Human Rights (U.S.), 1997. They understood that including aggression increased the likelihood that the big five states would insist on a strong role for the Security Council in controlling the court's docket.
20. Australia 1995.
21. Egypt 1995.
22. United Kingdom 1995.
23. Mexico 1995. Author's translation from Spanish.
24. United States 1995. The US delegate was referring colloquially to a treaty, the official name of which is the International Convention on the Suppression and Punishment of the Crime of Apartheid, adopted in 1973, entered into force in 1976. The United States offered a communicatively rational argument that drug crimes and terrorism cases required police and prosecution strategies that would be beyond the capability of the ICC.
25. Ireland 1997. The suggestion that countries who favored including more crimes might compromise on a mechanism that would allow the future consideration of additional crimes also reflected proposals that had been advanced by NGOs previously. See Lawyers Committee for Human Rights (U.S.) 1997.
26. China 1997; France 1997 and United States 1997.
27. Trinidad and Tobago 1997.
28. See Article 35 of ILC 1994 Draft statute, reprinted in Bassiouni, SICC, 1998, p. 665.
29. United Nations 1996.
30. China 1995.
31. China 1995.
32. Malaysia 1995.
33. Egypt 1995.
34. Mexico 1995.
35. Australia 1995.
36. Garcia, Martnez, and Darriba 1996. Circulated during the first Preparatory Committee meeting.
37. *Jus Cogens* are principles of international law that states have accepted are so fundamental that derogation from such a rule of law is never permitted under international law. These are also referred to as peremptory norms of international law. The Latin phrase means, literally, "compelling law."
38. Garcia, Martnez, and Darriba 1996.
39. Chile 1997. This remark is a year before Augusto Pinochet's detention in London, so it was not yet influenced by those events. The Chilean delegation was well aware of the pending investigations of Pinochet in Spanish courts.
40. Direct quotes are from the text adopted by the Preparatory Committee at its August 1997 session and are explained by the coordinator of this aspect of the negotiations, in Holmes 1999.
41. Presumably China was one of the final holdouts. The United States was prepared to accept the notion that the court could take jurisdiction when national courts were found "unwilling" to do so, as long as some other provision of the court's statute would have effectively allowed the United States to block prosecution of its own citizens, for example, a mechanism that required the UN Security Council to refer all cases before they could be considered. See U.S. statement before the UN from October 21, 1998, reprinted in Lee 1999.

42. The ABA ultimately urged ratification of the Rome Statute.
43. These references are to the post–Rome Statute statements of China and the United States.
44. Incidentally, the problems of trials in absentia was debated at length at this meeting, with the consensus being that fairness required the presence of the accused, except possibly in the most extreme of circumstances. Suikkari 1995, p. 216.
45. The British delegate noted that this was "a difficult matter and we must guard against putting political influence on the judicial process" (United Kingdom 1995). See also China 1995; Russian Federation 1995; and United States 1995.
46. Malaysia 1995.
47. Mexico 1995.
48. United States 1995.
49. Ibid.
50. Amnesty International, 1997a, p. 91. The UN General Assembly Resolution is A/45/121 14 December 1990.
51. Adrian Bos confirms that France maintained a position on the importance of the Security Council's being the mechanism to initiate cases that was essentially identical to that of the United States throughout the Preparatory Committee negotiations. Interview with Bos, May 14, 2002, in The Hague.
52. See Article 16, Rome Statute.
53. Interview with Helen Duffy, June 5, 2002, in The Hague; and interview with Lars Van Troost, May 3, 2002, in Amsterdam.
54. Interview with Troost, May 3, 2002, in Amsterdam.
55. That is, those without friends among the permanent five.
56. United States 1995.
57. Philippines 1997.
58. United Kingdom 1997. The UK also demonstrated a spirit of compromise at this point by endorsing the principle of having a pretrial chamber, even though such an institution does not exist in the common law.
59. United Kingdom 1997.
60. United States 1997.

Chapter 6

1. For instance, the *American Journal of International Law* published a series of summaries of the Preparatory Committee negotiations authored by the lead legal analyst for Amnesty International (Hall 1997, 1998a, 1998b, 1998c).
2. Interview with Adrian Bos, May 14, 2002, in The Hague.
3. In fact, Ambassador Scheffer once commented to the author that the fact that numerous NGO policy position statements were written and distributed did not mean that they influenced policy development in his office. In a government with an international legal affairs bureaucracy the size of that in the United States, it is not surprising that the policymaking would depend primarily on in-house analysis. But few governments have that luxury.
4. Rik Panganiban, "Like-Minded A to Z," *CICC Monitor—The Rome Treaty Conference*, 15, Rome, July 3, 1998, p. 1. The list included the following states; Andorra, Argentina, Australia, Austria, Belgium, Benin, Bosnia-Herzegovina, Brunei, Burundi, Canada, Chile, Costa Rica, Croatia, Czech Republic, Denmark, Egypt, Estonia, Finland, Gabon, Georgia, Germany, Ghana, Greece, Hungary, Ireland, Italy, Jordan, Latvia, Lesotho,

Liechtenstein, Lithuania, Malawi, Malta, Namibia, the Netherlands, New Zealand, Norway, the Philippines, Poland, Portugal, South Korea, Romania, Samoa, Senegal, Sierra Leone, Singapore, Slovakia, Slovenia, Solomon Islands, South Africa, Spain, Swaziland, Switzerland, Trinidad and Tobago, the United Kingdom, Uruguay, Venezuela, and Zambia.

5. HRW 1999. Available at http://www.hrw.org/worldreport99/special/icc.html.
6. Press Release: "Rights Group Praises Canadian Position on International Court," Richard Dicker, *Human Rights Watch*, June 15, 1998. Available at http://www.hrw.org/press98/june/cand0615.htm.
7. Press Release: "Rights Group Praises South Africa for Stand on International Criminal Court" Richard Dicker, Human Rights Watch, June 15, 1998. Available at http://www.hrw.org/press98/june/safr0615.
8. The author was able to attend similar meetings at the first meeting of that ICC's Assembly of State Parties in 2002. Typically a group of states would be brought together on a regional basis, and one or more experts from the NGO community would brief the interested states on issues that concerned the NGOs during that particular negotiating session. Other NGOs, particularly groups based in the states that were the target of persuasion, would be in attendance.
9. Pace 1998. An example of such a caucus was the faith-based caucus discussed in Chapter 4.
10. For a discussion of the organization of the conference by those most involved in the process, see Kirsch 1999 and Kirsch and Holmes 1999.
11. While the statute does make distinctions between crimes that can be committed in situations of international versus internal conflicts, it also provides for the ICC's jurisdiction over both types in some circumstances. For an extensive discussion of these issues see Lee 1999, Ch. 2.
12. Interview with Helen Duffy, June 5, 2002, in The Hague.
13. Letter to Secretary of Defense William Cohen from Kenneth Roth, executive director, HRW, April 10, 1998, quoting the policy *demarche* issued by the U.S. Department of Defense.
14. Press Release, "Human Rights Watch Condemns Pentagon Lobbying on the International Criminal Court" April 14, 1998, available at http://hrw.org/english/docs/1998/04/14/usint1086_txt.htm.
15. American behavior during the Rome negotiations suggests that U.S. officials were perfectly prepared to use such tactics. See discussion below at p. 120.
16. United Nations 2002, pp. 61–62.
17. Ibid, p. 61.
18. See also Boli and Thomas 1999 and Haas 1990.
19. United Nations 2002, p. 61.
20. Ibid, p. 62.
21. Ibid, p. 62.
22. Political scientists have developed an extensive and informative literature about the processes through which governments, bureaucracies, and other decision-making bodies make their decisions. That literature guided the analysis in this book. While the relevant literature is extensive, Allison 1971 is a classic in the field. On efforts to model the consequences of information flows on actors' attitudes and ultimately decisions, see Regenwetter, Falmagne, and Grofman 1999.
23. On analyzing the structural relationships of discourses, see Foucault 1972.
24. The most significant difference is probably that communicatively rational arguments are a broader category that include legal arguments but also all other forms of communication oriented toward reaching an understanding about how the world is, or about

how norms are or ought to be. Thus communicative action includes but is not limited to claims about existing legal rules.
25. Interview with Guariglia, May 21, 2002, in The Hague.
26. U.S. Ambassador for War-Crimes Issues David J. Scheffer (1997–2001), personal communication, March 6, 2003, Irvine, CA.
27. Interview with Niccolo Figa-Talamanca, June 11, 2002 in The Hague.
28. Interview with Cynthia Fairweather, May 28, 2002 in The Hague; and interview with Eve La Haye, July 2, 2002 in The Hague.
29. Interview with Adrian Bos, May 14, 2002 in The Hague.
30. ABA Task Force on an ICC and New York State Bar Association, "Joint Report with Recommendations to the House of Delegates: Establishment of an International Criminal Court," *International Lawyer* 27 (Spring 1993): 257.
31. Working Group on Improving the Effectiveness of the United Nations, "Report on Improving the Effectiveness of the United Nations in Advancing the Rule of Law in the World," *International Lawyer* 29 (Summer 1995): 300–1.
32. Amnesty International 1995 and Human Rights Watch 1996. These papers were discussed in Chapter 5.
33. Statement by David Scheffer, senior adviser and counsel to Ambassador M. K. Albright, U.S. permanent representative to the UN on the International Criminal Court, in the Sixth Committee, October 31, 1996, USUN press release #165 (96), p. 8.
34. Proposal of Germany, A/AC.249/1998/WG.3/DP.1 (1998). For discussion of this development see Wilmshurst 1999. For discussion of universal jurisdiction generally see also Paust 2000 and Ratner and Abrams 2001.
35. Two anonymous sources. According to one source, the German officials were not particularly impressed with the U.S. position and responded by requesting that the Americans be sure to pay their bills before leaving Germany.
36. Interview with Eve La Haye, July 2, 2002, in The Hague.
37. NGO issue papers had made the case for the more inclusive definition early on in the negotiating process; see, for instance, Amnesty International 1997.
38. "Definitions: Atrocious Acts, Withholding of Food Aid, and Sexual Violence Ignored by Canadian Compromise on Crimes Against Humanity, Warn Legal Experts," *On the Record* 11:1, published by The Advocacy Project, Washington D.C., July 2, 1998, p. 1, archived at http://www.advocacynet.org/news_view/news_84.html.
39. Canadian proposal quoted in ibid.
40. Ibid.
41. Ibid.
42. Ibid.
43. "French NGOs on the French Position," *On the Record*, The Advocacy Project, date and volume uncertain, p. 2. Also in this meeting the French insisted that the reservations should be permitted to the ICC statute and announced their intention to seek a high threshold of 60 or 80 state ratifications to trigger entry-into-force of the statute.
44. Ibid.
45. Article 7, The Rome Statute.
46. Ibid., Article 7, paragraph 1, line g.
47. "Aggression Splits the Rome Conference: Russia Straddles the Fence," *On the Record* 1:5, The Advocacy Project, Washington D.C., June 19, 1998. Available at http://www.advocacynet.org/news_view/news_78.html.
48. Ibid.
49. Because the Rome Statute entered into force in July 2002, proposed definitions of aggression will be open for adoption by the Assembly of State Parties in 2009.

50. This adverb was the subject of much debate during the Preparatory Committee meetings (Holmes, p. 50 in Lee 1999).
51. "Admissibility: US Pushing Hard to Sustain Challenge Proposal," *On the Record* 1:12, July 3, 1998, published by The Advocacy Project, Washington, D.C., available at www.advocacynet.org/news_view/news_85.html.
52. Ibid.
53. Personal communication, William R. Pace, November 10, 2000.
54. This issue is also discussed in Wippman 2004, p. 155.
55. For further discussion of this issue, see Struett 2005.
56. "French NGOs on the French Position," date and volume uncertain, p. 2.
57. Article 12, The Rome Statute.
58. Comments of Marc Perrin de Brichambaut, Director of Legal Affairs, French Foreign Ministry, cited in Alison Dickens, "A Conference of Difficulty, France Says," *Terraviva* Inter-Press Service, Rome, July 3, 1998.
59. Press Release: "E.U. Split Produces Weak Position on International Court," Richard Dicker, Human Rights Watch, June 15, 1998, available at http://www.hrw.org/press98/june/eu0615.htm.
60. It is interesting in this regard that the European Union does not seem to construct the British and French vetoes on the SC as being "their veto." Instead the majority of European nations seem to favor weakening the SC's role, at least as judged from the perspective of EU positions on the ICC.
61. Interview with Lars Van Troost, May 3, 2002, in Amsterdam.
62. During the Rome conference itself, the United Kingdom sometimes seemed to waiver in its commitment to an ICC prosecutor free of Security Council control. Some observers commented that this reflected a dispute between the Foreign Office and the Ministry of Defense, with the later fearing an independent prosecutor. NGOs were quick to note comments by British officials that reflected a weakening on this issue, and kept pressure on Blair's government to support the concept of an independent prosecutor in the final statute. See "'Rebellious' Rome Conference Demands Curbs on Security Council Veto Power: Britain Accused of Backtracking on Council Referral," *On the Record* 1:7, The Advocacy Project, Washington, D.C., June 23, 1998.
63. Yee 1999, p. 147. Yee was the head of Singapore's delegation to the ICC negotiations.
64. Personal communication, William R. Pace, Convenor, Coalition for an ICC; November 10, 2000.
65. Ken Roth of Human Rights Watch made this argument early at the Rome Conference; see *UN Diplomatic Conference of Plenipotentiaries on the Establishment of an International Criminal Court: Official Records,* Vol. II. P. 113. A/Conf.183/13.
66. *Terraviva* was published by Inter-Press Service, a nonprofit association of journalists accredited with UNESCO, with the support of NPWJ and the CICC. The article is "Burundi-Council Inaction on Genocide Shows Poor Record," *Terraviva*, no. 15, Rome, July 3, 1998, 1 and 4.
67. Ibid., 4.
68. Israel, Iraq, Yemen, Libya, and Qatar made a total of seven nations voting against the statute; there were 21 abstentions, and 120 votes in favor recorded.

Chapter 7

1. Cited in Power 2002, pp. 84, 533n65.
2. Article 126, The Rome Statute.
3. Interview with Lars Van Troost, May 3, 2002, in Amsterdam.

4. HRW is a New York–based international NGO that cooperated heavily with *Madres del Plaza del Mayo* based in Argentina, for instance.
5. For a political theory approach to thinking about the implications of the powers of the ICC and some possible implications of the ICC's political role in world politics, see Roach 2006.
6. Ratification data for both treaties is available at www.hrw.org.
7. For a preliminary effort to quantify various factors that significantly influence the decision to ratify the Rome Statute in particular states, see Struett and Weldon 2006.
8. Article 125 of the Rome Statute provided that states could sign the Rome Statute at any point after July 17, 1998, but before December 31, 2000. States which signed the statute could then ratify at a later time. After December 31, 2000, states could join the ICC by accession to the Rome Statute. Practically, there is little difference between accession and ratification of a multilateral treaty, but NGOs used the signature deadline to pressure states to act sooner rather than later in joining the Rome Statute.
9. China is the only permanent member that never signed. The United States withdrew its signature in April 2002.
10. Actually, these conferences continued after 2002. I simply bracket that point in time because that was the year that the statute entered into force.
11. "No Peace Without Justice"—International Conferences and Seminars, http://www.npwj.org/modules.php downloaded 2/28/05.
12. "No Peace Without Justice—Introducing No Peace Without Justice," http://www.npwj.org/modules.php?op=modload&name=Sections&file=index&req=viewarticle&artid=6&page=1. Downloaded 2/28/05.
13. Ibid.
14. In order: Nicaraguan Center for Human Rights; Women's Center of the University of the Regions; Unions of the Nicaraguan Caribbean Coast.
15. In order: The El Salvadoran Human Rights Commission; The Human Rights Institute of the Central American University; 23rd Century; Sustainable Peace; Center for the Promotion of Human Rights; Madeleine Lagadec, Legal Advocate for the Archbishop of San Salvador; the University of El Salvador; Minister of Justice for the Defense of Human Rights.
16. Committee for the Defense of Human Rights in Honduras.
17. In order: Group of Mutual Support; Myrna Mack Foundation; Rigoberta Menchu Tum Foundation; the Alliance against Impunity; Human Rights Legal Action Center; Institute of Human Rights of the University of San Carlos in Guatemala; Institute of Comparative studies of Criminology of Guatemala; Faculty of Human Rights of the University of Raphael Landívar; The Rope Association (a feminist group); the Human Rights Office of the Archbishop; the Social Work Office of the Archbishop; the National Human Rights Coordinatior of Guatemala; and the Inter-University Coalition for the International Criminal Court.
18. DECLARACION CENTROAMERICANA POR LA RATIFICACION DEL ESTATUTO DE ROMA, 14 March 2002, circulated by the Coalición Guatemalteca por la Corte Penal Internacional and reprinted in (ICC Digest 512, CICC).
19. In 2006, the Government of Guatemala addressed the ICC Assembly of State Parties as an observer and indicated that the government would be presenting the Rome Statute for consideration by the legislative branch in that country during 2007. "Intervencion de la Delegacion de Guatemala en su calidad de observador a la V Asamblea de Estados Parte del Estatuto de Roma—La Haya 23 de Noviembre de 2006." Available at http://www.iccnow.org/documents/Guatemala_GeneralDebate_23Nov06_Esp.pdf, accessed on August 18, 2007.
20. http://www.npwj.org.

21. ICC Digest #504, circulated by CICC, March 1, 2002. Released simultaneously as a CICC Press Release, Brussels, Belgium.
22. Ibid.
23. Ibid.
24. That analysis is based on the first 100 states to ratify the ICC statute through October 2005.
25. In her recently published work, Judith Kelley notes that she was unable to find a significant relationship between defense spending and ICC ratification, but that is because her model omits the important variable of the extent to which states already participate in supranational organizations (Kelley 2007, p. 579).
26. See Struett and Weldon (2006) for an ultimately somewhat unsatisfying effort to measure the state-by-state variation in pro-ICC NGO activity. A crucial problem is that the decentralized nature of NGO activities, with volunteers and paid staff working in multiple countries, it is virtually impossible to identify even simple measures, such as how much money particular NGOs spent on their ratification campaigns in particular states. While the information is sometimes available by organization, a total for what all relevant NGOs spent in a particular country on their pro-ratification efforts is difficult to ascertain. Also, much of NGOs' discursive activity was simultaneously directed at all states, so in such cases, there is no state-by-state variation in the strength of particular NGO efforts.
27. See, for instance, Amnesty International 2000.
28. Interview with Fabricio Guariglia, May 21, 2002, in The Hague.
29. CICC, http://www.iccnow.org/countryinfo/theamericas/argentina.html, downloaded on July 15, 2005.
30. CICC, http://www.iccnow.org/countryinfo/theamericas/argentina.html, downloaded on July 15, 2005.
31. Interview with Brigitte Suhr, March 30, 2002, in Los Angeles.
32. The full text of the ICC Act of 2001 passed by the British parliament is available at http://www.legislation.hmso.gov.uk/acts/acts2001/20010017.htm.
33. CICC, http://www.iccnow.org/countryinfo/europecis/unitedkingdom.html, downloaded on July 25, 2005.
34. CICC, http://www.iccnow.org/countryinfo/africa/uganda.html., viewed on July 27, 2005.
35. Information on the NGO expectations is reported at http://www.iccnow.org/countryinfo/africa/uganda.html.
36. HRW 2003, available at http://www.hrw.org/wr2k3/africa13.html.
37. On analyzing the use of communicative action in global public spheres, see also Mitzen 2005.
38. Insan Haklari Dernegi (Human Rights Association [of Turkey]).
39. Türkiye Insan Haklari Vakfi (Human Rights Foundation of Turkey).
40. Fédération Internationale des Ligues des Droits de l'Homme (International Federation for Human Rights).

Chapter 8

1. See, for instance, U.S. Department of State 2002.
2. For an alternative discussion of these issues, see Roach, 2006.
3. For a list of the hundreds of NGOs represented at the Rome conference by observers, see "The Final Act of the UN Diplomatic Conference of Plenipotentiaries on the

Establishment of an International Criminal Court: Annex IV," reprinted in Bassiouni 1998, pp. 109–12.
4. For instance, see statement by Bonafini and Petrini 1998.
5. Habermas 1996 and Rawls 2001, pp. 89–94.
6. The vote of 11 members of the UN Security Council in favor of granting the ICC jurisdiction over crimes committed in Darfur, Sudan, since July 1, 2002, demonstrates the breadth of international support at present for this still untested institution. UNSC Resolution 1593, March 31, 2005. Additional evidence of the diffuse perception of the court's legitimacy is the considerable diplomatic pressure that was put on the United States not to veto that resolution.
7. For a discussion of such criticisms, see Bass 2000 and Griffin 2001.
8. As of August 31, 2007.
9. Habermas 1996 and Rawls 2001.
10. Gutmann and Thompson 2004 and Habermas 1996.
11. It may be helpful to refer back to the main features of the court outlined in Chapter 1.
12. The U.S. objection is only to the first scenario. Sudan has argued that Security Council referral is an inappropriate extension of the UN bodies' legal authority, notwithstanding the ICTY and ICTR precedents.
13. Contrast Amann 2004 and Scharf 2001.
14. Article 46, The Rome Statute.
15. Struett 2004. See also Boli and Thomas, 1999.
16. Helen Duffy, Interview, June 5, 2002; Lars Van Troost, Interview, May 3, 2002.
17. For an authoritative review of the provisions of the Rome Statute and the text itself, including a discussion of the central complementarity provisions, see Lee 1999.
18. See Article 15, The Rome Statute.
19. Though making arrests and transferring suspects to the ICC may not be so isolated from political pressure because the court will rely on states for these functions. Judges are not normally eligible for reelection; see Article 36, Paragraph 9, The Rome Statute.
20. For a representative NGO statement on this issue, see for instance HRW 1998.
21. See Ratner and Abrams 2001, p. 190; Chihiro, Ando, Onuma, and Minear 1986, p. 29; and Kirchheimer 1995, pp. 368–71.
22. Alissa J. Rubin, "New Balkan Trend Turns Accused Sinners to Saints," *Los Angeles Times*, January 19, 2003, A1, A8–A9; and Cibelli and Guberek 2000.
23. Robertson 2000, pp. 188–96. Robertson notes that the 1977 Geneva Convention in some ways exacerbated the problem of distinguishing between international and internal armed conflict.
24. Articles 7 and 8, The Rome Statute.
25. For a representative statement of NGO views on this issue, see Amnesty International 1997a, p. 11.
26. Kirk 1998. Significantly, each of these states has battled internal armed insurrections in recent years.
27. But for the opposite view, see Wedgewood 1998.
28. Article 53 of the Rome Statute gives the prosecutor the authority to decline to pursue an investigation when such an investigation is not "in the interest of justice."
29. For an early statement of the possible advantages of international jurisdiction as opposed to prosecution in a transitional state, see Nino 1995.
30. See discussion of this issue in Schabas 2001, pp. 68–70 and Article 53 of the Rome Statute, which gives the prosecutor discretion to bring charges only when it is in the interest of justice.

31. As of this writing in August 2007, three situations have been referred by the territorial state parties to the attention of the court, from Uganda, the Democratic Republic of the Congo, and the Central African Republic; the situation in Sudan was referred by the UN Security Council. The prosecutor has decided on the basis of available evidence to open investigations in all four of these situations, and arrest warrants have been issued in each situation except the Central African Republic. At present one defendant is in custody.
32. One possible consequence of this fact is the need to consider a new realm of "pretransitional" justice. If a sitting authoritarian government has ratified the ICC statute, and it commits crimes against humanity on its own territory, it may be subject to ICC prosecution even before it loses power. Of course then the ICC itself has the potential to become a voice, in effect advocating a transition by indicting sitting leaders.
33. Article 46, The Rome Statute.
34. For example, the ICTY prosecutor's office has relied at times on evidence initially developed by NGOs. Interview with Niccolo Figa-Talamanca, June 11, 2002, in The Hague.
35. Brysk 1994, pp. 77–8, discusses Moreno-Ocampo's role in the legal effort to hold persons accountable for grave human rights abuses in Argentina.
36. The most logical ground for making this distinction is whether or not a Truth Commission has specifically granted amnesty in exchange for testimony as part of a judicial or quasijudicial process, thereby invoking the legal principle that defendants should not face "double jeopardy," in other words, be tried twice for the same alleged offence; the principle of "*Ne bis in Idem*" (not twice for the same) as it is defined in the ICC's Rome Statute. For further discussion, see Dugard 2002, p. 703.
37. Rosenau 1990 broadly discusses this trend.
38. Scheffer 1999b, pp. 533–4, explains the argument.
39. For instance, that argument has been made by the U.S. Ambassador for War Crimes Issues Pierre-Richard Prosper, Foreign Press Center Briefing (May 6, 2002), available at http://ftc.state.gov/9965.htm.
40. Werner 2004, p. 133 (emphasis added).
41. For an articulation of the view that sovereignty is an empirical phenomenon that is merely recognized by international law, see James 1986.
42. On the sociology of agents and structures, see Giddens 1984. With respect to states and international society, see Wendt, 1999.
43. For the opposite view that the ICC is a challenge to states' sovereign rights rather than a transformation of them, see Jensen 2004, pp. 170–1.
44. Tesón (2003) also extends the argument as a justification for humanitarian intervention in general in carefully defined circumstances.
45. See also Jensen 2004, pp. 327–8.
46. Convention on the Prevention and Punishment of the Crime of Genocide (entered into force January 12, 1951), available at http://www.preventgenocide.org/law/convention/text.htm.
47. Bassiouni 1999 and Paust 2000.
48. The Rome Statute, Part 2.
49. Report of the International Commission on Intervention and State Sovereignty, *The Responsibility to Protect* (December 2001), available at http://www.iciss.ca/pdf/commission-report.pdf.
50. UN Commission on Human Rights, 1998.
51. Article 17, The Rome Statute.

52. Regarding the duty to prosecute war crimes, see Ratner and Abrams 2001, p. 82. Regarding the duty to prosecute genocide, see Convention on the Prevention and Punishment of the Crime of Genocide, arts. 6–7, but be aware of numerous reservations to these provisions. See Ratner and Abrams 2001, pp. 39–40.
53. See the ICC website available at http:www.icc-cpi.int/cases.html discussing the investigations in Uganda and Congo; for investigations in Burundi, see http://globalsolutions.org/programs/law_justice/news/burundi.html.
54. Article 116, The Rome Statute.
55. Article 12, The Rome Statute.
56. Article 13, The Rome Statute.
57. Vienna Convention on the Law of Treaties, May 23, 1968, arts. 34–38, 1155 U.N.T.S. 331 (entered into force January 27, 1980), available at www.un.org/law/ilc/texts/treaties.htm.
58. Amann 2004, pp. 187–98. The governments of the United States, China, and India have also criticized the Rome Statute on essentially the same grounds advanced by Amann.
59. See Emmerich de Vattel, *The Law of Nations or the Principles of Natural Law*, Book 2, Ch. 8, para. 101–103, available at http://www.lonang.com/exlibris/vattel/index.html.
60. *Doe I v. Unocal*, 395 F.3d 932 (9th Cir. 2002).
61. *Doe I v. Unocal*, 395 F.3d 932 (9th Cir. 2002) at 948.
62. Article 10, The Rome Statute.
63. See, for example, John D. Negroponte, Letter from the Permanent Representative of the United States of America to the United Nations addressed to the President of the Security Council (October 7, 2001), available at http://www.un.int/usa/s-20010946.htm.
64. See, for example, Bradford 2004; Beard 2002.
65. See Newton 2001, pp. 27–28, describing the views of the proponents of the ICC that state sovereignty should be subordinated to the greater good of the world community. But see also Scheffer (1999b) describing the United States' position that the ICC interferes with state sovereignty.

Postscript

1. The recent ratification of the ICC by Japan will go a long way toward alleviating the ICC's budget problems.
2. Richard Norton-Taylor, "Lawyers for Families and Groups Present Evidence They Say Shows Government Acted Unlawfully on Iraq," *Guardian*, May 6, 2005.
3. Joshua Rozenberg, "Why Britain's Top Soldier Would Not End Up in the Dock over Iraq," *The Daily Telegraph*, May 2, 2005.
4. Ibid.
5. Norton-Taylor, "Lawyers for Families and Groups."
6. Rozenberg, "Britain's Top Soldier."

Bibliography

Abarinov, Vladimir. 1993. *The Murderers of Katyân.* New York: Hippocrene Books.
Abbott, Kenneth W., and Duncan Snidal. 1998. Why States Act through Formal International Organizations. *Journal of Conflict Resolution* 42 (1): 3–32.
Akhavan, Payam. 2001. Beyond Impunity: Can International Criminal Justice Prevent Future Atrocities? *American Journal of International Law* 95 (1): 7–31.
Albert, Steve. 1993. *The Case against the General: Manuel Noriega and the Politics of American Justice.* New York: Charles Scribner's Sons.
Alexy, Robert. 1989. *A Theory of Legal Argumentation: The Theory of Rational Discourse as Theory of Legal Justification.* Oxford: Oxford University Press.
Alker, Hayward R. Jr. 1988. The Dialectical Logic of Thucydides' Melian Dialogue. *American Political Science Review* 82 (3): 805–920.
Allison, Graham T. 1971. *Essence of Decision: Explaining the Cuban Missile Crisis.* New York: Little, Brown.
Amann, Diane Marie. 2004. The International Criminal Court and the Sovereign State. In Werner and Dekker, *Governance and International Legal Theory.*
Amnesty International. 1994a. Establishing a Just, Fair and Effective International Criminal Court. London.
———. 1994b. Memorandum to the International Law Commission: Establishing a Just, Fair and Effective Permanent International Criminal Tribunal. London.
———. 1995. The Quest for International Justice: Time for a Permanent International Criminal Court. London.
———. 1997a. The International Criminal Court: Making the Right Choices—Part I (AI Index: IOR 40/01/1997). January. London.
———. 1997b. The Quest for International Justice: Defining the Crimes and Permissible Defences and Initiating a Prosecution (AI Index: IOR 40/006/1997). February. London.
———. 1997c. The International Criminal Court: Making the Right Choices—Part II, Organizing the Court and Ensuring a Fair Trial (AI Index: IOR 40/011/1997). July. London.
———. 1998. The International Criminal Court: Ensuring Justice for Women. London.
———. 2000. The International Criminal Court: Checklist for Effective Implementation. London.
Aristotle. 1928. *Topica.* In *The Works of Aristotle,* translated by W. A. Pickard-Cambridge. Oxford: Oxford University Press.
Arthur, W. Brian. 1994. *Increasing Returns and Path Dependence in the Economy.* Economics, Cognition, and Society Series. Ann Arbor: University of Michigan Press.
Arts, Bas, Bob Reinalda, and Math Noortmann, eds. 2001. *Non-State Actors in International Relations.* Aldershot, UK: Ashgate.
Aust, Anthony. 2000. *Modern Treaty Law and Practice.* Cambridge: Cambridge University Press.

Australia. Statement by M. J. Baxter. 1995. On the Establishment of an International Criminal Court. Sixth Committee, United Nations General Assembly, New York. October 30.

Axelrod, Robert, and Robert O. Keohane. 1993. Achieving Cooperation under Anarchy: Strategies and Institutions. In Baldwin, *Neorealism and Neoliberalism*.

Baldwin, David A., ed. 1993. *Neorealism and Neoliberalism: The Contemporary Debate*. New Directions in World Politics. New York: Columbia University Press.

Bass, Gary Jonathan. 2000. *Stay the Hand of Vengeance: The Politics of War Crimes Tribunals*. Princeton Studies in International History and Politics. Princeton, NJ: Princeton University Press.

Bassiouni, M. Cherif. 1991. The Time Has Come for an International Criminal Court. *Indiana Journal of International and Comparative Law* 1, no. 1.

———. 1998. *The Statute of the International Criminal Court: A Documentary History*. Ardsley, NY: Transnational Publishers.

———. 1999. *Crimes against Humanity in International Criminal Law*. 2nd rev. ed. The Hague and Boston: Kluwer Law International.

Bassiouni, M. Cherif, and Christopher L. Blakesley. 1992. The Need for an International Criminal Court in the New International World Order. *Vanderbilt Journal of Transnational Law* 25 (2): 151–82.

Beard, Jack M. 2002. America's New War on Terror: The Case for Self-Defense under International Law. *Harvard Journal of Law and Public Policy* 25: 559–90.

Becker, David, Elizabeth Lira, María Isabel Castillo, Elena Gómez, and Juana Kovalskys. 1995. Therapy with Victims of Political Repression in Chile: The Challenge of Social Reparation. In Kritz, *Transitional Justice*.

Benedetti, Fanny, and John L. Washburn. 1999. Drafting the International Criminal Court Treaty: Two Years to Rome and an Afterword on the Rome Diplomatic Conference. *Global Governance* 5 (1): 1–38.

Bentham, Jeremy. 1786–1789. Principles of International Law. In *The Works of Jeremy Bentham*, edited by John Bowring. Edinburgh: Tait, 1843.

Biersteker, Thomas J., and Cynthia Weber, eds. 1996. *State Sovereignty as Social Construct*. Cambridge Studies in International Relations, no. 46. Cambridge: Cambridge University Press.

Boli, John, and George M. Thomas. 1999. *Constructing World Culture: International Nongovernmental Organizations since 1875*. Palo Alto, CA: Stanford University Press.

Bonafini, Hebe de, and Evel Petrini. 1998. Tribunal Internacional de Derechos Humanos. Rome: Asociación Madres de Plaza de Mayo.

Bos, Adrian. 2002. Interview by M. Struett. May 14. The Hague.

Bradford, William C. 2004. The Duty to Defend Them: A Natural Law Justification for the Bush Doctrine of Preventive War. *Notre Dame Law Review* 79: 1365.

Broms, Bengt. 1995. The Establishment of an International Criminal Court. In *Israel Yearbook on Human Rights*, edited by Y. Dinstein. Dordrecht, Netherlands: Martinus Nijhoff.

Brysk, Alison. 1994. *The Politics of Human Rights in Argentina: Protest, Change, and Democratization*. Palo Alto, CA: Stanford University Press.

Bull, Hedley. 1977. *The Anarchical Society: A Study of Order in World Politics*. London: Macmillan.

Bush, George Herbert Walker. 1991. State of the Union Address. Washington, D.C.

Buzan, Barry. 2004. *From International to World Society*. Cambridge: Cambridge University Press.

Byers, Michael. 1999. *Custom, Power, and the Power of Rules: International Relations and Customary International Law*. Cambridge and New York: Cambridge University Press.

Campbell, David. 1992. *Writing Security: United States Foreign Policy and the Politics of Identity*. Minneapolis: University of Minnesota Press.

Cassese, Antonio. 1996. Introduction. In *The Path to The Hague: Selected Documents on the Orignis of the ICTY*. The Hague: United Nations.

Cassese, Antonio, Paola Gaeta, and John R. W. D. Jones. 2002. *The Rome Statute of the International Criminal Court: A Commentary*. Oxford and New York: Oxford University Press.

Castelos, Montserrat Abad. 2003. Global Civil Society 2001. *European Journal of International Law* 14 (5): 1047–51.

Chen, Lung-chu. 1989. The Individual. In *An Introduction to Contemporary International Law: A Policy-Oriented Perspective*. New Haven, CT: Yale University Press.

Chihiro, Hosoya, N. Ando, Y. Onuma, and R. Minear, eds. 1986. *The Tokyo War Crimes Trial*. Tokyo: Kodansha.

Chile. Statement by P. F. Orrego-Vicuña. 1997. Establecimiento de una Corte Penal Internacional. Sixth Committee, United Nations General Assembly, New York. October 23.

China, People's Republic of. Statement by A. C. Shiqiu. 1995. On the Establishment of an International Criminal Court. Sixth Committee, United Nations General Assembly, New York. October 30.

———. Statement by M. D. Jeilong. 1997. On the Establishment of an International Criminal Court. Sixth Committee, United Nations General Assembly, New York. October 21.

Chiu, H. 1988. Book Reviews and Notes. *American Journal of International Law* 82: 892–95.

Cibelli, Kristen, and Tamy Guberek. 2000. *Justice Unknown, Justice Unsatisfied?: Bosnian NGOs Speak about the International Criminal Tribunal for the Former Yugoslavia*. Medford, MA: Tufts University Press.

Cohen, Roberta. 2004. The Guiding Principles on Internal Displacement: An Innovation in International Standard Setting. *Global Governance* 10 (4): 459–80.

Collier, Ruth Berins, and David Collier. 1991. *Shaping the Political Arena: Critical Junctures, the Labor Movement, and Regime Dynamics in Latin America*. Princeton, NJ: Princeton University Press.

Combs, Nancy Amoury. 2007. *Guilty Pleas in International Criminal Law: Constructing a Restorative Justice Approach*. Stanford: Stanford University Press.

Comisiâon Andina de Juristas. 2004. *La Corte Penal Internacional y los paâises andinos*. 2nd ed. Lima, Peru: Comisiâon Andina de Juristas.

Commission on Human Rights. 1998. The Guiding Principles on Internal Displacement. New York: United Nations.

Crawford, James. 2002. The Work of the International Law Commission. In Cassese, Gaeta, and Jones, *The Rome Statute of the International Criminal Court*.

Crawford, Neta C. 2002. *Argument and Change in World Politics: Ethics, Decolonization, and Humanitarian Intervention*. Cambridge Studies in International Relations, no. 81. Cambridge: Cambridge University Press.

Czartnetzky, John M., and Ronald J. Rychlak. 2003. An Empire of Law?: Legalism and the International Criminal Court. *Notre Dame Law Review* 79: 55–126.

Debrix, François, ed. 2003. *Language, Agency, and Politics in a Constructed World*. International Relations in a Constructed World. Armonk, NY: M. E. Sharpe.

Doebbler, Curtis F. J., and Maha W. Eid. 2004. American International Lawyers and the Use of Force. *Peace Review* 16 (3): 279–84.

Doty, Roxanne Lynn. 1996. *Imperial Encounters: The Politics of Representation in North-South Relations*. Minneapolis: University of Minnesota Press.

Douglas, Mary. 1986. *How Institutions Think*. The Frank W. Abrams Lectures. Syracuse, NY: Syracuse University Press.

Dubber, Markus D., and Mariana Valverde, eds. 2006. *The New Police Science: The Police Power in Domestic and International Governance*. Palo Alto, CA: Stanford University Press.

Duffy, Helen. 2002. Interview by M. Struett. June 5. The Hague.

Dugard, John. 2002. Possible Conflicts of Jurisdiction with Truth Commissions. In Cassese, Gaeta, and Jones, *The Rome Statute of the International Criminal Court*.

Egypt. Statement by D. N. Elaraby. 1995. On the Establishment of an International Criminal Court. Sixth Committee, United Nations General Assembly, New York. November 2.

Ehard, Hans. 1949. The Nuremberg Trial against the Major War Criminals and International Law. *American Journal of International Law* 43 (2).

Elsea, Jennifer. 2003. *International Criminal Court: Overview and Selected Legal Issues*. New York: Novinka Books.

Elster, Jon, ed. 1998. Deliberation and Constitution Making. In *Deliberative Democracy*. Cambridge: Cambridge University Press.

———. 2004. *Closing the Books: Transitional Justice in Historical Perspective*. Cambridge: Cambridge University Press.

———. 2006. Redemption for Wrongdoing: The Fate of Collaborators after 1945. *Journal of Conflict Resolution* 50: 324–338.

Evered, Timothy C. 1994. An International Criminal Court: Recent Proposals and American Concerns. *Pace International Law Review* 6 (1): 121–58.

Fairweather, Cynthia. 2002. Interview by M. Struett. May 28. The Hague.

Falk, Richard A., Friedrich V. Kratochwil, and Saul H. Mendlovitz. 1985. *International Law: A Contemporary Perspective*. Boulder, CO: Westview Press.

Ferencz, Benjamin B. 1980. *An International Criminal Court, A Step Toward World Peace: A Documentary History and Analysis*. 2 vols. Dobbs Ferry, NY: Oceana Publications.

———. 1992. An International Criminal Court: Where They Stand and Where They're Going. *Columbia Journal of Transnational Law* 30: 375–99.

Figa-Talamanca, Niccolo. 2002. Interview by M. Struett. June 11. The Hague.

Finnemore, Martha. 1993. International Organizations as Teachers of Norms: The United Nations Educational, Scientific, and Cultural Organization and Science Policy. *International Organization* 47 (4): 565–97.

———. 1996. Norms, Culture, and World Politics: Insights from Sociology's Institutionalism. *International Organization* 50 (2): 24.

Finnemore, Martha, and Kathryn Sikkink. 1999. International Norm Dynamics and Political Change. In *Exploration and Contestation in the Study of World Politics*, edited by P. J. Katzenstein, R. O. Keohane, and S. D. Krasner. Cambridge, MA: MIT Press.

Foucault, Michel. 1972. *The Archaeology of Knowledge*. New York: Pantheon Books.

Fox, Gregory H. 2000. The Right to Political Participation in International Law. In Fox and Roth, *Democratic Governance and International Law*.

Fox, Gregory H., and B. R. Roth, eds. *Democratic Governance and International Law*. Cambridge and New York: Cambridge University Press.

France. Statement by Republic of France. 1997. Creation d'une cour criminelle internationale. Sixth Committee, United Nations General Assembly, New York. October 23.

Franceshet, Antonio. 2002. Justice and International Organization: Two Models of Global Governance. *Global Governance* 8: 19–34.

Franck, Thomas M. 1988. Legitimacy in the International System. *American Journal of International Law* 82: 705–59.

Frost, Mervyn. 1996. *Ethics in International Relations: A Constitutive Theory*. Cambridge Studies in International Relations Series, no. 45. Cambridge and New York: Cambridge University Press.

Garcia, Josep M., Diana Martnez, and Javier Darriba. 1996. Commentaries to the Draft Statute of the International Permanent Criminal Court (IPCC): Pax Romana. Barcelona, Spain.

Geertz, Clifford. 1973. Thick Description: Toward an Interpretive Theory of Culture. In *The Interpretation of Cultures*. New York: Basic Books.

George, Alexander L., and Andrew Bennett. 2005. *Case Studies and Theory Development in the Social Sciences*. BCSIA Studies in International Security Series. Cambridge, MA: MIT Press.

Gerber, Steven. 1996. Complementarity: You Won't Find It in the Dictionary. *The ICC Monitor*, no. 1: 10.

Gerring, John. 2001. *Social Science Methodology: A Criterial Framework*. Cambridge and New York: Cambridge University Press.

———. 2004. What is a Case Study and What is it Good for? *American Political Science Review* 98 (2): 341–54.

Giddens, Anthony. 1984. *The Constitution of Society: Outline of the Theory of Structuration*. Berkeley, CA: University of California Press.

Goertz, Gary. 2003. *International Norms and Decision Making: A Punctuated Equilibrium Model*. Lanham, MD: Rowman & Littlefield.

Griffin, James Bount. 2001. A Predictive Framework for the Effectiveness of International Criminal Tribunals. *Vanderbilt Journal of Transnational Law* 34 (2): 405–449.

Guariglia, Fabricio. 1999. International Law Criminal Procedures: Investigation and Prosecution. In Lee, *The International Criminal Court*.

———. 2002. Interview by M. Struett. May 21. The Hague.

Guibentif, Pierre. 1996. Approaching the Production of Law through Habermas's Concept of Communicative Action. In *Habermas, Modernity and Law*, edited by M. Deflem. London: Sage.

Gupta, Joyeeta. 2004. Non-State Actors: Undermining or Increasing the Legitimacy and Transparency of International Environmental Law. In Werner and Dekker, *Governance and International Legal Theory*.

Gurmendi, Silvia A. Fernandez de. 1999. The Role of the International Prosecutor. In Lee, *The International Criminal Court*.

Gutman, Roy, David Rieff, and Kenneth Anderson. 1999. *Crimes of War: What the Public Should Know*. New York: W. W. Norton & Company.

Gutmann, Amy, and Dennis Thompson. 2004. *Why Deliberative Democracy?* Princeton, NJ: Princeton University Press.

Haas, Ernst B. 1990. *When Knowledge is Power: Three Models of Change in International Organizations*. Studies in International Political Economy, no. 22. Berkeley: University of California Press.

———. 1997. Reason and Change in International Life. In *Nationalism, Liberalism and Progress*. Ithaca, NY: Cornell University Press.

Habermas, Jürgen. 1984. *The Theory of Communicative Action*. 2 vols. Boston, MA: Beacon Press.

———. 1996. *Between Facts and Norms: Contributions to a Discourse Theory of Law and Democracy*. Studies in Contemporary German Social Thought. Cambridge, MA: MIT Press.

Hagan, John. 2003. *Justice in the Balkans: Prosecuting War Crimes in the Hague Tribunal*. Chicago Series in Law and Society. Chicago: University of Chicago Press.

Hall, Christopher Keith. 1997. The First Two Sessions of the UN Preparatory Committee on the Establishment of an International Criminal Court. *American Journal of International Law* 91 (1): 177–87.

———. 1998a. The Fifth Session of the UN Preparatory Committee on the Establishment of an International Criminal Court. *American Journal of International Law* 92 (2): 331–39.

———. 1998b. The Sixth Session of the UN Preparatory Committee on the Establishment of an International Criminal Court. *American Journal of International Law* 92 (3): 548–56.

———. 1998c. The Third and Fourth Sessions of the UN Preparatory Committee on the Establishment of an International Criminal Court. *American Journal of International Law* 92 (1): 124–33.

Hawkins, Darren. 2004. Explaining Costly International Institutions: Persuasion and Enforceable Human Rights Norms. *International Studies Quarterly* 48 (4): 779–804.

Hayward, Clarissa. 2007. Binding Problems, Boundary Problems: The Trouble with Democratic Citizenship. In *Identities, Affiliations, and Allegiances*, edited by S. Benhabib, I. Shapiro, and D. Petranovich. Cambridge: Cambridge University Press.

Hebel, Herman von. 2002. Interview by M. Struett. May 17. The Hague.

Hebel, Herman von, and Darryl Robinson. 1999. Crimes within the Jurisdiction of the Court. In Lee, *The International Criminal Court*.

Hobbes, Thomas, Richard E. Flathman, and David Johnston. 1997. *Leviathan: Authoritative Text, Backgrounds, Interpretations*. 1st ed. New York and London: W. W. Norton & Company.

Holloway, Steven. 1990. Forty Years of United Nations General Assembly Voting. *Canadian Journal of Political Science [Revue canadienne de science politique]* 23 (2): 279.

Holmes, John T. 1999. The Principle of Complementarity. In Lee, *The International Criminal Court*.

Hopf, Ted. 1998. The Promise of Constructivism in International Relations Theory. *International Security* 23 (1): 171–200.

Hosoya, Chihiro, N. Ando, Y. Onuma, and R. Minear, eds. 1986. *The Tokyo War Crimes Trial*. Tokyo: Kodansha.

Human Rights Watch. 1996. Commentary for the Preparatory Committee on the Establishment of an International Criminal Court. New York.

———. 1997. Nongovernmental Organization Action Alert: Establishing an Effective International Criminal Court. Edited by R. Dicker. New York.

———. 1998. *Justice in the Balance: Recommendations for an Independent and Effective International Criminal Court*. New York.

———. 1999. World Report 1999: Special Programs and Campaigns. New York.

———. 2001. Seminario Regional para la Ratificación e Implementación del Estatuto de la Corte Penal Internacional. Paper read at Resumen Ejecutivo. Buenos Aires.

———. 2003. World Report 2003: Africa: Uganda. New York.

Ireland. Statement by M. B. O'Donoghue. 1997. On the Establishment of an International Criminal Court. Sixth Committee, United Nations General Assembly, New York. October 21.

James, A. 1986. *Sovereign Statehood: The Basis of International Society*. London: Allen & Unwin.

Jensen, Rod. 2004. Globalization and the International Criminal Court: Accountability and a New Conception of State. In Werner and Dekker, *Governance and International Legal Theory*.

Jepperson, Ronald L. 1991. Institutions, Institutional Effects, and Institutionalism. In *The New Institutionalism in Organizational Analysis*, edited by W. W. Powell and P. DiMaggio. Chicago: University of Chicago Press.

Kairys, David. 1998. *The Politics of Law: A Progressive Critique.* 3rd ed. New York: Basic Books.

Keck, Margaret E., and Kathryn Sikkink. 1998. *Activists beyond Borders: Advocacy Networks in International Politics.* Ithaca, NY: Cornell University Press.

Kelley, Judith. 2007. Who Keeps International Commitments and Why? The International Criminal Court and Bilateral Nonsurrender Agreements. *American Political Science Review* 101 (3): 573–90.

Keohane, Robert O., and Lisa L. Martin. 2003. Institutional Theory as a Research Paradigm. In *Progress in International Relations Theory: Appraising the Field*, edited by C. Elman and M. F. Elman. Cambridge, MA: MIT Press.

King, Gary, Robert O. Keohane, and Sidney Verba. 1994. *Designing Social Inquiry: Scientific Inference in Qualitative Research.* Princeton, NJ: Princeton University Press.

Kirchheimer, Otto. 1995. Political Justice. In Kritz, *Transitional Justice*.

Kirk, Alejandro. 1998. Take It or Leave It. *Terraviva: The (Rome) Conference Daily Newspaper*, July 14.

Kirsch, Phillipe. 1999. The Development of the Rome Statute. In Lee, *The International Criminal Court.*

Kirsch, Phillipe, and John T. Holmes. 1999. The Rome Conference on an ICC: The Negotiating Process. *American Journal of International Law* 93 (2).

Klotz, Audie. 1995. *Norms in International Relations.* Ithaca, NY: Cornell University Press.

Klotz, Audie, and Cecelia Lynch. 2007. *Strategies for Research in Constructivist International Relations.* Armonk, NY: M. E. Sharpe.

Korey, William. 1998. *NGOs and the Universal Declaration of Human Rights: A Curious Grapevine.* New York: Palgrave Macmillan. 2001.

Krasner, Stephen D., ed. 1983. *International Regimes.* Ithaca, NY: Cornell University Press.

Kratochwil, Friedrich V. 1989. *Rules, Norms and Decisions.* Cambridge: Cambridge University Press.

Krieger, Heike. 1995. The Role of Criminal Law in Relation to the Peace and Security of Mankind and the Nature and Structure of an International Criminal Court. In *International Legal Issues Arising under the United Nations Decade of International Law*, edited by Najeeb Al-Nauimi and Richard Meese. The Hague: Martinus Nijhoff.

Kritz, Neil J., ed. 1995. *Transitional Justice: How Emerging Democracies Reckon with Former Regimes.* Vol. 1, *General Considerations.* Washington, D.C.: U.S. Institute for Peace Press.

La Haye, Eve. 2002. Interview by M. Struett. July 2. The Hague.

Lasswell, Harold. 1935. *World Politics and Personal Insecurity.* New York: Free Press. 1965.

Lawyers Committee for Human Rights (U.S.). 1997. The ICC Trigger Mechanism and the Need for an Independent Prosecutor. New York.

Lee, Roy S. 1999. *The International Criminal Court: The Making of the Rome Statute; Issues, Negotiations, Results.* The Hague and Boston: Kluwer Law International.

Liebowitz, S. J., Stephen Margolis, and Peter Lewin. 2002. *The Economics of QWERTY: History, Theory, and Policy.* New York: New York University Press.

Lukashuk, Igor I. 1994. The Nuremberg and Tokyo Trials: 50 Years Later. *Review of Central and East European Law* 20 (2): 207–16.

Lynch, Cecelia. 1999. *Beyond Appeasement: Interpreting Interwar Peace Movements in World Politics.* Ithaca, NY: Cornell University Press.

Malaysia. Statement by M. S. Thanarajasingam. 1995. On the Establishment of an International Criminal Court. Sixth Committee, United Nations General Assembly, New York. November 1.

Marquardt, Paul D. 1995. Law Without Borders: The Constitutionality of an International Criminal Court. *Columbia Journal of Transnational Law* 33: 73–148.
Martin, Raymond. 1997. The Essential Difference Between History and Science: Paradigms of Interpretation. *History and Theory* 36 (1): 1–14.
Meron, Theodor. 1997. Answering for War Crimes: Lessons from the Balkans. *Foreign Affairs* 76, no.1.
Mexico. Statement by Representante de Mexico. 1995. Establecimiento de una Corte Penal Internacional. Sixth Committee, United Nations General Assembly, New York. November 2.
Meyer, Howard. 2002. *The World Court in Action: Judging among the Nations*. Lanham, MD: Rowman & Littlefield.
Meyer, John W., George M. Thomas, Francisco O. Ramirez, and John Boli, eds. 1987. *Institutional Structure: Constituting State, Society, and the Individual*. Newbury Park, CA: Sage.
Milliken, J. 1999. The Study of Discourse in International Relations: A Critique of Research and Methods. *European Journal of International Relations* 5 (2): 225–54.
Mitzen, Jennifer. 2005. Reading Habermas in Anarchy: Multilateral Diplomacy and Global Public Spheres. *American Political Science Review* 99 (3): 401–17.
Moghalu, Kingsley Chiedu. 2006. Saddam Hussein's Trial Meets the "Fairness" Test. *Ethics & International Affairs* 20 (4): 517–25.
Morgenthau, Hans Joachim. 1948. *Politics among Nations: The Struggle for Power and Peace*. 1st ed. New York: A. A. Knopf.
Morton, Jeffrey S. 2000. *The International Law Commission of the United Nations*. Columbia: University of South Carolina Press.
Murphy, Sean D. 2000. Democratic Legitimacy and the Recognition of States and Governments. In Fox and Roth, *Democratic Governance and International Law*.
Nanda, Ved P. 1998. The Establishment of a Permanent International Criminal Court: Challenges Ahead. *Human Rights Quarterly* 20: 413–28.
Nau, Henry R. 2002. *At Home Abroad: Identity and Power in American Foreign Policy*. Cornell Studies in Political Economy. Ithaca, NY: Cornell University Press.
Newton, Lieutenant Colonel Michael A. 2001. Comparative Complementarity: Domestic Jurisdiction Consistent with the Rome Statute of the International Criminal Court, *Military Law Review* 167: 20–73.
Nino, Carlos S. 1995. Response: The Duty to Punish Past Abuses of Human Rights Put into Context: The Case of Argentina. In Kritz, *Transitional Justice*.
O'Brien, Robert, Ann Marie Goetz, Jan Aart Scholte, and Marc Williams, eds. 2000. *Contesting Global Governance: Multilateral Economic Institutions and Global Social Movements*. Cambridge: Cambridge University Press.
Oliver, C. 1991. The Jurisdiction (Competence) of States. In *International Law: Achievements and Prospects*, edited by M. Bedjaoui. Dordrecht, Netherlands: Martinus Nijhoff.
Olson, Kevin. 2003. Do Rights Have a Formal Basis? Habermas' Legal Theory and the Normative Foundations of the Law. *Journal of Political Philosophy* 11 (3): 273–94.
Orentlicher, Diane F. 1999. Politics by Other Means: The Law of the International Criminal Court. *Cornell International Law Journal* 32: 489–97.
Pace, William R. 1998. Globalizing Justice. *Harvard International Review* 20 (2): 26–29.
Pace, William R., and Jennifer Schense. 2002. The Role of Non-Governmental Organizations. In Cassese, Gaeta, and Jones, *The Rome Statute of the International Criminal Court*. Oxford: Oxford University Press.
Pace, William R., and Mark Thieroff. 1999. Participation of Non-Governmental Organizations. In Lee, *The International Criminal Court*.

Pace, William R., and Sir Peter Ustinov. 1996. Views of the World Federalist Movement on the Establishment of a Permanent International Criminal Court. New York: World Federalist Movement.

Panganiban, Rik. The NGO Coalition for an International Criminal Court. In *UN Chronicle* 34, no. 4: 36.

Paust, Jordan J. 2000. *International Criminal Law: Cases and Materials.* 2nd ed. Carolina Academic Press Law Casebook Series. Durham, NC: Carolina Academic Press.

Perry, Michael J. 1998. *The Idea of Human Rights: Four Inquiries.* New York: Oxford University Press.

Persico, Joseph E. 1994. *Nuremberg.* New York: Penguin.

Philippines, The. Statement by A. R. Ilustre-Goco. 1997. On the Establishment of an International Criminal Court. Sixth Committee, United Nations General Assembly, New York. October 23.

Powell, Walter W., and Paul DiMaggio. 1991. *The New Institutionalism in Organizational Analysis.* Chicago: University of Chicago Press.

Power, Samantha. 2002. *A Problem from Hell: America and the Age of Genocide.* New York: Basic Books.

Ratner, Steven R., and Jason S. Abrams. 2001. *Accountability for Human Rights Atrocities in International Law: Beyond the Nuremberg Legacy.* 2nd ed. Oxford and New York: Oxford University Press.

Rawls, John. 2001. *Justice as Fairness: A Restatement.* Edited by E. Kelly. Cambridge, MA: Belknap Press.

Regenwetter, M., J. C. Falmagne, and B. Grofman. 1999. A Stochastic Model of Preference Change and Its Application to 1992 Presidential Election Panel Data. *Psychological Review* 106 (2): 362–84.

Reus-Smit, Christian. 2001. Human Rights and the Social Construction of Sovereignty. *Review of International Studies* 27 (4): 20.

Risse, Thomas. 2000. "Let's Argue!" Communicative Action in World Politics. *International Organization* 54 (1): 1–39.

Risse-Kappen, Thomas, Steve C. Ropp, and Kathryn Sikkink. 1999. *The Power of Human Rights: International Norms and Domestic Change.* Cambridge Studies in International Relations, no. 66. New York: Cambridge University Press.

Roach, Steven C. 2006. *Politicizing the International Criminal Court: The Convergence of Politics, Ethics, and Law.* Lanham, MD: Roman & Littlefield.

Robertson, Geoffrey. 2000. *Crimes Against Humanity: The Struggle for Global Justice.* New York: New Press.

Roht-Arriaza, Naomi. 2005. *The Pinochet Effect: Transnational Justice in the Age of Human Rights.* Pennsylvania Studies in Human Rights. Philadelphia: University of Pennsylvania Press.

Rosenau, James N. 1990. *Turbulence in World Politics: A Theory of Change and Continuity.* Princeton, NJ: Princeton University Press.

Rosenstock, Robert. 1994. Remarks Made at Pace University School of Law. *Pace International Law Review* 6: 83–86.

Rubin, Alfred P. 1994. Essays: An International Criminal Tribunal for Former Yugoslavia? *Pace International Law Review* 6: 7–17.

Ruggie, John Gerard. 1993a. *Multilateralism Matters: The Theory and Praxis of an Institutional Form.* New Directions in World Politics. New York: Columbia University Press.

———. 1993b. Multilateralism: The Anatomy of an Institution. In Ruggie, *Multilateralism Matters.*

———. 1996. *Winning the Peace: America and World Order in the New Era.* New York: Columbia University Press.

———. 1998. *Constructing the World Polity: Essays on International Institutionalization.* The New International Relations. London and New York: Routledge.

Russian Federation. Statement by Representative of Russia. 1995. On the Establishment of an International Criminal Court. Sixth Committee, United Nations General Assembly, New York. November 2.

Sandholtz, Wayne, and Alec Stone Sweet. 1998. *European Integration and Supranational Governance.* Oxford and New York: Oxford University Press.

Schabas, William. 2001. *An Introduction to the International Criminal Court.* Cambridge and New York: Cambridge University Press.

Scharf, Michael P. 1994. Getting Serious about an ICC. *Pace International Law Review* 6 (1): 103–20.

———. 1997a. *Balkan Justice.* Durham, NC: Carolina Academic Press.

———. 1997b. The Prosecutor v. Dusko Tadic: An Appraisal of the First International War Crimes Trial since Nuremberg. *Albany Law Review* 60 (3): 861.

———. 2001. The ICC's Jurisdiction over the Nationals of Non-Party States: A Critique of the US Position. *Law and Contemporary Problems* 64 (1): 52.

Scheffer, David J. 1998. Developments at the Rome Treaty Conference: Testimony of David J. Scheffer. In *Senate Foreign Relations.* Washington, D.C.: G.P.O.

———. 2000. Statement before the Sixth Committee of the UN General Assembly on the International Criminal Court. New York: US Department of State.

———. 1997. U.S. Policy and the Proposed Permanent International Criminal Court. *US Department of State Dispatch* 8 (10): 20–22.

———. 1999a. The United States and the International Criminal Court. *American Journal of International Law* 93 (1): 10.

———. 1999b. US Policy and the International Criminal Court. *Cornell International Law Journal* 32 (3): 528–34.

Searle, John R. 1995. *The Construction of Social Reality.* New York: Free Press.

Shaw, Karena. 2003. Whose Knowledge for What Politics? *Review of International Studies* 29 (Special Issue): 199–221.

Sjöstedt, Roxanna. 2007. The Discursive Origins of a Doctrine: Norms, Identity, and Securitizations under Harry S. Truman and George W. Bush. *Foreign Policy Analysis* 3 (3): 233–54.

Smith, Bradley F. 1982. *The American Road to Nuremberg: The Documentary Record, 1944–1945.* Palo Alto, CA: Hoover Institution Press.

Smith, Steve. 2004. Singing Our World into Existence: International Relations Theory and September 11. *International Studies Quarterly* 48 (3): 499–515.

Solingen, Etel. 1998. *Regional Orders at Century's Dawn: Global and Domestic Influences on Grand Strategy.* Princeton Studies in International History and Politics. Princeton, NJ: Princeton University Press.

Spiropoulos, Jean. 1950. Documents of the Second Session Including the Report of the Commission to the General Assembly. In *Yearbook of the International Law Commission.* New York: United Nations.

Stone, Julius, and Robert Woetzel, eds. 1970. *Toward a Feasible International Criminal Court.* Belgrade, Yugoslavia: Federation of Jurists.

Stone Sweet, Alec. 1999. Judicialization and the Construction of Governance. *Comparative Political Studies* 32 (2): 147–84.

Stone Sweet, Alec, and Tom Brunell. 1998. "Constructing a Supranational Constitution: Dispute Resolution and Governance in the European Community." *American Political Science Review* 92, no. 1: 63–81.

Struett, Michael. 2004. NGOs, the International Criminal Court, and the Politics of Writing International Law. In Werner and Dekker, *Governance and International Legal Theory*.
———. 2005. The Transformation of State Sovereign Rights and Responsibilities under the Rome Statue for the International Criminal Court. *Chapman Law Review* 8 (1): 179–99.
Struett, Michael, and Steven Weldon. 2006. Explaining State Decisions to Ratify the International Criminal Court Treaty. Paper read at American Political Science Association annual meeting, Philadelphia, PA, August 30–September 2.
Suhr, Brigitte. 2002. Interview by M. Struett. March 30. Los Angeles.
Suikkari, Satu. 1995. Debate in the United Nations on the International Law Commission's Draft Statute for an International Criminal Court. *Nordic Journal of International Law* 64: 205–21.
Terry, Deborah J., and Michael A. Hogg. 2000. *Attitudes, Behavior, and Social Context: The Role of Norms and Group Membership*. Mahwah, NJ: Lawrence Erlbaum Associates.
Tesón, Fernando R. 1998. *A Philosophy of International Law*. Boulder, CO: Westview Press.
———. 2003. The Liberal Case for Humanitarian Intervention. In *Humanitarian Intervention: Ethical, Legal, and Political Dilemmas*, edited by J. L. Holzgrefe and R. O. Keohane. Cambridge: Cambridge University Press.
Trinidad and Tobago. Statement by M. G. A. Ramoutar. 1997. On the Establishment of an International Criminal Court. Sixth Committee, United Nations General Assembly, New York. October 21.
Troost, Lars Van. 2002. Interview by M. Struett. May 3. Amsterdam.
United Kingdom. Statement by Representative of the United Kingdom. 1995. On the Establishment of an International Criminal Court. Sixth Committee, United Nations General Assembly, New York. November 2.
———. Statement by Representative of the United Kingdom. 1997. On the Establishment of an International Criminal Court. Sixth Committee, United Nations General Assembly, New York. October 23.
United Nations. 1954. Report of the 1953 Committee on International Criminal Jurisdiction. *Official Records, Ninth Session*. New York: General Assembly.
———. 1996. Official Records of the General Assembly: Fifty-first Session. *Supplement No. 22*. New York: United Nations.
———. 1996. Report of the Preparatory Committee on the Establishment of an International Criminal Court. Vol. 1, *Proceedings of the Preparatory Committee during March–April and August 1996*. Vol. 2, *Compilation of Proposals*. New York.
———. 2002. *United Nations Diplomatic Conference of Plenipotentiaries on the Establishment of an International Criminal Court, Rome, 15 June–17 July 1998: Official Records*. Vol. 2, *Summary Records of the Plenary Meetings and of the Meetings of the Committee of the Whole*. New York: United Nations.
United States. Statement by J. S. Borak. 1995. On the Establishment of an International Criminal Court. Sixth Committee, United Nations General Assembly, New York. November 1.
———. Statement by B. Richardson. 1997. On the Establishment of an International Criminal Court. Sixth Committee, United Nations General Assembly, New York. October 23.
———. Department of State. Statement by M. Grossman. 2002. American Foreign Policy and the International Criminal Court. Center for Strategic and International Studies, Washington, D.C., May 6.
Van Esch, Femke. 2001. Defining National Preferences: The Influence of International Non-State Actors. In Arts, Reinalda, and Noortmann, *Non-State Actors in International Relations*.

Van Evera, Stephen. 1997. *Guide to Methods for Students of Political Science*. Ithaca, NY: Cornell University Press.

Walker, R. B. J. 1993. *Inside/Outside: International Relations as Political Theory*. Cambridge Studies in International Relations, no. 24. Cambridge and New York: Cambridge University Press.

Waltz, Kenneth Neal. 1979. *Theory of International Politics*. 1st ed. Boston, MA: McGraw-Hill.

———. 1986. Anarchic Orders and Balance of Power. In *Neorealism and its Critics*, edited by R. Keohane. New York: Columbia University Press.

Wapner, Paul Kevin. 1996. *Environmental Activism and World Civic Politics*. SUNY Series in International Environmental Policy and Theory. Albany, NY: State University of New York Press.

———. 2000. The Normative Promise of Non-State Actors: A Theoretical Account of Global Civil Society. In *Principled World Politics: The Challenge of Normative International Relations*, edited by P. Wapner and L. E. J. Ruiz. Lanham, MD: Rowman & Littlefield.

Weber, Max. 1957. *The Theory of Social and Economic Organization*. Translated by A. M. Henderson and T. Parsons. Glencoe, IL: Free Press.

Wedgewood, Ruth. 1998. Fiddling in Rome: America and the International Criminal Court. *Foreign Affairs* 77, no. 6: 20–24.

Weiss, Thomas G., and Cindy Collins. 2000. *Humanitarian Challenges and Intervention*. 2nd ed. Dilemmas in World Politics. Boulder, CO: Westview Press.

Wendt, Alexander. 1999. *Social Theory of International Politics*. Cambridge Studies in International Relations, no. 67. Cambridge and New York: Cambridge University Press.

Werner, Wouter. 2004. State Sovereignty and International Legal Discourse. In Werner and Dekker, *Governance and International Legal Theory*.

Werner, W. G., and I. F. Dekker, eds. *Governance and International Legal Theory*. Leiden and Boston: Martinus Nijhoff.

Wilmshurst, Elizabeth. 1999. Jurisdiction of the Court. In Lee, *The International Criminal Court*.

Wippman, David. 1999. Atrocities, Deterrence, and the Limits of International Justice. *Fordham International Law Journal* 23: 473–488.

———. 2004. The International Criminal Court. In *The Politics of International Law*, edited by C. Reus-Smit. Cambridge: Cambridge University Press.

Wittgenstein, Ludwig. 1968. *Philosophical Investigations*. Oxford: Basil Blackwell.

Woetzel, Robert K., Foundation for the Establishment of an International Criminal Court, and Johnson Foundation. 1973. *A Report of the First and Second International Criminal Law Conferences*. Racine, WI: Johnson Foundation.

Yee, Lionel. 1999. The International Criminal Court and the Security Council: Articles 13(b) and 16. In Lee, *The International Criminal Court*.

Young, Iris Marion. 1996. Communication and the Other: Beyond Deliberative Democracy. In *Democracy and Difference: Contesting the Boundaries of the Political*, edited by S. Benhabib. Princeton, NJ: Princeton University Press.

Zinn, Howard. 1997. *The Zinn Reader: Writings on Disobedience and Democracy*. New York: Seven Stories Press.

Index

Abu Ghraib, 2
Ad hoc Committee on the Establishment of an International Criminal Court, 78, 88, 100, 105, 187
Africa, 6, 69, 89, 111, 132, 135, 137, 140, 142–3
agent-structure problem, 18
Aguirrezabal, Irune, 142
Aideed, Mohammad, 74–5
Albright, Madeleine, 74–5, 193
Alexy, Robert, 10, 38–41, 45, 79, 91, 185
Alfaro, Ricardo, 59–60, 65
Allied war crimes (World War II), 85
American Bar Association, 54, 100, 119, 127, 188, 191, 193
American Journal of International Law, 59, 191
American Society for the Judicial Settlement of International Disputes, 51
American Society of International Law, 54, 59
amnesty, 147, 164, 167, 198
Amnesty International, 91–2, 94–8, 103–4, 111, 119–21, 123, 128, 139, 144, 150, 158–9, 189, 191, 193, 196–7
  discursive practices of, 29, 34, 42, 86–8
Andorra, 191
Annan, Kofi, 114–5
Arbour, Louise, 104
Argentina, 117, 127, 134, 136, 143–5, 185, 191, 195, 198
  ICC implementing legislation, 145
  ratification, 144
argumentation, 39
  discursive, 7, 36, 55
  normative, 21, 29, 36
  rational, 2, 6, 11, 20, 22, 29, 35, 37–8, 50, 55, 84, 101, 106, 115–6, 123, 125–6, 129, 152, 190, 192

Aristotle, 38, 185
Asia, 6, 11, 132, 136, 137, 140, 141, 142
Assembly of State Parties, xiii, 156, 183, 192–3, 195
Atomic Energy Commission, 56
Australia, 44, 93, 97, 135–6, 190–1
Austria, 191
authoritarian regimes, 134, 163, 166
authority 2, 3, 5–6, 8–12
  ICC, 12, 93, 165
  judicial, 10, 12, 84, 93, 99
  NGO, 26, 81
  prosecutors, 151, 165
  rational-legal, 153
  state, 3, 163
  supranational, 50, 73
  See also power
Axis powers (World War II), 53, 59
Axworthy, Lloyd, 111

Bahai International Community, 80
Bass, Gary Jonathan, 50–2, 74, 77, 160–1, 188, 197
Bassiouni, Cherif, 72, 74, 77, 93, 105–6, 117, 133, 187–8, 190, 197–8
Belgium, 148, 191, 196
Belize, 142, 147
Benin, 191
Blair, Tony, 26, 34, 128, 145, 181, 194
Boli, John, 22, 25, 31, 54–5, 132, 184, 192, 197
Bolivia, 144
Bonino, Emma, 139
Bos, Adrian, xiii, 119, 187–9, 191, 193
Bosnia-Herzegovina, 77, 89, 118, 121, 181, 191
Boyce, Lord Michael, 181
Brazil, 57
British Grotius Society, 54

Brunei, 141, 191
Brussels, 142. *See also* European Union.
Bull, Hedley, 17, 19, 21, 184
Bureau of the Preparatory Committee, 110, 119
Burundi, 128, 173, 191, 194, 199
Bush administration (G. W.), 2, 24, 34, 176, 185
Bush, George H. W., 68, 70, 74, 187, 188
Bush, George W., 24, 34

Cambodia, 53, 138, 141
Camus, Albert, 13, 183
Canada, 98, 102, 110–1, 122–3, 135–6, 143, 191
Caribbean, 74, 93–4, 143, 195
CARICOM, 94
Carnegie, Andrew, 51
Cassese, Antonio, 87
CCIA/ World Council of Churches, 80
Central African Republic, 198
Central America, 68, 140–1, 195
Chile, xiv, 56, 98, 136, 142, 144, 163–4, 167, 190–1
China, 11, 24, 42, 59, 73, 94, 96–7, 100–1, 129, 160, 188, 190–1, 195, 199
Churchill, Winston, 51
civil society, 13, 33, 46, 51, 64–5, 141, 149
  discourse and, 50, 64–5, 146
  global, 12, 14, 21, 34, 57, 115
  representatives of, 54, 65, 78, 115
  transnational, 6
clemency, 164
Clinton administration, 70, 75, 175, 187
Clinton, William Jefferson, 69, 107, 187
Coalition for an ICC (CICC), 7, 25, 27, 94, 124, 129, 191, 194–96
  list-serv, 43–4
  lobbying, 43, 77, 86, 99–101 104, 107, 110–13, 117–19, 122, 128, 135, 137, 142–50, 157
  members, 78, 80, 154
  purpose, 77–9
  secretariat of, 78–9, 113
Code of Crimes against the Peace and Security of Mankind, 71
code of law (crimes), 54, 60
codification, 56–7, 120, 157
Cohen, William, 192

Cold War, 4, 11, 25–7, 53, 55, 58–60, 64, 68, 70–1, 76, 85, 143
Colombia, 3, 56, 142, 144
Committee of the Whole of Rome, 126. *See also* Rome Conference of Plenipotentiaries on the Establishment of an ICC
communicative action, 10, 27, 29, 62, 64–5, 77, 118, 148, 152–7
  orientation, 10, 22
  requirements for, 33, 38–41, 184
  theory, 10, 20, 30–6, 41–2
complementarity, 15, 89–90, 95–9, 112–14, 124–5, 143, 145, 147–8, 152–3, 155–8, 162–5, 175–8, 184, 197, 180
  definition of, 8, 95, 124
constructivism, 13, 26, 32–3, 112, 132, 169
  methodology, 10, 14, 50
  ontology, 10, 50, 186
Convention Against Torture of 1984, 4, 7, 76
Convention on the Prevention and Punishment of the Crime of Genocide of 1948. *See* Genocide Convention
Convention on the Suppression and Punishment of the Crime of Apartheid of 1973, 94, 190
Costa Rica, 141, 191
Council of the European Union, 142
Crawford, Neta, 7, 18, 29, 31, 65
Crimean War, 51
crimes
  against humanity, 1–8, 19, 53–5, 60, 65, 71, 89, 91–6, 100, 107, 114, 119–22, 128, 143, 146, 151, 159–60, 162, 165, 168, 172–3, 175, 178, 188, 193, 198
  against the peace, 57, 60, 71 (*see also* crimes of aggression)
  of aggression, 3, 8, 11, 59, 63, 77, 85, 92–5, 100, 123, 128, 131, 181, 186, 190, 193
  categories of, 1, 93, 102, 119
  core, 9, 93–7, 120, 127, 160
  definitions, 87, 90, 119, 149, 152, 188
  drug trafficking, 90, 93–5, 123, 188
  gender, 121
  genocide (see genocide)
  hijacking, 123
  hostage taking, 91

murder, 3, 38, 91
nuclear weapons, 90, 93, 95, 123
piracy, 61, 120
terrorism, 53, 90, 93–5, 123, 187, 189–90
torture, 2, 4, 7, 76, 91
treaty, 93–4, 188–9
victims of, 34, 42, 52, 63, 65, 93, 115, 149, 163–7
war, 1–8, 11, 19, 24, 28–9, 42, 49–53, 55, 57–9, 64–5, 71, 74, 77, 87, 89, 91–5, 100, 107, 114, 117, 120–2, 125–9, 131, 143, 146, 151, 153, 159–62, 165, 168, 172–8, 180, 185, 193, 198
criminalization, 48
criminal prosecutorial responsibility, 163
critical theory, 10, 32, 185
Croatia, 191
Cuba, 56
customary international law. *See* international law
Czech Republic, 191

decolonization, 7, 31, 53, 65, 169
deliberative democratic theory, 42
Democratic Republic of Congo, 173, 198–9
Denmark, 191
discourse analysis, 10, 26, 30–4, 83, 185
discursive practices, 2, 9–11, 13–16, 31, 33, 35–7, 46, 49, 67–8, 83–4, 91, 106, 109, 112, 131–2, 157, 168
Draft Convention on the Crime of Genocide of 1947, 56
Draft Statute for an International Criminal Court of 1953, 55, 61–3
Dugard, John, 164, 198
Durkheim, Emile, 18, 20

East Timor, 53
Economic and Social Council of the United Nations (ECOSOC), 56
Ecuador, 144
Egypt, 93, 97, 101, 110, 190–1
Elements of Crimes, 6, 125, 183
El Salvador, 140, 144, 195
Estonia, 191
ethics, 7, 31, 36, 45, 80, 105–6, 185
Europe, 5, 26, 51, 74, 89, 135–7, 147–50, 175, 196
Eastern, 6, 111, 132
Western, 29, 111, 118, 132, 143

European Parliament, 138, 142
European Union, 128, 132, 138–9, 142, 147–9, 184, 194
extradition, 61, 72, 75, 98

Faith-based Caucus for an International Criminal Court, 80, 189, 192
Falk, Richard A., 17, 171,
Fédération International des Ligues des Droits de l'Homme (FIDH), 147–50
Fiji Islands, 141
Finland, 53, 191
Finnemore, Martha, 26–7, 46, 132, 184, 186
Fligarta v. Pena-Irala, 24
force, use of, 3, 5–6, 17, 68, 70, 73–4, 160, 169, 171, 180
collective, 102

Foucault, Michel, 46, 192
four policemen, 54
France, 11, 56, 58–60, 64, 74, 78, 94, 104, 121–3, 126–9, 144, 190–1, 194
free-riding, 28

Gabon, 191
General Assembly. *See* United Nations
Geneva Conventions, 58, 91, 122, 160, 172, 189, 197
genocide, 1, 3–6, 8, 11, 19, 55, 59–60, 63, 65, 71, 77, 89–96, 100, 107, 119–21, 128, 143, 151, 159, 162, 165, 168, 178, 194
Convention of 1948, 4, 9, 56, 69–70, 119–20, 131, 133, 170, 172, 187, 198–9
Georgia, 191
Germany, 52, 59, 71, 85, 88, 98, 110, 120, 123–4, 126, 185, 188, 191, 193
National Socialist Party of, 52, 85, 186
Ghana, 110, 191
global community, 161, 167
global culture, 26
global governance, 1–2, 10, 12, 16–17, 25, 46–8, 68
Goldstone, Richard, 75
Greece, 64, 123, 191
Guariglia, Fabricio, 117, 173–4, 189, 193, 196
Guatemala, 140–1, 195
Guiding Principles on Internal Displacement, 172
Gurmendi, Silivia, 151

Hass, Ernst, 132, 186, 192
Habermas, Jurgen, 10, 15, 20–2, 32–3, 35, 37–42, 62, 84, 154, 179, 184–7, 197
   theory of democracy, 62, 64–5
The Hague, 26, 51, 68, 72, 88, 137, 166, 188–9, 191–2, 196, 198
Hague Peace Conferences of 1899 and 1907, 51
Hall, Christopher, 104, 191
Hankey, Lord, 58
Helms, Senator Jesse, 69
Hitler, Adolf, 3, 50
Honduras, 141–4, 195
Hopf, Ted, 32–3, 185
humanitarian law, international, xiii, 2–5, 10, 16, 23, 51, 91–2, 102, 107, 111, 121, 125, 154, 160, 165, 170, 176–7
human rights, 12, 26, 29, 63, 77–8, 80, 87, 89, 94, 103, 110–11, 113, 115, 123, 126, 128, 131, 133, 135, 144–7, 149–50, 151–2, 154, 156, 160, 163–4, 166, 169, 172, 173, 189–98
Human Rights Watch (HRW), 77, 78, 79, 89, 94, 111, 113–14, 119, 139–40, 145–6, 154, 192, 194–7
Hungary, 53, 191
Hussein, Saddam, 74, 188

ICC Monitor, 96, 191. *See also* Coalition for an ICC
impunity, 3, 6–7, 28–9, 52, 62, 79–80, 84–5, 89, 92, 95–7, 102, 105, 114, 123–4, 131, 143, 147–8, 151, 153, 160–2, 177–8
India, 24, 44, 56, 73, 160, 199
Indonesia, 141
institutionalization, 1, 19, 24, 53, 70, 153, 158
internal armed conflict, 51, 91, 94, 113, 146, 160, 197
International Association for Religious Freedom, 80
International Association of Penal Law, 57, 77
International Commission of Jurists, 78, 87, 111
International Commission for Penal Reconstruction and Development, 54
International Committee of the Red Cross, 87, 139, 141

International Court of Justice (ICJ), 51, 62, 68, 71, 100
International Covenant on Civic and Political Rights (ICCPR), 133
International Covenant on Economic, Social, and Cultural Rights (ICESCR), 133
international criminal code, 5, 56, 90
International Criminal Court (ICC)
   accountability of, 154,
   authority, 121, 165
   complementarity (*see* jurisdiction of the ICC)
   compromises, 7, 44–5, 78, 85, 94, 98–9, 104, 106–7, 109, 113–5, 122–9, 131, 185, 190, 191, 193
   criticism of, 155, 162
   effectiveness, 81, 95, 155
   feasibility, 67
   features, 8–10, 100, 112, 122, 155
   funding, 76, 139, 173
   implementing legislation, 142–6
   intervention in domestic conflict, 174
   jurisdiction of (*see* jurisdiction of the ICC)
   legitimacy, 151–68, 172–78
   limitations, 49, 106, 161
   military resistance to, 114
   permanence of, 3, 5, 9, 12, 24, 35, 50, 56–7, 60, 72, 85, 89, 95, 102, 153, 158–61
   prosecution, 102, 114, 124, 128, 181, 198
   prosecutor, 2, 36, 101, 103, 121, 124, 127, 146, 155–6, 161–67, 172–4, 177, 194
   prosecutorial independence, 103, 151, 154
   purpose of, 50, 89, 92, 95, 101, 165
   ratification of, 11, 27, 132, 137–9, 142–3, 147, 149, 199
   Registrar of, 8, 183
   rejection of in 1950s, 53, 56
   signatories to,135–6
   state consent to jurisdiction of, 97, 113, 126
   state incentives under the, 143, 166, 172–3
   statute of (*see* Rome Statute of the ICC)
   trigger-mechanism (*see* jurisdiction of the ICC)
   universal participation, 106, 147

international criminal law, 18, 61, 70, 72, 81, 84, 93, 109, 119, 121, 134, 173–4
  ad hoc enforcement of, 177
  code, 5, 54, 56, 71, 90
  enforcement of, 4, 12, 17, 20, 23–4, 43, 48, 51, 55, 74, 96, 98, 125, 129, 170
  institutionalization of, 18–19, 53, 64, 157–60
  judicialization, 27, 63, 167
  violation, 15, 28, 84, 171
International Criminal Tribunal for Rwanda of the UN (ICTR), 4, 19, 24, 25, 88–9, 104, 128, 181, 197. *See also* Rwanda
International Criminal Tribunal for the former Yugoslavia of the UN (ICTY), 4, 25, 52, 75, 87–9, 98, 104. *See also* Yugoslavia
International Federation for Human Rights, 111, 196
international governmental organization (IGO), 25, 55, 107
  founding, 55
  legitimization of, 54
International Herald Tribune, 44
International Institute of Higher Studies in Criminal Sciences, 77, 188
international law
  customary, 5, 119, 170, 176, 187, 189
  legitimacy of, 175, 179
  norms, 5, 6, 84
  potential of, 70
  principles of, 42, 120, 190
  rules, 97, 116, 168–9, 175–7
  treaty-based, 5, 90, 159
  violations of, 2, 5, 23–4, 50, 90–1, 175
International Law Association, 57, 71, 188
International Law Commission (ILC), 10–1, 39, 43, 54–60, 64–5, 71–8, 85–6, 90, 92, 97, 104–5
International Military Tribunal for the Far East (IMTFE), 53, 57–8
International Monetary Fund (IMF), 64
international nongovernmental organization (INGO). *See* nongovernmental organizations, international
International Peace Bureau, 87
International Penal Court, 54

international relations (IR), discipline of, 10, 17, 21, 26, 32, 46–7, 57, 73, 169, 187–8
Inter-Parliamentary Union, 57
intersubjectivity, 10, 14–15, 18, 30, 33, 37, 67, 157, 184
Iran, 68, 136
Iraq, 2–3, 53, 73–4, 121, 180–1, 188, 194, 199
Ireland, 94, 190–1
Israel, 136, 194
Italy, 53, 99, 106, 137, 191

Japan, 55, 99, 132, 139, 199
Jensen, Rod, 198
Jepperson, Ronald L., 153
John Birch Society, 69
Jordan, 135, 191
jurisdiction of the ICC, 9, 19, 52, 81, 104–7, 147, 177, 186, 188, 190, 193, 197
  automatic (*see* inherent)
  complementarity of, 8, 72, 90, 95–8, 112–13, 125–7, 143, 148, 155, 161–2, 165, 172
  court (prosecutorial) referral of, 9
  inherent, 9, 92, 96, 97, 120
  international criminal, 57, 61, 67
  in 1953 draft statute, 61–3
  "non-consensual," 175
  "opt-in," 71–2, 85, 92
  "opt out," 131
  over persons, 8, 74, 109
  Security Council referral of, 9, 53, 101, 103, 104
  state consent to, 3, 63, 73, 75, 85, 93, 97, 100, 113, 153
  state referral of, 2, 8, 9, 101, 103
  subject-matter, 1, 5, 6, 8, 56, 61, 84, 89–95, 100, 107, 119–20, 123, 160
  temporal, 9
  territorial, 8, 24, 76, 85, 137, 180–1
  trigger-mechanism, 87, 90, 99–103, 112, 126
  universal, 9, 24, 36, 56, 59, 76, 85, 120, 125–7, 131, 193
jus cogens, 97–8, 190
Justice in the Balance, 113

Kaiser Wilhelm II, 50, 51
Katyn Massacre, 64, 184
Kirkpatrick, Jeanne, 69–70
Knox, Philander, 51
Kratochwil, Friedrich V., 10, 14, 17, 19–20, 29, 31, 35, 37–8, 83, 171, 184–5, 189
Kuwait, 73

Laos, 141
Latin America, 6, 93, 111, 132, 135, 137, 141, 143–44
Latvia, 191
law
    human rights, 154
    Natural, 19, 199
    treaty, 6, 125, 152
    of war, 3–5, 23, 91, 170, 176
    See also international criminal law
Lawyers Committee for Human Rights, 78, 111, 189–90
Lawyers for Nuclear Policy, 78
League of Nations, 1, 68
Lee, Roy S., 95, 100, 110, 119, 124, 129, 183–4, 190, 192, 194, 197
Lemkin, Ralph, 56
Lesotho, 191
Leviathan, 3
Libya, 74–5, 194
Lieber Code, 51
Liechtenstein, 192
lifeworld, 20, 41, 85, 185
like-minded group, 71, 94, 110–11, 117, 119, 127–8, 135–6, 144, 191
Lincoln, Abraham, 51
Lithuania, 192
Lockerbie, Scotland, 53, 75
London Naval Conferences, 51
Lord's Resistance Army (LRA), 2, 146–7
    See also Uganda

MacArthur Foundation, 74
Malawi, 192
Malaysia, 93, 97, 101, 141, 189–91
Mali, 138
Malta, 192
Marshall Islands, 141
Mexico, 93, 97, 101, 138, 144, 160, 190–1
Milošević, Slobodan, 74, 89, 163, 181
Morgenthau Jr., Henry, 85

Mouvement National Judiciare Français, 54
multilateral negotiations, 16, 70, 74, 187

Namibia, 192
NATO, 64
"*Ne bis in idem*," 198
Negroponte, John, 199
neoliberal theory, 10, 16, 28, 184
Netherlands, 74, 110, 137, 148, 192
Nicaragua, 68, 140, 195
nongovernmental organizations (NGO), 2, 6–7, 9, 11–16, 21–3, 25–31, 34–7, 39, 42–6, 48–50, 52–5, 57, 59, 64, 67–8, 72–81, 83–107, 109–29, 131–49, 151–78, 184, 187–8
    advocacy, 13–14, 28–9, 132
    authority, 22, 26
    Coalition, 7, 25, 27, 34, 43–4, 78–80, 98, 104, 110–13, 115, 117, 124, 129, 132, 134, 140, 149–50, 188–90, 194 (*see also* Coalition for an ICC)
    discursive practices, 2, 7, 9–16, 25–6, 20, 28, 30–1, 33, 35–7, 39, 45–6, 49–50, 67–68, 83–4, 91, 106, 109, 112, 131–4, 157–8, 168, 177, 184, 196–9
    educational work, 136, 147
    efficacy, 13–14, 27, 30, 74, 113, 129
    influence, 2, 26, 29–31, 34–5, 46, 48, 90, 157
    international (INGO), 11, 22, 25–6, 49, 54–5, 75, 132, 139–40, 144, 148, 154, 184, 195
    legitimacy, 16, 156
    lobbying, 57, 78, 86, 104, 114, 139, 144
    networks, 28–9, 132
    Northern-based, 132, 148
    persuasion, 25, 29–30, 44, 84, 116, 152, 192
    power, 22
    ratification campaigns, 11, 132, 134, 141, 143–8, 196
    roles, 7, 22–3, 45, 57, 73, 77, 79, 107, 117, 143, 156, 184
    Southern-based, 132, 148
    strategy of, 79, 89
    topoi and, 83–5, 89

No Peace Without Justice, 78, 118, 121, 138–9, 142, 194–5
Noriega, Manuel, 24, 74, 186
norms, 4–7, 10, 17–28, 35–7, 39–42, 46, 51–5, 59–60, 62–5, 79, 83–5, 89, 96, 103, 106, 115, 128, 152–4, 156–9, 162, 168–9, 171–3, 176, 178–80, 186, 190, 193
   definition, 18, 37–8
   diffusion, 26
   entrepreneurs, 17, 21
   functions, 18
   international, 17, 19, 24, 36–7, 51–3, 59, 62, 64, 84, 106, 169, 176, 178
   legal, 19, 21–2, 40, 62–3, 154, 156, 179
   legitimacy of, 15, 20, 54, 79
   maintenance, 21
   promotion, 21
   sovereignty, 10, 12–15, 168, 173
   universal, 15, 26, 55, 60, 153, 158–9, 180
   validity, 20–2, 35, 37, 41, 154, 186
North Carolina, 69
Norway, 110, 123, 192
Nullum crimen sine lege, 159
Nuremburg tribunal, 4, 10, 24, 58, 85, 93, 158, 161

Ocampo, Louis Moreno, 2, 167, 198
ontology, 17–18, 21, 30, 75
Organization of Economic Cooperation and Development, 132

Pace, William, 12, 77–9, 102–3, 111–12, 186, 189, 190, 192, 194
Pakistan, 123
Palau, 141
Panama, 56, 74, 141, 144, 188
Parliamentarians for Global Action, 78, 142
path-dependent, 35
Pella, V. V., 57
People's Republic of China, 42
Philippines, 138, 191–2
Pinochet, Augusto, 24, 114, 136, 163, 164, 190
"Plan for a World Criminal Code," 57
Poland, 56, 58, 64, 192
political problems, 58
   global, 22, 31
political will-formation, 22

politicization of trials, 59, 68–9, 100, 104
Portugal, 144, 192
Portuguese language, 44, 140
positivism, 14, 18, 32
Pot, Pol, 3, 50
power, 1, 3–9, 11, 15, 17, 21–3, 25–6, 29, 31, 33–5, 39, 42, 45, 50–1, 53–4, 61, 65, 68, 70–4, 81, 84, 98–9, 101–2, 105–6, 109, 111, 115, 120, 123–4, 127, 132–3, 146, 152–3, 155, 157–8, 161, 163–6, 170–1, 174, 176, 178, 181, 184, 189, 195, 198
   administrative, 8
   discursive, 22, 27, 31
   distribution of, 31–2, 50, 53
   European, 74
   judges, 15
   persuasive, 29, 81
   police, 23, 115, 164, 171, 184
   proprio motu, 127, 155
   prosecutors, 15, 127, 173–4, 177
   state, 6, 115
   UN Security Council, 123, 129, 188
"pre-transitional" justice, 198
process tracing, 10, 13, 30, 34–5, 37, 83, 183
Prosper, Pierre-Richard, 185, 196
Proxmire, William, 69–70, 131, 187
public spheres, 22, 196

Qatar, 194
Quaddafi, Muammar, 74
Quaker UN Office, 80

rational choice, 33
rational discourse, 11, 19, 31, 35, 37, 40–1, 46, 77, 85, 91, 186
   coding, 45
   communicative, 2, 6, 11–12, 20, 27, 29, 31, 34–6, 38–9, 41–2, 45–6, 62, 64–5, 77, 79, 81, 84, 85, 88, 91, 101, 105–6, 110, 112, 114–16, 118, 123, 125, 129, 134, 148, 153, 154, 156–57, 177, 179, 184, 186–87, 190, 192–93, 196
   conceptualization of, 35–41
   justification, 63, 89
   purposive, 38
   Western, 26

Ratner, Steven R., 90, 133, 193, 197, 199
Rawls, John, 157, 197
  "veil of ignorance," 157
reconciliation, 164, 178
Red Cross, 51, 87, 111, 115, 139, 141.
    See also International Committee of
    the Red Cross.
regime theory, 10. See also neoliberal theory
retribution, 50, 164
Reus-Smit, Christian, 169
Richardson, Bill, 107
Risse, Thomas, 10, 33–4
Robertson, Geoffrey, 1, 183, 187, 197
Robinson, A. N. R., 67
Romania, 53, 57, 192
Rome Conference of Plenipotentiaries on
    the Establishment of an ICC, 11, 39,
    55, 78–80, 84–6, 88–9, 95, 99, 104,
    106–7, 109–22, 124, 127–9, 131, 133,
    135, 144, 193–4, 196
  aftermath, 69, 111–12, 131
  compromises, 44–5, 114, 131
  delegates, 11, 81, 110–11, 113, 115–19,
      121, 124, 127–9
  drafting committee, 117
  "near consensus," 113, 129
  negotiations, 69, 77, 109–29
  outcome, 23
Rome Statute of the ICC, 1–3, 5–6, 8–9,
    12–14, 16–17, 21, 23, 27, 36, 43, 48,
    61, 62, 67, 71–5, 77, 84–5, 88–9, 98,
    100, 109–16, 118–28, 131, 133–7,
    140–5, 147 152–7, 159, 161, 165, 168,
    170, 173–4, 176–8, 185, 187–8, 191,
    193–5, 197–9
  adoption, 6, 11, 23–4, 26, 43, 48, 61, 71,
      97, 105–6, 134–5
  Article 1,   8, 109
  Article 7,   119, 121–2, 193
  Article 8,   121
  Article 12,   194, 199
  Article 15,   183–4, 197
  Article 17,   8, 98–9, 124, 198
  Article 18,   109
  Article 36,   183–4, 197
  Article 46,   197–8
  Article 53,   165, 197
  Article 124, 127, 131
  Article 126, 194
  deference, 124, 153

implementation, 25, 111, 139, 141, 147
negotiations, 7–9, 11–12, 15–16, 20–1,
    24, 30, 35–6, 39–40, 42–6, 68–70,
    72–4, 76–81, 83–107, 109–29, 133,
    136, 151–7, 159–60, 162, 173, 177,
    179, 185, 187, 189–92, 194
NGO influence and, 1, 7, 26, 29, 31, 46,
    141, 146, 157
Part 9, 173
preparation, 79, 95, 107
ratification, 1, 6–9, 11–12, 21, 23, 27, 34,
    44, 76, 80, 85, 124, 127, 131–49,
    154, 174, 191, 193, 195–6, 199
rejection, 15, 97, 105
signature campaigns, 2, 11, 88, 131,
    134–7, 139, 195
"situations," 2, 143, 162
sovereignty, 5–6, 10, 93, 95–7, 100, 124,
    145, 147
support, 9, 11, 15–16, 25, 27, 84, 107,
    109, 113, 117, 122–3, 125–6, 129,
    131, 134–7, 139, 141–6, 149,
    161,163, 166, 175, 177
Roosevelt, Franklin D., 54, 68
Root, Elihu, 51
Rosenau, James N., 198
Rosenstock, Robert, 71, 187–8
Roth, Kenneth, 192, 194
Rubin, Alissa J., 43, 197
Ruggie, John, 14, 16, 18, 54, 67–8, 186–7
rule of law, 1–2, 13, 70, 115, 158,
    174, 190, 193
Russia, 52, 58, 85, 97, 100–1, 123, 127,
    129, 160, 188, 189, 191, 193
  legal scholars, 85
  See also Union of Soviet Socialist
      Republics
Russian Federation. See Russia
Rwanda, 3–4, 19, 24–5, 53, 89

Samoa, 141, 192
sanctions, 3, 6, 154, 157, 173
Saudi Arabia, 56
Schabas, William, 183, 197
Scharf, Michael, 43, 74–5, 88–9, 99–100,
    161, 188, 197
Scheffer, David, 70, 117–18, 125, 156–6,
    175, 186, 191, 193, 198–9
Scotland, 75
Searle, John, 17–18, 184

security, 3, 43, 46, 57, 59, 60, 71, 73, 177, 184
  human, 28
  international, 9, 23, 100, 102–3, 125, 180
Senate Foreign Relations Committee, 69
Senegal, 192
Sierra Leone, 53, 118, 137, 192
Sikkink, Kathryn, 13, 17–18, 26–9, 31, 46, 77, 132, 134, 184–5
Singapore, 99, 104, 107, 110, 128–9, 141, 192, 194
Singapore Compromise, 104, 107, 128–9
  NGO involvement, 104
Slovakia, 192
Slovenia, 192
social facts, 14, 184
  definition, 18, 32
social reconstruction, 164
Société Française de Droit International, 54
sociological institutionalism, 10, 26, 132
Solomon Islands, 192
Somalia, 3, 74–5
Soros Foundation, 74
South Africa, 44, 111, 192
South African Truth and Reconciliation Commission, 164, 167
South America, 111, 137, 143
South East Asia, 140
Southern Asia, 137
South Korea, 110, 126–7, 132, 185, 192
sovereignty, 5–7, 10, 43, 48, 49–51, 56, 58–63, 70, 93, 95, 97, 100, 124, 145, 147, 165, 167–74, 176–7, 184, 196, 199
  absolutist view, 43, 51
  de facto, 169, 177
  definition, 167–70
  loss of, 93
  social construction, 164, 168–9
  state autonomy, 65, 168–9, 171, 177
  territory and, 7, 96, 168, 171, 173
  See also states
Spain, 138, 144, 192
Spanish language, 44, 190
Spiropoulos report, 57, 186
Srebrenica Massacre, 181
Stalin, Josef, 3, 52

states
  accountability of, 3, 171
  as actors, 14, 21, 25, 27, 49, 132
  authority of, 3, 73, 80, 96, 153, 157, 163, 167, 169
  definition of, 3
  discursive positions of, 49
  juridical equality, 170
  legal personality, 63
  marginalized, 34
  sanctioned violence, 3–4, 6, 23, 28, 48, 86, 89, 146, 164, 170
  sovereignty, 5–7, 10, 43, 48–51, 56, 58–63, 70, 93, 95–7, 100, 124, 145, 147, 165, 167–73, 176–7, 198–9
  totalitarian, 171
strategic action, 10, 11, 22, 38, 41, 81, 114, 120, 129, 154, 156, 184
structures, social, 17–18, 198
  communication, 50, 64
Sudan, 117, 146, 156, 197–9
  Darfur, 197
Suhr, Brigitte, 196
supranational authority, 5, 50, 73, 171
Swaziland, 192
Sweden, 60
Switzerland, 192

Tadic, Dusko, 88–9
Taft, William Howard, 51
Terraviva, 128, 194
Thailand, 141
Theory of Communicative Action, 10, 20, 32–3, 35
third-party dispute resolution, 160
Times (London), 58–9
Tonga, 141
topoi, 11, 29, 37–9, 83–5, 89, 119–20, 122, 131, 185
  definition, 29, 38
  and the ICC Treaty negotiations, 83–4, 89, 122
  and international law, 85, 119–20, 122
  use, 83–4, 89
totalitarian states, 154, 171
transitional governments, 167
Transnational Advocacy Networks, 27–9, 132

treaties, 1, 4, 8–9, 11–13, 15–16, 19–20, 22–3, 25, 36–7, 47, 50, 53, 57, 61, 71, 73, 75–7, 81, 83, 85, 88, 90–1, 93–6, 100, 103, 105, 114, 116, 125–6, 131–5, 137, 139, 141–2, 144–5, 148, 152, 154–6, 159, 170–2, 175, 180, 187–91, 195
tribunals, 2, 4, 10, 19–20, 24–5, 28, 50–6, 58, 69, 71–2, 74–7, 85, 87–9, 93, 99, 102–3, 107, 119, 121, 128, 153, 156, 158–62, 165–66, 175, 181, 188
   ad hoc war crime, 4–5, 19, 52, 87, 89, 102–3, 121, 153, 159, 161–2, 165, 175 (*see also* International Criminal Tribunals)
   authority of, 64, 84, 93, 99, 124, 165
   establishment of, 71, 76, 98, 119
   international criminal, 4, 10, 25, 51, 54, 71–2, 74, 76, 89, 102
   jurisdiction of, 88
   legitimacy of, 197
   military, 24, 53, 58, 102, 158
   Nuremberg, 4, 10, 24, 39, 50, 52–2, 56–9, 64, 74, 85, 93, 98, 123, 158–9, 161, 165, 186
   Tokyo, 3, 58–9, 85, 93, 158–9, 161
   weakness of, 89, 154, 178
Trinidad and Tobago, 94, 190, 192
Troost, Lars Van, 128, 191, 194, 197
Truman, Harry S., 49, 57, 186
truth commissions, 107, 156, 158–9, 165
Turkey, 147–8, 150, 196
Tuvalu, 141

Uganda, 2, 134, 145–6, 173, 183, 196, 198–9
   investigations, 173, 199
   ratification campaign, 134, 145–7
UN Congress on the Prevention of Crime and the Treatment of Offenders, Eighth, 103
UN Delegations, 57, 86
UN Diplomatic Conference of Plenipotentiaries on the Establishment of an ICC, 88. *See also* Rome Conference of Plenipotentiaries on the Establishment of an ICC
UNESCO, 194
United Kingdom, 60, 78, 93, 101, 106–7, 123, 126–8, 134, 145, 180–1, 190–2, 194
   ICC Act of 2001, 145, 196
   military, 181
   Parliament, 196
   ratification campaigns, 143, 196
United Nations, 1, 9, 19, 24, 33–4, 43, 53–61, 64–5, 71, 77, 102–3, 107, 117, 146, 171, 174, 186, 189–90, 192–3, 199
   budget, 76
   Charter, 1, 9, 24, 54, 61, 75–6, 102–4, 128, 176, 183
   ICC Preparatory Committee, 87–9, 94, 96–9, 102–4, 106, 110–12, 114, 119–20, 124–7, 187, 190–1, 194
   personnel, 110, 118, 157
   "State-building," 171
   war crime tribunals, 107 (*see also* International Criminal Tribunals)
United Nations Commission on Human Rights, 172, 198
United Nations General Assembly, 36, 43, 54–8, 60–1, 71–7, 85, 87, 92, 100, 103–4, 107, 110, 188–9, 191
   resolutions of, 60, 103, 110, 189, 191
   Sixth Committee of, 43, 54, 57, 58, 60, 76–8, 86, 92, 96, 100–1, 187–8, 193
United Nations Security Council, 9, 24, 26, 33, 36, 43, 53, 70, 74–6, 89, 93–4, 100–104, 107
   authority, 93, 100, 102
   decision-making process, 33, 101
   ICC, relationship to, 9, 35, 53, 70, 73–4, 76, 93–4, 101–4, 107, 112–13, 121–123, 125, 127–9, 165, 174, 188, 190, 194
   permanent members, 74, 94, 121, 129, 134, 137, 165
   referrals, 101, 103–4
United States, 2, 10, 11, 24, 34, 36, 44, 50–1, 53–4, 56–7, 59–60, 68–71, 73–5, 77–8, 92, 94, 96, 100–2, 104–7, 118, 120–1, 123–6, 128–9, 136, 142, 149, 153, 157, 161, 165, 168, 175–7, 181, 185, 187–8, 190–1, 195, 197, 199
   federal courts, 24
   and the Genocide Convention, 9, 56, 69–70, 120, 133, 170, 172, 187

Government, 56, 71, 74–5, 94, 112, 118–19, 123, 154, 156–7, 168, 175–6, 185, 199
ICC opposition, 2, 10, 24, 69, 71, 73–5, 77–8, 94, 96, 100–2, 105–6, 118, 120–121, 123–6, 128–9, 132, 142, 149, 153, 157, 161, 168, 175–7, 181, 185, 188, 190–191, 195, 197, 199
ICC policy, 107, 116
preemptive force, 176
Universal Declaration of Human Rights, 63
UN Secretariat, 76, 115, 186
Uruguay, 56, 144, 187
Union of Soviet Socialist Republics, 53, 54, 59, 60, 64, 186

Venezuela, 144, 192
Vienna Convention on the Law of Treaties, 199
Vietnam, 141
Von Pufendorf, Samuel, 19, 20, 184

Waltz, Kenneth, 32, 184
Weberian view, 14
Wilmshurst, Elizabeth, 126–7, 193
Wilson, Woodrow, 68, 86
World Conference on Human Rights, 77
World Court, 51, 52. *See also* International Court of Justice
World Federalist Association(U.S.), 77, 96
World Federalist Movement, 77, 87, 102
"world polity theory," 26. *See also* sociological institutionalism
World War I, 51
World War II, 49, 51, 52, 53, 54, 55, 64, 73, 102, 161, 186

Yemen, 194
Yugoslavia, 4, 19, 24,25, 73, 74, 158, 161, 163, 188

Zambia, 192